From the Gracchi to Sulla

Second Edition

LACTOR Sourcebooks in Ancient History

For more than half a century, *LACTOR Sourcebooks in Ancient History* have been providing for the needs of students at schools and universities who are studying ancient history in English translation. Each volume focuses on a particular period or topic and offers a generous and judicious selection of primary texts in new translations. The texts selected include not only extracts from important literary sources but also numerous inscriptions, coin legends and extracts from legal and other texts, which are not otherwise easy for students to access. Many volumes include annotation as well as a glossary, maps and other relevant illustrations, and sometimes a short Introduction. The volumes are written and reviewed by experienced teachers of ancient history at both schools and universities. The series is now being published in print and digital form by Cambridge University Press, with plans for both new editions and completely new volumes.

Osborne	*The Athenian Empire*
Osborne	*The Old Oligarch*
Cooley	*Cicero's Consulship Campaign*
Grocock	*Inscriptions of Roman Britain*
Osborne	*Athenian Democracy*
Santangelo	*Late Republican Rome, 88-31 BC*
Warmington/Miller	*Inscriptions of the Roman Empire, AD 14-117*
Treggiari	*Cicero's Cilician Letters*
Rathbone/Rathbone	*Literary Sources for Roman Britain*
Sabben-Clare/Warman	*The Culture of Athens*
Stockton	*From the Gracchi to Sulla*
Edmondson	*Dio: the Julio-Claudians*
Brosius	*The Persian Empire from Cyrus II to Artaxerxes I*
Cooley/Wilson	*The Age of Augustus*
Levick	*The High Tide of Empire*
Cooley	*Tiberius to Nero*
Cooley	*The Flavians*
Cooley	*Sparta*

From the Gracchi to Sulla

Sources for Roman History, 133-80 BC

Second Edition

Translated and edited by
D. L. STOCKTON
University of Oxford

CAMBRIDGE
UNIVERSITY PRESS

CAMBRIDGE
UNIVERSITY PRESS

Shaftesbury Road, Cambridge CB2 8EA, United Kingdom

One Liberty Plaza, 20th Floor, New York, NY 10006, USA

477 Williamstown Road, Port Melbourne, VIC 3207, Australia

314–321, 3rd Floor, Plot 3, Splendor Forum, Jasola District Centre, New Delhi – 110025, India

103 Penang Road, #05–06/07, Visioncrest Commercial, Singapore 238467

Cambridge University Press is part of Cambridge University Press & Assessment, a department of the University of Cambridge.

We share the University's mission to contribute to society through the pursuit of education, learning and research at the highest international levels of excellence.

www.cambridge.org
Information on this title: www.cambridge.org/9781009383059

DOI: 10.1017/9781009383042

First published 2023
First paperback edition 2024

A catalogue record for this publication is available from the British Library

ISBN   978-1-009-38305-9   Paperback

TABLE OF CONTENTS

	Page
Preface	4
Introduction	5
Brief Notes on the Sources and Authorities	8
THE SOURCES	13
Index of Passages Quoted	175
Index of Names and Places	179

PREFACE

Due acknowledgement must be paid here to the book on which this collection of translations is based: E. W. Gray's second edition of *Sources for Roman History*, 133-70 B.C. (Clarendon Press, Oxford, 1960). The first edition by A. H. J. Greenidge and A. M. Clay was published as long ago as 1903, and I am happy to note the agreeable coincidence that Dr. Greenidge was then, as I am now, tutor in ancient history at Brasenose College.*

I have not followed the pattern of 'Greenidge and Clay' in every detail. Some pieces included there are omitted here, rather more pieces have been added or extended. In particular, I have often chosen to vary the layout of passages within particular years so as to face the reader with more continuous excerpts from certain authors. But this present book is in substance a translation of what is to be found there, and without it the labour would have been Herculean.

As with 'Greenidge and Clay', so too here the evidence is arranged by consular years, and generally by subject-matter within those years. Though convenient for some purposes, not least that conflicts or variations between different sources stand out clearly, this arrangement inevitably leads to "bittiness", and renders the flavour and emphasis and value of individual authors elusive. This defect I have tried to palliate a little by citing more continuous and extensive excerpts in several instances.

All the translations are my own, so the blame for errors and infelicities can be laid squarely on my own shoulders. I hope there are not too many of these. I am most grateful to Mr. Alan Towey of Harrow School for compiling the Indices.

Brasenose College, Oxford,   D. L. Stockton
June 1981.

---

*Mr. Mark Greenstock of Harrow School, a former pupil of mine who engaged me for this task in his capacity as General Editor of LACTORs, completes a Brasenose trio.

INTRODUCTION

The period of history that stretches from the tribunate of Tiberius Sempronius Gracchus to the dictatorship of Lucius Cornelius Sulla Felix constitutes the first stage of what Sir Ronald Syme has aptly named 'the Roman revolution', the first half of the century which witnessed the collapse and demise of the Roman Republic and the inception of the Augustan Principate. I may perhaps be allowed to repeat here what I have already written elsewhere:*

'The history of the tumultuous and exciting last century of the Republic of Rome centres around the fight of the great families of the senatorial ruling nobility to hold their controlling position against the assaults of their opponents. The attack was launched with verve and skill by the brothers Tiberius and Gaius Gracchus. The questions they raised, the issues they fought, the proposals they championed were to remain central to Roman politics for the next century: agrarian reform, social justice, the right of Rome's Italian allies and partners in conquest, the food supply, the administration of justice, the curbing of the arbitrary power of consuls and senate. They rested their position on the uncompromising basis of the sovereignty of the *populus Romanus*. They failed themselves to storm the citadel, but it was along the line of advance they had mapped out that later assaults were pressed home. At the end of the second century Saturninus renewed the attack. Cicero was nearly seven years old when, like the Gracchi before him, Saturninus went down in face of the force deployed by the ruling oligarchy, who when it come to the point of decision were prepared to fight rather than be legislated out of power. Cicero was already a youth and studying at Rome when the murder of Livius Drusus the Younger sparked off the Social War. In 88 Sulpicius Rufus assumed the mantle of Drusus, and from 87 Cinna and Carbo seized and held power. But first in 88 and then again in 82 Sulla led his armies against Rome to overthrow his opponents. The arrangements which he made during his later period of dominance ruthlessly restored the senatorial position and left the nobility in tight control of Rome. But the forces of reform were too deeply seated in the widespread and serious social and economic grievances of large sections of the populace to be long repressed. In 70 ... the tribunate recovered its Gracchan strength, ready to be deployed for new attacks.'

Despite its interest and importance, however, the history of these years is patchy and controversial. We lack a dependable continuous literary source to hold it together, to serve as a secure framework into which we can fit the substantial amount of miscellaneous information which we have. By accident of survival, our continuous accounts, above all that of Livy, but including also such works as those of Diodorus Siculus and Cassius Dio, remain only in excerpts or fragments or wretched short summaries of uncertain reliability. The first book of Appian's *Civil Wars* has luckily been spared, but that book is by way of being an introduction to the whole work, and is deliberately and consciously selective in its treatment of issues and episodes, leaping from high

* Cicero: *A Political Biography* (Oxford, 1971) pp. 21–22.

point to high point, uneven in the quality of the sources on which it depends. Plutarch's *Lives* of the leading men of this period are invaluable, but they are the work of a biographer and not an annalistic or general historian, and are marked by an understandable looseness in precise chronology.

It cannot be too strongly emphasised that the quality of the authors cited in the pages that follow varies enormously, not only between each other but also between different sections of an individual author's work, depending on his interest or on the nature of the source or sources he himself happens to be using at the time. Far and away our best guide is Cicero. Born in 106 BC, he was as a young man close to leading politicians who were thirty or more years his senior. His great idol Lucius Licinius Crassus, for example, was born in 140 BC and in due course married the daughter of Q. Mucius Scaevola (consul 117 BC), a cousin of P. Mucius Scaevola who was consul in 133 BC and of Publius' brother who was adopted into the Crassus family as P. Licinius Crassus Mucianus and himself held the consulship in 131 BC. This Lucius Crassus as a young man prosecuted the renegade Gracchan Papirius Carbo and in 106 BC was a leading and vocal supporter of Servilius Caepio, a role he was to repeat for the younger Drusus in 91 BC, having meanwhile shared the consulship with another Scaevola in 95 BC and the censorship in 92 BC with that Domitius Ahenobarbus who twelve years earlier had been a prominent reforming tribune in 104 BC. Apart from his intercourse with men of that standing and experience, Cicero was also of course able to read many works and occasionally consult public records no longer available to us. But even with a man like Cicero (or other near-contemporaries like Julius Caesar or Sallust) interest may be narrow or capricious, accidentally or deliberately selective, and there may be personal axes to grind, and hence we must be on the watch for deliberate slanting or suppression of the truth (*suggestio falsi* and *suppressio veri*), a not uncommon feature of the activities of orators and historians. (Just so nowadays, we do not necessarily or perhaps even usually assume that what a politician of one party has to say when promoting his own party's policies or running down those of the opposition party should be accepted as 'the truth, the whole truth, and nothing but the truth'.)

Cicero himself once observed that 'anybody who supposes that he has my personal signed guarantee for the things I say in my speeches in the courts is seriously in error: they are all of them suited to particular cases and instances'. He then went on to speak with humorous admiration of the good sense of another of his boyhood idols, the great orator Marcus Antonius (consul 99 BC), who used to say that he had never had any of his own speeches 'published' because he wanted to be free to deny later anything which it might turn out he had better not have said (*pro Cluentio* 139–40).

Much of our material has to be garnered from detached comments and brief asides, casual references and stray snippets, scraps of speeches and fragmentary inscriptions, which we have to try to fit into such framework as Appian and Plutarch and others provide. And much of our information in the following pages comes from men writing long after, sometimes several centuries after, the events to which they refer, men who frequently display a sad lack of critical acumen or even interest in their selection and assessment and use of the available evidence: and where they were getting their 'facts' from is generally a mystery. The briefest of glances at what, for instance, Appian and Velleius Paterculus have to tell us about Tiberius Gracchus' programme reveals behind the former a source or sources of the highest quality and in the latter a casual and superficial oversimplification that leaves one wondering if anything Velleius writes is worth bothering very much about.

Having said all that, it is a case of *'Spartam nactus es, hanc exorna!'*, which means that we have to stop complaining and get on to do the best job we can with the materials available. All history has to start with facts and dates, and these we must find and determine by comparing and weighing the evidence we have. The 'facts' presented in this collection are not intended to be self-sufficient, but to supplement the reading of standard text-books and even provide a check on what is to be found there. Much is necessarily and willingly left to the schoolmaster or schoolmistress to explain and elucidate. The high points are obvious: the exciting movement of the tribunates of the two Gracchi; the growing disarray of the last decade of the second century BC, the rise of Marius and the bid of Lucius Appuleius Saturninus to pick up the Gracchan threads once again; the still somewhat opaque thrust of the tribunate of Drusus the Younger in 91 BC, and the Social War which his death sparked off as Rome's Italian allies, weary of unproductive political essays, took up arms to extort the equality of status and opportunity which they so richly deserved; the merging of that Social War into a Civil War, when Roman fought Roman as he was to do again in the civil wars of the two decades that followed Caesar across the Rubicon; the firm and thorough work of the 'deadly reformer' Sulla, which ends this book and which was to collapse in ruins ten years later. No doubt it is for these episodes that this collection will chiefly be used. But, while 'history books begin and end', as Collingwood reminds us, 'the events they describe do not'. Small patches and pools of information lying between these larger episodes may illuminate them, the diligent accumulation of stray facts and names can help to build a background to them and to the society which gave them birth. Thus Sallust's monograph on *The Jugurthan War*, for all its narrow major theme, can provide something in some ways of a 'portrait of an age' and illustrate the assumptions of a whole generation. Finally, we ought not to forget that men were not and are not forever living in the violent throes of political crises of the greatest moment. There are often also the 'quiet' times, when life resumes a more even tenor, when politics display a preoccupation with the contest for office and the fruits of office, wealth and prestige, influence and patronage and distinction, a preoccupation that formed the enduring leitmotif of the concerns and activities of the ruling class of Republican Rome as of other times and places. Of course, the big divisive issues had not gone away, they had become latent or quiescent. But that truth, like many others, is easy to detect by hindsight, but was to discern for those who were alive at the time and had no access to our crystal ball in which their present and future are visible to us as the past.*

---

* (Note: spellings of proper names in this book are often inconsistent, reflecting the inconsistency in the original texts.)

BRIEF NOTES ON THE SOURCES AND AUTHORITIES

APPIAN was born in Alexandria towards the end of the 1st. century AD. After holding local office there he moved to Rome where he practised as an advocate, later entering government service as an imperial procurator. His *Romaica* is divided into subject patterns, including the *Civil Wars* in five books, the first of which covers the period from Tiberius Gracchus to 70 BC, *Mithridatica*, and *Celtica*, etc.

ASCONIUS. Q. Asconius Pedianus was born in Padua in 9 BC and lived until AD 76. All that survives of his work is part of his commentary on Cicero's speeches (the *in Pisonem, pro Scauro, pro Milone, pro Cornelio*, and *in toga candida*), which he composed to help his sons' education, drawing chiefly for his exposition on Cicero's own writings.

ATHENAEUS. His *Deipnosophistae ('The Scholars' Banquet')* dates from about AD 200, and is essentially a collection of snippets on a very wide range of varied subjects – he cited over 1,250 authors!

CAESAR. Gaius Julius Caesar, the later dictator, was born in 100 BC. Consul in 59 BC and subsequently governor of Gaul, his *de bello Gallico* was published probably in 50 BC – the eighth and final book being the work of one of his subordinate commanders, Aulus Hirtius, consul in 43 BC. The three books of his *Civil War* take the narrative from his crossing of the Rubicon in January 49 BC down to the beginning of the fighting at Alexandria the following autumn: the work was pretty certainly left unfinished at his death in 44 BC. It was continued in three works by other (contemporary) hands: the *Alexandrian War*, the *African War*, and the uncouth, ill-written, and very scrappy *Spanish War*.

CASSIODORUS held high office under the Gothic kings of the 6th. century AD. His *Chronicle* is a brief summary of Roman History down to AD 519.

CASSIUS DIO Cocceianus was born in Asia Minor, the son of Cassius Apronianus, governor of Cilicia and also of Dalmatia. After a suffect consulship in AD 205 he was colleague as consul of the Emperor Alexander Severus in AD 229. His *Roman History* went from the earliest beginnings down to AD 229. Much of it is lost, and for our period we have largely only fragments and excerpts.

L. CASSIUS HEMINA was a Roman annalist of the mid-second century BC, whose work survives only in sparse fragments.

CATO. Marcus Porcius Cato ('Cato the Censor', 'The Elder Cato') was born in 234 BC; though not of a senatorial family, he rose to be consul in 195 BC. His *On Agriculture* was written about 160 BC, a practical guide to husbandry with the well-to-do non-subsistence farmer in mind. His *Origines* covered Roman History from earliest times down to 149 BC, the year of his death; but of this work only fragments survive.

CICERO. Marcus Tullius Cicero was born in Arpinum in Central Italy in January 106 BC. Like the elder Cato, his was a non-senatorial family, but he became consul in 63 BC. Besides his speeches and dialogues and essays, nearly

1,000 letters survive written by or to him. In this book the various works are individually dated. He was proscribed and killed in 43 BC. (See also SCHOLIASTS.)

CIL. The *Corpus Inscriptionum Latinarum*, a collection of surviving Latin inscriptions.

de viris illustribus. A work sometimes attributed to Aurelius Victor, this is a ragbag of stories and anecdotes about famous men of the Republican period. It was compiled probably in the 4th. century AD.

Digest. The *Digest* (or *Pandects*) is a collection of passages from the writings of the classical jurists compiled by order of the Emperor Justinian in the early 6th. century AD.

DIO CASSIUS (See under CASSIUS DIO.)

DIODORUS SICULUS in the second half of the 1st. century BC cobbled together a *World History* extending down to 54 BC. Of its forty books not all survive intact, and for this period we have generally to rely on fragments and excerpts.

DIONYSIUS OF HALICARNASSUS lived and taught at Rome in the Augustan period. His *Roman Antiquities* went down to the outbreak of the First Punic War in twenty books, of which the first ten survive. It is very much a moralising work, but contains much valuable information.

EPITOME OF LIVY (See under LIVY.)

EUSEBIUS. Bishop of Caesarea in Palestine in the early 4th. century AD, his works include a *Chronicle* with chronological tables from Abraham onwards.

EUTROPIUS was an imperial official in the 4th. century AD. His *Breviary* covered (in ten books) Roman History from the foundation of the city down to AD 364. For the Republican part, he drew his material from Livy or a Livian *Epitomator*.

FESTUS was roughly contemporary with Eutropius, like him an imperial official, and also the author of a *Breviary* of Roman History. He too drew his material from the Livian well.

FIR. The *Fontes Iuris Romani*, a collection of surviving Roman laws, etc. edited by the German scholar Bruns.

FIRA. The *Fontes Iuris Romani Anteiustiniani*, a similar collection by the Italian scholar Riccobono.

FLORUS in the early 2nd. century AD wrote an *Epitome* of Roman History with special emphasis on wars. He was less wholly dependent on Livy than either Eutropius or Festus or Orosius.

FRONTINUS. Sextus Iulius Frontinus lived from about AD 30 to AD 104. A partisan of Vespasian's, he was suffect consul in the seventies and then governor of Britain, conquering Wales and founding Caerleon. Appointed chief of the Roman Metropolitan Water Board by Nerva in AD 97, he wrote an excellent historical and technical manual *On the Aqueducts*. His *Strategems* is a manual of strategic and tactical instruction for the use of army officers, illustrated by examples from Greek and Roman history.

AULUS GELLIUS was a writer of the 2nd. century AD of whose personal background we are largely ignorant. His *Attic Nights* consisted of twenty books, most of which happily survive. It is a delightful sort of commonplace book on a very wide range of topics, a collection he began in his student-days at Athens and continued thereafter. It contains very valuable citations from earlier writers whose work has been lost.

ad Herennium. The earliest extant Latin work on Rhetoric, addressed to Gaius Herennius, it was in late antiquity taken to be a work of Cicero's, which it is not. It is a systematic and technical manual dating from the very early 1st. century BC.

INSCRIPTIONS. As well as the *CIL, FIR,* and *FIRA,* already listed, we have the *ILS (Inscriptiones Latinae Selectae:* ed. Dessau); *ILLRP (Inscriptiones Latinae Liberae Rei Publicae:* ed Degrassi); *II (Inscriptiones Italiae)*; *IGRR (Inscriptiones Graecae ad res Romanas pertinentes)*; *SEG (Supplementum Epigraphicum Graecum)*; *MAMA (Monumenta Asiae Minoris Antiqua)*; and the *Fasti Consulares* and *Fasti Triumphales,* lists of consuls and triumphators.

JULIUS VICTOR wrote in the 4th. century AD on *The Art of Rhetoric.*

JUSTIN. Marcus Justinus Junianus in the 3rd. century AD wrote an *Epitome* of the *Historiae Philippicae* of the Augustan writer Pompeius Trogus.

JUSTINIAN, the famous emperor of the early 6th. century AD, commissioned massive legal compendia, the *Digest* and *Codex* and *Institutes.*

LICINIANUS. Granius Licinianus in the 2nd. century AD wrote an annalistic handbook of Roman History which survives only in bitty fragments very scattered in date.

LIVY. Titus Livius of Padua lived either from 59 BC to AD 17 or from 64 BC to AD 12. His history of Rome *ab urbe condita* was written in annalistic form and totalled 142 books, of which only 35 have survived (Bks.1–10 and 21–45). His reputation was high from his own lifetime onwards, and shortened or 'pocket' versions were made, one *Epitome* being already in circulation in Martial's day (late 1st. century AD). For the missing books covering the period 133-80 BC we can refer to the surviving *Epitome* (or *Perioche*) of these books. This particular version is probably of late imperial date, and pretty certainly an abbreviation not of Livy himself but of an already existing Epitome. The reduction is drastic, a whole book of Livy often being compressed into a dozen or two lines of summary, little more than a bare list of contents. The *Epitomator*'s accuracy, carefulness, and judgement are all sadly of the poorest.

MACROBIUS in the late 4th. or early 5th. century AD wrote the *Saturnalia,* an academic symposium covering a wide range of topics.

MEMNON lived in Heraclea Pontica in early imperial times, and wrote a history of his city which includes some information on Roman history.

OBSEQUENS. Julius Obsequens, probably in the 4th. century AD, compiled a collection of prodigies, much of his information going back ultimately to Livy.

ORF. The *Oratorum Romanorum Fragmenta,* a collection of excerpts from and testimonia about Roman orators of the Republican period (excluding Cicero), edited by Malcovati.

OROSIUS. Paulus Orosius in the early 5th. century AD was a pupil of St. Augustine, who persuaded him to write the *Historiae adversus Paganos,* from the creation of the world to the founding of Rome and then the history of Rome down to AD 417. Again, he used a lot of Livian material.

PLINY. Gaius Plinius Secundus ('Pliny the Elder') was born at Comum in North Italy in AD 23/24 and died during the course of the eruption of Vesuvius (he was commander of the fleet at Misenum) in AD 79. He saw military service and held high equestrian offices. His *Natural History* comprises 37 books and is a mine of miscellaneous information.

PLUTARCH was born in Boeotia in Greece and died sometime after AD 120 at an age of something over seventy. He was a voluminous writer. His best-known and most enduringly popular work was his collection of biographies or *Lives* of famous Greeks and Romans; but he wrote many other works both philosophical and antiquarian.

QUINTILIAN. Marcus Fabius Quintilianus came of Hispano-Italian stock, became a famous teacher, and was probably the first state-appointed and salaried 'professor' of rhetoric at Rome. His famous *Institutio Oratoria* was published towards the very end of the 1st. century AD.

SALLUST. Gaius Sallustius Crispus was born into the local aristocracy at Amiternum around 86 BC. He was tribune of the plebs in 52 BC, when he was on the other side from Cicero and Milo. A partisan of Caesar's in the Civil War, he was praetor in 47 BC, later governing Africa Nova, after which he only narrowly escaped conviction on an extortion charge. He retired from public life and turned to the writing of history, dying in about 35 BC. Early monographs on *Catiline* and the *Jugurthan War* (both extant) were followed by a full-scale history (the *Historiae*) which began in 78 BC (the year of Sulla's death) and may not have got much beyond about 67 BC by the time Sallust died; but this, his major work, survives only in excerpts, fragments, and citations.

SCHOLIASTS is the name given to ancient commentators on particular texts. The Ciceronian scholiasts are all available in the collection *Ciceronis Orationum Scholiastae* edited by Stangl, and cited by the pages of his edition; thus (e.g.) Schol. Bob. p.172 St. = Scholia Bobiensia on page 172 of Stangl's edition. Asconius, however (see his entry) is generally cited by the pages of Clark's Oxford Text of Asconius: e.g. Asconius 25C = page 25 in Clark's edition.

SENECA. Lucius Annaeus Seneca was born into a well-to-do Hispano-Italian family at Cordoba in Spain sometime between 4 BC and AD 1. The Emperor Claudius appointed him tutor to the young Nero, and when Nero became Emperor in AD 54 his power was for some years considerable as an *éminence grise* behind the young Emperor. But his influence waned in the early sixties, and in AD 65 he was forced to commit suicide for alleged involvement in an unsuccessful conspiracy against Nero. Apart from his verse, his published works were basically 'philosophical'.

STRABO wrote his *Geography*, which also contains historical information, in the reign of Augustus.

SUETONIUS. Gaius Suetonius Tranquillus, at one time a young protégé of the younger Pliny, joined the imperial service, and under Trajan and Hadrian in the early 2nd. century AD held in turn three of the highest posts in the imperial private secretariate, secretary *a studiis, a bibliothecis*, and *ab epistulis*. Of his works most survive only in bits, with the exception of his *Lives of the Caesars* (*de vita Caesarum*), a set of biographies of Julius Caesar (the first few chapters of this *Life* are lost) and of the eleven emperors from Augustus to Domitian.

TACITUS. Cornelius Tacitus was born probably about AD 56 of wealthy Celtic or Gallic stock, into a family which had been given the Roman citizenship some generations back. His father, a high equestrian officer, once served as procurator of Gallia Belgica and paymaster-general to the Rhine army; Tacitus himself married the daughter of the famous Julius Agricola, governor of Britain, member of another romanised Celto-Gallic family from Fréjus in Provence. Consul-suffect in AD 97, he was later governor of the province of Asia, probably in AD 112/3. Early works of his were the *Dialogus de oratoribus, de vita Julii Agricolae* (a biography of his father-in-law), and *de origine et situ Germanorum*. His great works were the *Histories*, covering the period AD 69 to (probably) the death of Domitian in AD 96, of which only the first four books and a scrap of the fifth survive; and the *Annals*, starting from the death of Augustus and going down to AD 68, where again we have not the whole work, for of its sixteen books parts of 5 and 6 are missing, the whole of 7–10, and 16 breaks off in AD 66.

VALERIUS MAXIMUS published his handbook of historical examples in the reign of Tiberius, probably sometime after AD 31. His work is an odd mish-mash of scattered information of widely varying degrees of accuracy, judgement, and critical insight.

VELLEIUS PATERCULUS was roughly a contemporary of Valerius Maximus. After an early career in the army, he entered politics and became a praetor along with his brother in AD 15. He may have been involved in Sejanus' downfall in AD 31; but two Vellei Paterculi, perhaps his sons, were suffect consuls in AD 60 and 61. His praenomen is uncertain. His *Historiae Romanae* was in two books, the first (of which much is missing) going down to the fall of Carthage in 146 BC, the second continuing down to AD 30. Which sources he drew on for his material is far from clear.

THE SOURCES

133 BC   Consuls: P. Mucius Scaevola, L. Calpurnius Piso Frugi

(a) 'A house divided against itself'

SALLUST, *Jugurthine War* 41.2–42.1

Before the destruction of Carthage (*146 BC*), the Roman Senate and the Roman People managed the affairs of state in quiet and restrained co-operation, and there was no internecine struggle for glory or domination. Fear of external enemies ensured that they conducted themselves sensibly. But, once that apprehension had vanished, in came arrogance and lack of self-restraint, the children of success. So it was that the peace which they had longed for in their times of travail proved, when once it had been attained, only too harsh and bitter. For the nobility proceeded to convert the dignity of their position, and the People their liberty, into self-indulgence, every man seeking to twist and turn and force it to his own selfish advantage. As a result the whole nation was split into two divisions, and Rome was torn to pieces in the middle.

However, the nobility drew superior strength from its cohesion, while the strength of the commons was diluted and dissipated by their sheer numbers, and so was less effective. Domestic and foreign affairs were in the hands of a small group who also controlled the Treasury, the provinces, the great offices of state; theirs too the glories and the triumphs. The People were worn down by military service and poverty; the spoils of war were seized by the generals and shared with only a few, while the parents and little children of the ordinary soldiers were driven from their homes by rich neighbouring landowners. So power and greed ran riot, contaminated and pillaged everything, and held nothing sacred or worthy of respect, until they plunged themselves to their own destruction.

As soon as men emerged from the ranks of the nobility who put true glory above unjust power, the state began to be convulsed by an earthquake of civil strife. For, when Tiberius and Gaius Gracchus, whose forebears had done much to add to Rome's dominion in the Punic and other wars, came forward to champion the freedom of the common people and set about exposing the crimes of the privileged few, the nobility, reeling back shaken and wounded, fought back against their activities first by way of the allies and the Latins, then by way of the Roman knights, who had been split away from the mass of the commons by hopes of co-operation with the nobles. First Tiberius was killed, then Gaius too a few years later when he started along the same path, and with him M. Fulvius Flaccus.

(b) The background to Tiberius Gracchus' agrarian legislation

PLUTARCH, *Ti. Gracchus* 8.1–3

When the Romans acquired land from their neighbours in war (*during the course of their conquest of Italy*), some of it they sold, but some of it they made public and distributed to landless needy citizens to cultivate on payment of a small rent to the state Treasury. When the rich began to offer higher rents and drive out the poor, a law was passed barring any individual from holding more than 500 *iugera** of land. For a short while this enactment restrained the acquisitiveness of the rich and protected the poor, who were able to stay on the land they had rented and work their original individual plots. But as time passed their well-to-do neighbours took over the tenancies under fictitious names, and in the end held most of the land in their own names. Thus driven out, the poor no longer readily presented themselves for military service and began to stop raising families, with the result that a scarcity of free-born men became apparent throughout Italy, which became full of gangs of foreign slaves used by the rich to cultivate their land after the citizens had been driven out. Scipio's friend Gaius Laelius had made a move to remedy this state of affairs, but faced with the opposition of powerful interests and alarmed by the outcry, he desisted, and so won his nickname of 'Laelius the wise' (*Laelius Sapiens*).

APPIAN, *Civil Wars* 1.7–8

As step by step the Romans subdued Italy in warfare, they were in the habit of confiscating tracts of conquered territory and establishing urban settlements, or sending out colonists of their own to occupy already existing settlements, planning to use these as strongpoints.

The cultivated areas of the land thus acquired by right of conquest on various occasions they either divided among the colonists, or sold it or leased it. But as regards the areas which at the time lay uncultivated because of the fighting – and these were generally the most extensive – they announced that for the time being anyone who wished to cultivate this land might do so for the time being in return for a charge based on the yearly crop, ten per cent on cereal crops and twenty per cent on fruit crops, and they also laid down a poll-charge on any beasts, both large and small, that were pastured. Their aim in this was to encourage the fertility of the Italian race, a race they reckoned to be the most hard-working of peoples, to ensure a plentiful supply of domestic allies.

But things turned out quite otherwise. The rich got hold of the great part of this undistributed land, and, encouraged with the passage of time to believe that nobody would ever now take it away from them, they went on to acquire neighbouring lands and the smallholdings of the poor, partly by purchase and persuasion and partly by force, cultivating wide estates in place of single farms and using slaves as field-workers and herdsmen to avoid having free labourers dragged off from their farm-work to serve in the army. At the same time this slave-ownership brought them a lot of profit from the high birth-rate among their slaves, whose numbers increased since they were not exposed to the risks of military service. In consequence the powerful men became extremely rich and the slave population multiplied throughout the land, while the Italians diminished in numbers and quality, worn down by poverty and taxes and conscription. Even if they chanced to have any respite from these burdens, they spent their time in idleness, since the land was held by the rich, and the rich used slaves to work the land in place of free men.

The Roman people were upset by these developments: Italy would no longer

* one *iugerum* = ⅝ of an acre.

provide them with a plentiful supply of allies; their dominion itself might be endangered by such vast numbers of slaves. But no plan could be thought of to set things right, since it was neither easy nor altogether just to deprive so many people of such extensive possessions which had been held so long, and of the trees they had planted on them, the buildings they had put up and the equipment they had collected; until at long last the tribunes brought in a law that allowed no individual to hold more than 500 *iugera* of this land or pasture more than 100 large or 500 small beasts; and on top of that they fixed a figure for the number of free-born men who had to be employed and who could keep an eye on and report what was going on.

Such then was the scope of what was enacted, and oaths were taken to uphold it and penalties laid down for transgressions of the rules, the supposition being that the excess holdings would quickly be sold back to the poor in small parcels. But no respect was shown for the laws or the oaths: even those few who appeared to show respect fraudulently passed the land over to relatives, while most paid not the slightest heed.

LIVY 6.35.5

C. Licinius and L. Sextius were elected tribunes (*for 367 BC*) and promulgated a law dealing with the limits on land-holdings (*de modo agrorum*) to the effect that no individual might possess more than 500 *iugera*.

LIVY 10.13.14

In this year (*298 BC*) many prosecutions were brought by the plebeian aediles for possessing land in excess of the legal limit; scarcely any of those charged were acquitted, and a strong shackle was put on unrestrained greed.

LIVY 35.10.11–12

That year (*193 BC*) saw a notable aedileship of M. Aemilius Lepidus and L. Aemilius Paulus; they convicted a large number of cattle-ranchers, and from the fines erected gilded shields on the roof of the Temple of Jupiter and constructed two porticoes.

CATO, *For The Rhodians* (167 BC)

"Is there any law so harsh as to declare: If anyone shall have conceived a wish to do such-and-such, he is to pay a large fine; if anyone shall have conceived a wish to hold more than 500 *iugera*, the penalty shall be such-and-such; if anyone shall have conceived a wish to have too large a number of cattle, he is to be mulcted of so much? We all *want* to have more of everything, and there is no crime in just wishing."

CASSIUS HEMINA fr. 17P *(writing in or about the middle of the second century BC)*

...Those who were driven from the public land because of their poverty ...

(c) Some alleged motives for Tiberius Gracchus' programme

PLUTARCH, *Ti. Gracchus* 8.3–9.1

Most allege that Tiberius was spurred on by the rhetorician Diophanes of

Mitylene and the philosopher Blossius of Cumae .... Some put a share in the blame on his mother Cornelia for often upbraiding her sons with her being well-known as the mother-in-law of Scipio Aemilianus and not yet as the mother of the Gracchi. Others say that a certain Spurius Postumius was responsible: Postumius was the same age as Tiberius and his keen rival in repute as a public speaker, and when Tiberius got back from his military service and found Postumius far ahead in reputation and influence and the focus of admiration he decided, it seems, to surpass Postumius by taking up a startling policy which aroused great expectations.

But in a book written by his (*younger*) brother Gaius we are told that it was while Tiberius was travelling through Etruria (*Tuscany*) on his way to Numantia that he noticed how empty the countryside was and that all the field-workers and herdsmen were foreign slaves, and that it was then that there first came into his head the idea of the political programme that proved the beginning of countless ills for the two brothers. But Tiberius' enthusiasm and ambition were above all fired by the popular slogans scrawled on porticoes and walls and public monuments appealing to him to give the public land back to the poor.

Not that Tiberius devised the agrarian law all by himself, for he had the help and advice of brilliant and distinguished leading Romans, among them the chief pontiff Crassus and the jurisconsult Mucius Scaevola, who was consul at the time, and Appius Claudius, the father of Tiberius' wife.

CICERO, *de haruspicum responsis* 43 (56 BC)

Tiberius Gracchus incurred resentment for his part in the Numantine treaty, which he had helped to negotiate while serving as quaestor to the consul C. Mancinus (*137 BC*); and the harsh line which the Senate took in disavowing this treaty made him indignant and apprehensive, and the whole business drove this gallant and distinguished man to abandon the sobriety (*gravitas*) of his forebears.

CICERO, *Brutus* 103 (46 BC)

Tiberius had entered on his tribunate angry with the *boni* because of the resentment caused by the Numantine treaty.

CICERO, *Lucullus* 13 (46 BC)

It is said that those two learned and distinguished brothers, P. Crassus and P. Scaevola, were responsible for Tiberius' laws, Crassus indeed – it is plain to see – quite openly, Scaevola – so it is suspected – more covertly.

(d) Some of Tiberius' public arguments for his agrarian bill

APPIAN, *Civil Wars* 1.9.1–2

When he was tribune Tiberius spoke with grave eloquence on the subject of the Italian people: they were superb soldiers and of kindred stock, but little by little they were being ground down to impoverishment and declining numbers, with no hope of any remedy for their plight. He had harsh things to say too about the slave population as being of no use as soldiers and never to be trusted by their masters, adducing arguments from the calamity recently suffered by the slave-owners in Sicily at the hands of their slaves, who had for their part increased in numbers through employment on the land, and Rome's war against those slaves, difficult and far from short, but developing rather into a long-drawn-out struggle with all sorts and shapes of dangers.

APPIAN, *Civil Wars* 1.11.1

His aim was not economic but human wealth.

PLUTARCH, *Ti. Gracchus* 9.4

Tiberius was fighting for a just and noble cause with a power of words fit to embellish a far less worthy object, and he was a force to be reckoned with and unchallengeable whenever the people crowded round the speakers' platform and he spoke on the subject of the poor: 'Even the wild beasts of Italy at least have their lairs and their nests; but the men who fight and die for their country go destitute, the sky their only covering, drifting homeless and shelterless with their wives and little children. The generals are lying when they call on the rank and file to fight Rome's enemies in defence of hearth and home and holy places; of all those many men there is none who has a family shrine, an ancestral tomb; they fight and die to safeguard the comfort and wealth of others; "masters of the world" they are called – and yet they have not a single clod of earth to call their own.'

APPIAN, *Civil Wars* 1.11.1–4

Tiberius advanced many arguments in favour of his proposal, and in particular he demanded to know: Was it not right that what belonged to all should be shared by all? Did not a citizen always deserve more consideration than a slave? Was not the man who served as a soldier more useful than the man who did not? Was not the man who had a stake in his country more loyal to its common interests?

....Rome held most of the world by war and conquest, and had hopes of winning the rest: now all was at hazard – either to win the whole world by the quality of her manpower or lose to enemies what she already possessed because of weakness and selfishness ... The rich should think on these things and be ready if need be to bestow this land themselves as a free gift on men who would rear children to realise these hopes, and not lose sight of the wood for the trees.

(e) The provisions of the agrarian bill

APPIAN, *Civil Wars* 1.9.3

Tiberius set out to revive the law against any individual's holding more than 500 *iugera*, but he was more generous than the old law in that he added half that amount for children. The excess land recovered was to be distributed among the poor by an elected commission consisting of three men who were to change places among themselves every year.

APPIAN, *Civil Wars* 1.11.5

(*In return for surrendering the excess holdings which they had improved*) the rich were getting each of them a special bonus of a free and perpetually secure title to

500 *iugera*, and a further half of this amount for each of their children if they had any.

PLUTARCH, *Ti. Gracchus* 9.2

Never was a milder or more indulgent law passed against such flagrant misconduct and greed: those who deserved to be tried and punished for breaking the law, and compelled to surrender the land which they were illegally cultivating, were to be given a reward for giving up the land which they had unjustly acquired and making room for citizens who stood in need of succour.

EPITOME OF LIVY, Bk. 58

Tiberius Sempronius Gracchus sought to pass a law in the teeth of opposition from the Senate and the equestrian order that no individual could possess more than 1,000* *iugera* of public land.

CICERO, *de lege agraria* 2.81 (63 BC)

Neither the two Gracchi nor Sulla ventured to touch the Campanian Land.

A reference in line 14 of the Lex Agraria *of 111 BC (Bruns FIR 11) to a particular category of landholdings of 'not more than 30 iugera' has sometimes been seen as indicating the maximum size of allotments under Tiberius Gracchus' agrarian law. But the inference cannot be proved, and other explanations are available.*

(f) Opposition to the bill

CICERO, *pro Sestio* 103 (56 BC)

Tiberius Gracchus sought to carry an agrarian law. It appealed to the common people. It looked likely to safeguard the fortunes of the poor. The best people threw their weight against it because they saw it was a source of discord and believed that to remove the rich from their long-held possessions was to rob the state of its defenders.

APPIAN, *Civil Wars* 1.10.1–6

This (*the election of an agrarian commission of three*) it was that most upset the rich, making them no longer able to ignore the law, as in the past, on account of the commissioners. Nor could they buy the land from the poor, because Tiberius had provided against this by forbidding sales. So they collected together and complained loudly and reproached the poor: they had worked for a long time to improve the land with plantations and buildings; some of them had paid good prices to buy it – were they to lose their money along with their land? Some had family tombs on their land, had accepted it as their portion of the family estate, had spent their wives' dowries to buy it or given it as dowries for their own daughters. Money-lenders pointed to loans they had made on the security of these lands. All in all there was much weeping and wailing and gnashing of teeth.

On the other hand the poor bewailed their reduction from a decent livelihood to extreme indigence and consequent childlessness, since they could not afford

---

* This figure may be corrupt – the MSS readings vary. But the author *de viris illustribus* 64 also has a figure of 1,000 *iugera*.

to raise families. They enumerated the campaigns they had served in to win this very land, and expressed their indignation at being deprived of their share in the common wealth, and reproached the rich for employing slaves – an untrustworthy and vicious breed and hence unemployable as soldiers – instead of free citizens who fought in the army.

Amidst these mutual recriminations and complaints there poured in another great crowd of men with similar anxieties from the colonies and municipalities and wherever else there existed some share in this land, and they lined up behind one side or the other.

APPIAN, *Civil Wars* 1.12

Tiberius ordered the clerk to read out the bill, but one of the other tribunes, Marcus Octavius, who had been put up to block it by the men of property – and at Rome a veto always defeats an affirmative proposal – ordered the clerk to be silent. Whereupon Tiberius adjourned the meeting to the next market-day....

(*To this second meeting*) he came backed by a sufficient force of men calculated to browbeat Octavius into compliance, and with threats bade the clerk read out the bill to the assembly. The clerk began to do so, but on Octavius' command he stopped. Then, as the tribunes fell to mutual recrimination and the crowd began to get noisy, the leading citizens appealed to the tribunes to submit their differences to the Senate. Tiberius seized on this suggestion, supposing that all men of good will must approve of his bill, and hurried off to the Senate House. There, however, amidst their small numbers he met with abuse from the rich; so he at once rushed back to the Forum and announced that on the next market-day he would call for a vote both on his agrarian bill and on Octavius' tribunate and whether it was right that a tribune who was working against the people should continue in his office.

(*When at this third assembly 17 of the 35 tribes had voted for Octavius' deposition and only one more tribe was needed to supply a majority*) Tiberius made a final emotional appeal to Octavius not to stop a project so righteous and so obviously advantageous to all Italy nor frustrate the enthusiastic desire of the people, whose earnest wishes he should rather as a tribune be ready to yield to in some measure*, nor let himself be stripped of his office with contumely. So saying, and calling Heaven to attest his reluctance to dishonour a colleague, since he failed to persuade Octavius, he continued with the voting. At once Octavius reverted to private status, and slipped hurriedly away. Quintus Mummius was elected tribune in his place, and the land bill was voted into law.

PLUTARCH, *Ti. Gracchus* 10–12

Abandoning argument, the rich turned to one of the tribunes, Marcus Octavius. He was a friend and contemporary of Tiberius, and hence to begin with tried to hold back out of regard for him; but in the end the insistent pleas of many powerful men drove him to oppose Tiberius, and he set about blocking his bill.

* In this connection, one may note what Polybius (6.16.5) had to say in his account of the workings of the Roman constitution written some 15 to 20 years before Tiberius' tribunate: 'The tribunes of the plebs are always duty-bound to carry out the will of the People, and above all to make what the People wants their target.'

(Among the tribunes the decisive role is played by the one who uses his veto, for the remaining nine can get nothing done if one tribune vetoes.)

Irritated by this, Tiberius withdrew his generous bill and substituted one more congenial to the masses and now harsher towards the rich, ordering them to quit those parts of the land which they had acquired in contravention of the earlier laws. (*A lively public debate then ensued between the two men in the course of which*) Tiberius appealed to Octavius to give up his contentiousness and offered to pay him the value of his personal holdings out of his own pocket, for all that he was not a very rich man. When Octavius refused, Tiberius issued an edict forbidding all other magistrates to transact any public business. He also put his personal seals on the Treasury in the Temple of Saturn to stop the quaestors making payments in or out, and announced penalties for any praetor who disregarded his edict, with the result that they all gave up transacting their normal business.

(*The first assembly called to vote on the agrarian bill broke up in disorder and Tiberius was persuaded to take the dispute to the Senate*) but, when the influence of the rich in that body ensured that nothing was settled, despairing of any other way of securing a vote on his bill, he turned to an unconstitutional and improper action, the removal of Octavius from office. He told Octavius first to take a vote on whether he (*Tiberius*) should remain in office, undertaking to step down at once if the citizens should so decide. When Octavius rejected this offer, he warned that he would himself call for a vote on Octavius, if after due consideration he would not change his mind, and thereupon dismissed the assembly.

The people met next day, and Tiberius got to his feet and once again tried to persuade Octavius; when he would not be moved, Tiberius put the proposal to strip him of his tribunate .... 17 of the 35 tribes voted for the proposal, and with only one more needed to make Octavius a private citizen, Tiberius called a halt and again made urgent appeals to Octavius .... But Octavius told Tiberius to do what he would. The law was thus carried, and Tiberius told one of his freedman attendants to drag Octavius from the tribunes' platform .... The crowd made a threatening move but the rich ran to link arms to help him, and Octavius managed to get clear and escape the mob, although one of his faithful attendants lost his eyes as he stood in front trying to protect his master – which was all not to Tiberius' liking, who rushed to the spot once he saw what was happening.

(g) The agrarian commission

APPIAN, *Civil Wars* 1.13.2

The first men elected to distribute the land were Gracchus himself, the author of the law, his brother Gaius, and his father-in-law Appius Claudius; for the people were still afraid that the object of the law would not be properly carried out unless Tiberius himself together with all his family was put in charge.

PLUTARCH, *Ti. Gracchus* 13.1

Three men were elected to carry out the adjudication and distribution of lands:

Tiberius himself and his father-in-law Appius Claudius and his brother Gaius, who was away from Italy serving under Scipio Aemilianus at Numantia.

*About a dozen markers (*termini, cippi*) have been found in various parts of Italy with the names of the commissioners, giving them the title of commissioners 'for adjudicating and assigning lands' (IIIviri a(gris) i(udicandis) a(dsignandis)). One was found near Capua in Campania. (See Degrassi,* Inscriptiones Latinae Liberae Rei Publicae, *vol. I, pp. 269–75, for details.)*

(h) The developing quarrel

APPIAN, *Civil Wars* 1.13.3–4

Tiberius was immensely popular because of his law, and was escorted home in triumph as the founder, not of one city or a single race, but of all the peoples of Italy. Afterwards his victorious supporters went back to the country districts from which they had come in to support his programme, while the losers stayed behind nursing their grievances and talking about how once he had reverted to private status Tiberius would be sorry for his actions in doing violence to the sacred and inviolate office of a tribune and sowing so many seeds of future strife in Italy.

PLUTARCH, *Ti. Gracchus* 14–15

Attalus Philometer had died, and Eudemus of Pergamum arrived in Rome with the king's will, which named the Roman People as his heir. Courting popular favour, Tiberius at once published a proposal that when the royal moneys were received they should be made available to provide capital and stock for those citizens who obtained allotments of land; as for the cities of the Attalid kingdom, that was no business of the Senate – he would himself bring proposals before the People. This really led to a head-on collision with the Senate, where Pompeius got up and said that he knew – he lived near Tiberius – that Eudemus had presented him with a royal diadem and robe of purple as the king of Rome. Quintus Metellus also rounded on Tiberius: whenever Tiberius' father had been walking home after a dinner when he was censor people used to douse their lights for fear that their dining and drinking might be thought immoderately prolonged, and now the son was lighted home at night by the hooligan dregs of the common people.

Titus Annius challenged Tiberius to an inquiry as to whether he had not done dishonour to a colleague whose office was sacred and by law inviolate .... and he asked: 'If you decide to disgrace me and abuse me, and I appeal to one of your colleagues, and he come to my rescue, and you get angry, will your strip him of his office too?' This question is said to have left Tiberius at a loss for an answer and reduced his bold eloquence to silence. So on that occasion he dismissed the assembly. But, perceiving that not only the powerful but the mass of the people too were disturbed by his handling of Octavius – for down to that day the prestige of the tribunes had been too great and honourable to be done away with and abused – (*he gave a reasoned public defence of his conduct*). A tribune was sacrosanct and inviolate in that he was solemnly pledged to the people and stood at their head; but, should he shift his stance and do them wrong and check their strength and set their vote at naught, then he stripped himself of office by failing to do what he had been elected to do. If a tribune wanted to demolish the

Capitol or burn down the dockyard, he must be allowed to do it: he was a tribune, albeit a wicked tribune; but if he sought to destroy the people, he was not a tribune. If the people could commit a consul to prison, it was surely monstrous that they could not deprive a tribune of his powers if he used them against the people's interests: both tribune and consul alike were elected by the people....If it was right for a man to be elected tribune by a majority of the tribes, it must surely be even more right for him to be deprived of his office by the unanimous decision of all the tribes.

EPITOME OF LIVY, Bk. 58

Tiberius became so angry with his opponents that he had a law passed to annul the powers of his colleague M. Octavius who was championing the other side, and had himself and his brother Gaius and his father-in-law Appius Claudius elected as the three commissioners for land-distribution. He also published a second agrarian bill to bring more land within his scope, empowering the same three men to adjudicate which was public land and which private. Then, when it turned out that there was not enough land available for distribution, to avoid annoying the commons, whose greed he had inflamed to hopes that there would be plenty, he announced that he would bring in a bill to divide the moneys left to the Roman People by King Attalus of Pergamum among those who were expected to be given land-grants under the agrarian law. This succession of insults deeply shocked the Senate, above all the former consul Titus Annius: when he had wound up his attack on Tiberius in the Senate, he was haled off by Tiberius and denounced to the people, whereupon he launched a public attack on Tiberius from the speakers' platform.

CICERO, *de legibus* 3.24 (52–44 BC)

Tiberius was himself overthrown by the tribune whose veto he had disregarded and whom he had removed from office. For what else was his undoing but his abrogation of an obstructive colleague's powers?

CICERO, *Brutus* 95 (46 BC)

What broke Tiberius Gracchus was the resolute obduracy which Marcus Octavius displayed in the noblest of causes.

(i) Tiberius' attempted re-election, and his death

APPIAN, *Civil Wars* 1.14–16

It was now summer, and the tribunician elections were imminent. As the day drew near, the rich were openly backing Tiberius' bitterest enemies. Afraid of what might happen to him if he were not elected to a second tribunate for the coming year, he appealed to his countrymen supporters to come in for the voting; but they were busy with their summer work, so with time running out he was forced back onto the city poor, tramping all over Rome asking each individually to consider the danger he was in on their account and vote for him. When the voting began the first two tribes declared for him, but the rich objected that it was unconstitutional for a man to hold the tribunate two years running. The tribune Rubrius, on whom the lot had fallen to preside that day, was in two minds about this, so Mummius, the tribune who had been elected to replace Octavius, told him to surrender the presidency to himself. Rubrius was prepared to do so, but the other tribunes objected and held that the lots must be drawn again....As the dispute became bitter, a discomfited Tiberius adjourned the meeting to the following day....

Tiberius mustered his supporters while it was still dark, and told them a special signal which would be given if it were to come to open fighting; they seized the Capitoline temple, where the count was to take place, and occupied the middle ground of the assembly. When he met obstruction from the tribunes and the rich who would not allow a vote to be taken on his election, he raised the signal. (*A violent and confused mêlée then ensued with improvised weapons*) and there were wild rumours that Tiberius had deposed all his fellow-tribunes – they were nowhere to be seen, which made this plausible – and had declared himself tribune for the next year without election.

Meanwhile the Senate was meeting in the Temple of Fides. I find it astonishing that they never thought of appointing a dictator to deal with this emergency....Whatever decision they did reach, they marched off up to the Capitol with the Chief Pontiff Scipio Nasica at their head shouting out for everyone who wished to save his country to fall in and follow him....As he neared the temple and set about the Gracchans, they fell back out of awe for his elevated rank and at the spectacle of the Senate following behind. Scipio's people wrested the cudgels from the Gracchans' own hands and broke up benches and other assembly paraphernalia and belaboured them and drove them back over the steep rim of the hill. Many Gracchan supporters perished in this affray, and Tiberius himself was killed at the feet of the statues of the kings as he crouched near the door of the temple. That night all the bodies were thrown into the Tiber.

PLUTARCH, *Ti Gracchus* 16–19

Seeing the threatening coalition that was building up against him, Tiberius' friends urged him to try for a second tribunate for the coming year; and he at once set to winning over the masses with further laws reducing the period of military service, allowing appeal to the People from court decisions, adding an equal number of knights to the court-panels, at that time exclusively senatorial in composition, and in general cutting down the power of the Senate, motivated more by passion and a spirit of contention than by calm calculation of what was right and sensible. As the votes were being cast and he and his supporters realised that his opponents were winning – for not all the voters were present at the assembly – after first trying to win time by personal attacks on the tribunes they dismissed the assembly with orders that it should meet the next day...

(*That night was marked by many ill omens, but in the morning a reluctant Tiberius was persuaded by his friends to attend the assembly.*) To start with he got a rapturous reception, his arrival was greeted with loud and friendly cheering, and he climbed the hill among enthusiastic greetings as men clustered round to protect him. When Mucius* again commenced the voting, however, none of the customary formalities could be gone through thanks to the uproar raised by

---

* Mucius was, according to Plutarch, the man elected to take Octavius' place as tribune. Appian gives his name as Mummius, Orosius gives it as Minucius. We cannot say which is the correct name.

people on the outskirts of the crowd, where a lot of shoving and scuffling was going on as hostile elements tried to force a way in and join the assembly. Amid all this Fulvius Flaccus, a distinguished senator, unable to make himself heard, signified by his gestures that he wanted a private word with Tiberius, who ordered the crowd to make a path for him. Getting through with difficulty, Flaccus told Tiberius that in the Senate the rich, unable to prevail on the consul, were planning to take matters into their own hands and kill him, and had many slaves and friends waiting fully-armed to help them.

When Tiberius passed this on to his companions, they at once began to gird up their gowns, and took the pikes which the attendants used to hold back the crowd and broke them up and shared them out among themselves so as to use the pieces to ward off any attack. Those some way away were puzzled and wanted to know what was happening, so Tiberius put his hand to his head as a visible indication that his life was in danger – for he could not make himself heard. But his opponents, seeing this gesture, rushed off to the Senate with the news that Tiberius was asking for a crown....The whole House was in an uproar, and Scipio Nasica* called on the consul to 'save Rome and destroy the tyrant'. The consul's restrained reply was that he would not initiate violence or kill any citizen without due trial, but that if Tiberius should persuade or force the assembly to reach any unlawful decision he would hold it invalid. Nasica jumped up and shouted: 'Since our chief magistrate is a traitor, let everyone who wants to defend the laws follow me.' So saying he wrapped the hem of his toga over his head and set off for the Capitol. Every senator who followed his lead wrapped his own gown round one arm, and they pushed aside all who stood in their path – their high rank overawed everyone, who all ran away and trampled on each other in their flight; the senators' followers carried clubs and staves which they had brought with them from home, but they themselves seized legs and other pieces from broken benches and climbed towards Tiberius, belabouring those who stood in front of him, who took to their heels and were killed. As Tiberius himself tried to escape someone grabbed his clothing; he slipped out of his toga and ran off in his tunic, but tripped over some of his people who had fallen in front of him, and fell. As he got up, the first blow was clearly seen to be struck by one of his fellow-tribunes, Publius Satureius, who hit him over the head with the leg of a stool. Lucius Rufus claimed the credit for the second blow, as if it were something to boast about. Three hundred others died, all from blows with clubs and stones, none from cold steel.

VELLEIUS PATERCULUS, 2.2.2–2.3.2

One hundred and sixty two years ago (*in 133 BC*) Tiberius Gracchus abandoned the *boni* and promised citizenship to the whole of Italy, and at the same time by also publishing agrarian proposals turned everything upside down and led his country into terrible blind dangers. When his colleague Octavius stood up for the common good he removed him from office, and he made himself and his

---

* P. Cornelius Scipio Nasica (consul 138 BC, and Chief Pontiff till his death in 132 BC) was Tiberius Gracchus' cousin. According to Plutarch, he had led the opposition to the agrarian bill in the Senate and was responsible for the Senate's allocating the commissioners insultingly inadequate working funds. He was himself allegedly a very large holder of public land.

father-in-law the ex-consul Appius and his still very young brother Gaius commissioners for distributing land and founding colonies. Thereupon P. Scipio Nasica, though he was but a private citizen holding no magistracy... wrapped the edge of his toga round his left arm, and standing at the top of the steps on the upper part of the Capitoline called on all those who wished to save the state to follow him. Then the optimates, the senators and the more numerous and better section of the knights, and those of the commons who had not been infected by Tiberius' pernicious plans, rushed on Gracchus as he stood in the open with his gangs, haranguing a crowd gathering from pretty well all Italy. Tiberius ran away down the slope, but was hit with a bit of wood from a bench, and so brought to an untimely end a life which he could have lived out in true glory.

CASSIUS DIO *fragment* **83**

Gracchus introduced some laws offering relief to the common soldier, and he sought to transfer the law-courts from the Senate to the knights....When the end of his tribunate drew near and he was threatened with attack from his enemies once he gave it up, he attempted to get elected for the following year along with his brother, and have his father-in-law elected consul.

(j) Epilogue

PLUTARCH, *Ti. Gracchus* **21.1–3**

The Senate, aware of the need to conciliate popular feeling, put up no opposition to the distribution of the land, and allowed the assembly to elect another commissioner to take Tiberius' place. The result was the election of Gracchus' kinsman P. Crassus – his daughter Licinia was Gaius Gracchus' wife....But the people were angry at Tiberius' death and clearly seeking a chance for revenge, and Nasica was already being threatened with indictments; so, fearing for his safety, the Senate invented an appointment for him in the province of Asia. Wherever he went he was hissed and booed and reviled, for people did not hide their hatred....So he slipped away out of Italy, although as Chief Pontiff he had very important religious duties. Not long afterwards, after some restless wandering, he died near Pergamum.

CICERO, *de domo* **91** (56 BC)

I chose not (*in 58 BC*) to try to defend the national interest against armed violence since I could look for no official support – not that I disapproved of the action of the gallant P. Scipio when, for all that he held no official powers, he used force against Tiberius Gracchus; no, but Scipio's action was promptly supported by the then consul, P. Mucius (*Scaevola*), who in a whole string of senatorial decrees not only defended what Nasica had done but even added lustre to it. In my own case, however, even if you were killed, Clodius, I would have had to fight it out in open warfare with both the consuls, or, if you stayed alive, with all three of you.

CICERO, *de oratore* **2.285** (55 BC)

When M. (*Fulvius*) Flaccus delivered a scurrilous attack on Scipio Nasica and proposed P. Mucius Scaevola as judge, 'I enter a formal objection under oath,' said Nasica; 'Scaevola is not a fair man.' As the Senate murmured in shocked disapproval, 'Ah, gentlemen,' said Scipio, 'it is not merely on the grounds that he is not fair to me – he is never fair to anybody'.

VALERIUS MAXIMUS 5.3.2e

Who does not know that Scipio Nasica earned as much glory as a private citizen as the two Scipiones Africani did in command of armies, when he refused to sit by and allow Tiberius Gracchus' foul hand to throttle the life out of his country? But the totally unjust estimation of his splendid qualities by his fellow citizens meant that he too had to leave Rome under the pretext of a legateship. He withdrew to Pergamum, and there spent what remained of his life with no regret for his ungrateful fatherland.

*Cicero (*de re pub. *1.6) also speaks of the 'hostile resentment' (*invidia*) which Nasica incurred for his action.*

132 BC   Consuls: P. Popillius Laenas, P. Rupilius

(a) Special Court set up to try Tiberius Gracchus' supporters

SALLUST, *Jugurthine War* 31.7

After the murder of Tiberius Gracchus, who they said was aiming to make himself king, a special court was set up against the Roman commons.

CICERO, *de amicitia* 37 (44 BC)

Gaius Blossius of Cumae, a protégé of your family, Scaevola, came to see me (*Gaius Laelius*) to plead for mercy when I was a member of the committee advising the consuls Laenas and Rupilius. The reason he gave for asking me to show leniency was that he held Tiberius Gracchus in such high regard that he thought it his duty to do anything Tiberius told him. 'What', said I, 'even if he told you to set fire to the Capitol?' 'He would never have given such an order', replied Blossius, 'but, if he had, I would have obeyed.'....This madman, in fear of a fresh inquiry, fled to Asia, joined our enemies, and paid a heavy and well-deserved penalty for his crimes against our country.

VALERIUS MAXIMUS 4.7.1

When the Senate instructed the consuls Rupilius and Laenas to proceed in the traditional way against those who had supported Gracchus....(*there follows the story about Blossius' exchange with Laelius: see above*).

PLUTARCH, *Ti. Gracchus* 20.2–3

Some of Tiberius' friends were driven into exile without trial, others were seized and put to death, among them the rhetorician Diophanes....Blossius of Cumae was brought before the consuls and in answer to questioning admitted that he had acted under Tiberius' orders. 'What', asked Nasica, 'if he had ordered you to set fire to the Capitol?' At first Blossius sought to deny that Tiberius would ever have given such an order, but after he had been pressed frequently on this point by many of those present, 'Well', he said, 'if he had ordered it, I would have accepted that it was a perfectly proper thing to do; for he would never have given such an order had it not been for the good of the people.' Blossius got away and later joined Aristonicus in Asia, where he took his own life when Aristonicus' revolt collapsed.

See further below, 123 BC and exile of Popillius Laenas.

(b) An inscription found near Forum Popillii in Lucania (Val di Diano)

DESSAU *ILS* 23

I made a road from Regium to Capua, and along that road I set up all the bridges, milestones and posting-stations....As praetor in Sicily I also hunted down the runaway slaves of the Italians, and I handed 917 back to their owners. I was also the first man to compel herdsmen to give place to arable farmers on the public land. Here I built a market-place and public buildings.

The identity of the (unnamed) author of this inscription is uncertain. He could be either P. Popillius Laenas (praetor by 135 BC, consul 132 BC) or T. Annius Rufus (praetor by 131 BC, consul 128 BC).

(c) The end of the slave war in Sicily

OROSIUS 5.9.7

When the consul Rupilius took over the command, he captured Tauromenium and Henna, the securest strongholds of the rebel slaves. It is reported that more than 20,000 slaves were butchered on that occasion.

DIODORUS SICULUS 24.2.23

Rupilius with a small force overran the whole of Sicily faster than anyone had expected and completely freed the island of brigandage.

131 BC   Consuls: P. Licinius Crassus Mucianus, L. Valerius Flaccus
**   Censors: Q. Caecilius Metellus Macedonicus, Q. Pompeius**

(a) Tribunician activities of C. Papirius Carbo*

CICERO, *de oratore* 2.170 (55 BC)

And take this remark of Crassus (*consul 95 BC*) when he was a young man: 'The mere fact that you defended Opimius, Carbo, did not make people take you for one of the *boni*. It was very obvious that you were playing a part, that you were after something – because you repeatedly condemned Tiberius Gracchus' murder in your public harangues, because you had a hand in the death of P. (*Cornelius Scipio Aemilianus*) Africanus, because you carried that law of yours when you were tribune, because you have always been at odds with the *boni*.'

CICERO, *de legibus* 3.35 (52–44 BC)

There are three ballot laws. First, the Gabinian Law (*139 BC*) which applied the ballot to voting at magisterial elections, carried by an obscure man of no

---

* The date of the tribunate of Carbo could be either 131 or 130 BC: the available evidence does not enable us to make a confident choice between one year or the other.

account. Two years later came the second, the Cassian Law (*137 BC*), extending it to voting at trials before the People, carried by L. Cassius, a noble, but, if you will forgive my saying so, a noble who was at odds with the *boni* and kept a demagogic ear wide open to catch any silly ideas that were going around. The third is the law which Carbo carried prescribing the use of the ballot in voting on legislative proposals; Carbo was a disruptive and disreputable character, whose later volte-face back to the side of the *boni* could not save him from his doom at their hands.

CICERO, *de amicitia* 95 (44 BC)

What honeyed words Gaius Papirius poured into the ears of the listening throng when he was trying to carry a law about the re-election of tribunes of the plebs! Our people argued against it, but I (*the speaker is Gaius Laelius, and the dramatic date of the dialogue is 129 BC*) will say nothing of my own part, I would much rather talk about Scipio (*Aemilianus*). Ye gods, what power there was in his speech on that occasion, what majesty!...But you were both of you there, and his speech is available to be read. As a result, this 'popular' law was defeated by the popular vote.

EPITOME OF LIVY, Bk. 59

When Carbo was tribune, he proposed a law that any man might be elected tribune as often as he chose. P. Africanus delivered a very powerful speech against this proposal, in the course of which he declared that the killing of Tiberius Gracchus had been justified. Gaius Gracchus spoke on the other side, in favour of the bill, but Scipio won the day.

VELLEIUS PATERCULUS 2.4.4

When the tribune Carbo demanded to know what Scipio Aemilanus thought about the killing of Tiberius Gracchus, Scipio's answer was that, if Gracchus had been aiming at supreme power, his killing had been justified. When the whole crowd burst into an uproar, 'I have far too often', said Scipio, 'faced the armies of our enemies and been unshaken by the din they raised for me to be disturbed by the clamourings of a crowd like you, mere stepchildren of Italy'.

For much the same story, see Cicero, de oratore *2.106 and* pro Milone *8.*

(b) The Censorship

EPITOME OF LIVY, Bk. 59

The count of citizens totalled 317,823, not including widows or boys and girls in wardship. The censor Q. Metellus moved that everyone should be compelled to take a wife and raise children. His speech survives, and the Emperor Augustus Caesar later read it out in the Senate, when he was engaged on his own marriage legislation, as specially appropriate to his own times.

AULUS GELLIUS, *Attic Nights* 1.6 (*citing fragment from Metellus' speech*)

'If, citizens, we could live our lives as bachelors, we should be free from all such trials and tribulations. But since Nature has so ordered things that, while we cannot live with our wives comfortably enough, without them life is impossible, we must set our own short-lived gratification on one side and take thought for lasting salvation.'

(c) The war in Asia

STRABO 14.1.38

...The town of Leucae, which Aristonicus induced to rebel after the death of Attalus Philometer. Aristonicus was apparently of the royal line, and planned to win the kingdom for himself. He was then defeated in a naval engagement near Cumae by the Ephesians and driven out, retreating deep inland, where he quickly collected a large number of poor men and of slaves whom he promised to free. He called them *Heliopolitai* (*'Citizens of the Sun'*). He first fell upon Thyateira, then captured Apollonia, then attacked other strongpoints. But he did not last very long; the cities quickly sent a strong force, and King Nicomedes of Bithynia and the kings of Cappadocia sent help. Then five legates arrived from Rome, followed by an army under the consul Publius Crassus, and later Marcus Perperna, who ended the war, capturing Aristonicus and sending him to Rome....Perperna fell ill and died, and Crassus was killed in fighting near Leucae. Then the consul Manius Aquilius arrived with ten legates and organised the province on the system that still survives.

JUSTIN 36.4.6

Aristonicus was an illegitimate son of Eumenes by his mistress Ephesia, herself a musician's daughter. After Attalus' death, he invaded Asia as if it were his own kingdom by right of birth.

DIODORUS SICULUS 34.2.26

Aristonicus was joined by the slaves, driven to desperation by their maltreatment. They did terrible damage to many cities.

STRABO 14.1.38

Five envoys arrived in Asia from Rome, and they were followed by an army under the consul Publius Crassus.

EPITOME OF LIVY, Bk. 59

The consul P. Licinius Crassus set out to fight Aristonicus, although he was Chief Pontiff and no previous holder of that office had ever before left Italy.

CICERO, *Philippics* 11.18 (43 BC)

When P. Licinius and L. Valerius were consuls, a war had to be fought against Aristonicus. The Roman People was asked who was to take command. Crassus, consul and Chief Pontiff, threatened to fine his colleague Flaccus, who was the Priest of Mars, if he neglected his sacred duties. The People remitted the fine, but instructed the Priest to obey the Pontiff. But even then the Roman People declined to give the command to a non-magistrate, although Africanus, who had celebrated a triumph over the Numantines the previous year, was available. For all his unmatchable reputation as a great general, only two tribes voted for him. Thus the Roman People preferred to entrust the conduct of the war to the consul Crassus rather than to the private citizen Africanus.

EUTROPIUS 4.20

When the Pontiff P. Licinius Crassus was sent to fight Aristonicus, the kings gave him unlimited support: Rome received help from King Nicomedes of Bithynia, Mithridates of Pontus (with whom there was later a very serious war), Ariarathes of Cappadocia, and Pylaemenes of Paphlagonia. Despite this, Crassus was defeated in the field and killed.

JUSTIN 34.4.8

Crassus, more intent on plunder than on fighting, gave battle at the very end of the year, but disposed his forces clumsily. He was beaten, and paid for his rash greed with his own blood.

130 BC   Consuls: L. Cornelius Lentulus, M. Perperna.

Lentulus died in office, and was succeeded by Ap. Claudius Pulcher, to be distinguished from Ap. Claudius Pulcher, consul in 143 BC (agrarian commissioner, and father-in-law of Tiberius Gracchus), who was probably his cousin.

The war in Asia

EUTROPIUS 4.20

The consul Perperna was due to succeed Crassus in Asia. Hearing the bad news from there, he arrived with all speed, and defeated Aristonicus in the field. Aristonicus took refuge in Stratoniceia, which Perperna besieged, and starved him into surrender. While in prison, Aristonicus was garrotted by order of the Senate, since no triumph could be celebrated, Perperna having died at Pergamum on his way back to Rome.

129 BC   Consuls: C. Sempronius Tuditanus, M'. Aquillius

(a) Opposition to the activities of the agrarian commission

APPIAN, *Civil Wars* 1.18–20

As the possessors neglected to register their holdings, the agrarian commissioners (*Gaius Gracchus, M. Fulvius Flaccus, and C. Papirius Carbo – the latter two elected to replace Claudius and Crassus, both now dead*) issued an announcement inviting anyone to come forward and lay information. Straightaway a whole crop of difficult litigation sprang up. Wherever other adjoining land had been sold or divided among Rome's allies, the whole area was subjected to an inquisition as to the title owing to the measuring out of the public land to discover how it had been sold or divided. Not everybody still had the original conveyances or title-deeds, and even those which did come to light were vague. As the current survey proceeded, some found themselves being moved from land with plantations and buildings to bare land, others from cultivated land to uncultivated land, or land that was marshy or undrained; the original surveys had not been done with great care, the land having originally been so much war-booty. The earlier declaration that anyone who chose might cultivate unassigned land had encouraged many to bring under cultivation tracts immediately adjoining their own property, thus blurring the demarcation between the two, and the sheer passage of time had brought changes everywhere. Hence the illegal aggrandisements of the rich, though extensive, were difficult to identify with precision. So it was nothing short of a massive game of musical chairs, with everybody being moved out of his own place and settled down in somebody else's.

All this then, and the rapid decisions made by the commissioners in their adjudication, proved intolerable to the Italians, who appealed to Cornelius Scipio (*Aemilianus*), the destroyer of Carthage, to defend them against the injustices they were suffering. Having enjoyed their willing support in the wars he had fought, Scipio was reluctant to ignore this appeal. He took the matter to the Senate. He did not openly criticise Gracchus' law because of popular feeling, but he did stress its troublesome aspects, and moved that the adjudications should not be left to be conducted by the commissioners, on the grounds that they were distrusted by the claimants, but entrusted to others.

In this he won his point, being reckoned a just man; and Tuditanus, one of the two consuls in office, was appointed to adjudicate these issues. But he had barely begun to touch his task when, appreciating its troublesomeness, he went off to fight a war in Illyria, using this as an excuse for his not deciding the disputes, and the agrarian commissioners were reduced to inactivity since nobody approached them to have an issued adjudicated. As a result popular dislike and resentment arose against Scipio – a man to whom they had displayed great favour and whom they had often supported against the powerful and had twice elected consul in defiance of the normal rules, and now saw acting against the people on behalf of the Italians. Observing this, his political enemies began to proclaim that he was set on abolishing Gracchus' law root and branch, and planning to resort to armed strife and bloodshed to achieve this end.

These allegations alarmed the people, until finally Scipio, having one evening set by him a notebook in which he planned that night to compose a speech to deliver to the people, was later found dead without any visible marks of violence. Whether this was the work of Cornelia, Gracchus' mother, and whether in this she was abetted by Sempronia, Gracchus' sister, the ill-favoured, childless, unloved and unloving wife of Scipio, or whether, as some think, he took his own life because he could see that he would not be able to fulfil what he had promised, is unknown. Some say that under torture his slaves declared that some strangers had come into the back of the house by night and smothered him, but that this information was not acted on because of the continuing ugly mood of the populace, who were glad that he was dead.

EPITOME OF LIVY, Bk. 59

Disturbances were provoked by the three commissioners who had been elected to distribute the land, Fulvius Flaccus, Gaius Gracchus, and C. Papirius Carbo. They were opposed by P. Scipio Africanus. One day this brave and gallant gentleman arrived home, and next morning he was found dead in his bed.

Suspicion chiefly fell on his wife Sempronia, for having poisoned him, because she was the sister of the Gracchi with whom Africanus had been at odds. However, no formal enquiry was held into his death; and, once he was gone, the triumviral disturbances blazed up more fiercely.

VALERIUS MAXIMUS 4.1.12

Metellus Macedonicus had quarrelled bitterly with Scipio Africanus....Nevertheless, when he heard the cry go up that Scipio was dead, he rushed out into the street and declared, sad of face and broken-voiced: 'To me, citizens, to me! Rome's walls are breached. A crime of violence has been done to Scipio Africanus as he lay abed in his own home.'

The finger of suspicion for Scipio's death was pointed also at Fulvius Flaccus, and even Gaius Gracchus himself (Plutarch, Gaius Gracchus 10), and at Papirius Carbo (Cicero, ad familiares 9.21.3; ad Q.F. 2.3.3). A passage from the funeral speech delivered by Laelius which is cited by the Bobbiensis scholiast on Cicero (p.118 Stangl) seems to point to natural causes, but the text is uncertain: see Badian, JRS 46 (1956) 220.

CASSIUS DIO fr. 83.2

Once Scipio had been removed, the cause of the powerful was once again weakened, with the result that the agrarian commissioners had Italy at their mercy, so to speak, to plunder as they would.

(b) Some comments on the general political situation

Cicero's dialogue On the Republic *is set in the year 129 BC not long before Scipio's death, and takes the form of a discussion between Scipio, Laelius and other close friends. Laelius is speaking:*

CICERO, de re publica 1.31 (52 BC)

The death of Tiberius Gracchus and already before that the whole pattern of his tribunate has split a united people into two. The spiteful detractors of Scipio, taking their lead from Publius Crassus and Appius Claudius, still now that those two are dead control the other division of the Senate which disagrees with all of you (*Scipio and his friends*) on the prompting of Metellus (*Macedonicus*) and P. Mucius (*Scaevola*). Our allies and the Latins have been provoked, treaties have been violated, every day three revolutionary agrarian commissioners are up to some new devilry, decent men of property have been evicted from their lands, yet they will not allow the one man who can (*i.e. Scipio*) to rescue the state from these great perils that threaten it.

CICERO, de re publica 3.41

...Tiberius Gracchus persevered on behalf of the citizens of Rome but paid no heed to the rights and treaties of allies and Latins. If this practice, this lack of self-restraint, should begin to become more widespread, if our dominion should cease to be based on law and come to rely on force, so that those who have up till now given us their willing obedience should be held subject through fear....then I am concerned for our posterity and for Rome's own immortality, which could abide for evermore, if only we were to live by our ancestral institutions and practices.

(c) Proposal to pass a bill in the plebeian assembly to exclude senators from membership of the equestrian centuries in the centuriate assembly

CICERO, *de re publica* 4.2

(....*the equestrian centuries*) where the Senate also casts its votes. Just now too many people are stupidly eager to abolish this advantageous arrangement, and searching for a novel sort of bribe by way of some plebiscite or other for surrendering the public horse.

(d) Asia organised as a province

FLORUS 1.35

Aquilius finished off the last stages of the war in Asia, compelling some cities there to capitulate by – a dreadful deed – poisoning their water-supplies. This tactic hastened his victory, and besmirched it.

STRABO 14.1.38

Manius Aquillius arrived accompanied by ten legates and organised the province in the form which it still preserves to this day (*viz., the early Principate*).

The years 128 and 127 BC contain no material worthy of inclusion.

126 BC   Consuls: M. Aemilius Lepidus, L. Aurelius Orestes

(a) The aliens expulsion law of M. Junius Pennus

CICERO, *Brutus* 109 (46 BC)

Marcus Pennus   your kinsman, Brutus – when he was tribune crossed swords with Gaius Gracchus, who was slightly younger than himself. For, when M. Lepidus and L. Orestes were consuls, Gracchus was only a quaestor and Pennus was a tribune. He was the son of the Marcus Pennus who had been consul with Q. Aelius (*167 BC*); a man of the highest promise, he died while holding the aedileship (*c. 123 BC*)

CICERO, *de officiis* 3.47 (44 BC)

It was a wicked thing to bar any state to non-citizens and physically expel them, as Pennus did in our fathers' day, and Papius more recently (*65 BC*). Of course, it is perfectly justifiable to forbid a non-citizen to masquerade as a citizen, as was done by the law carried by those wisest of consuls, Crassus and Scaevola (*95 BC*); but to forbid non-citizens to enter or live in a state is downright uncivilised.

FESTUS p.388L = *ORF²* p.180

Gaius Gracchus, in a passage of the speech which he composed on the law of Pennus and non-citizens, talks of "those nations which have lost their independence through, apart from anything else, greed and stupidity".

(b) Gaius Gracchus quaestor

CICERO, *de divinatione* **1.56** (45–44 BC)

This same Coelius has written of how Gaius Gracchus told a lot of people that, when he was in two minds about standing for the quaestorship, his brother Tiberius appeared to him in a dream, and asked him: "Why this hesitation? Like it or not, you are fated to meet the same death as I did." This, Coelius writes, he heard with his own ears from Gaius before he had become tribune, and Gaius had told many others too.

PLUTARCH, *C. Gracchus* **1–2**

Gaius Gracchus made other orators seem children compared with himself, and once more the men in power became alarmed, and there was much talk among them of how they would not let Gaius proceed to a tribunate. Then, as luck would have it, the lot fell to Gaius when he was quaestor to accompany the consul Orestes to Sardinia. This delighted his enemies; but it did not displease Gaius either, for he liked the military life and was as well fitted for fighting in the field as in the law-courts,,,

In Sardinia he displayed all-round ability, and far surpassed all the other younger men in battles against hostile tribes, in the justice of his dealings with Rome's subjects, and in loyal devotion to his commander-in-chief, while in commonsense and frugality and sheer hard work he outstripped even his seniors. That winter in Sardinia was hard and sickly. Orestes requisitioned supplies of clothing for his men from the local communities, but they appealed to Rome to be relieved of this burden, and the Senate granted their request and ordered Orestes to look elsewhere for clothing for his troops. With Orestes at a loss and the men suffering badly, Gaius went round the Sardinian towns and persuaded them voluntarily to send clothing and other help to the soldiers. This was reported back to Rome, and worried the Senate: it looked like the opening shots in a campaign of demagoguery. And when a delegation arrived from King Micipsa in Africa with an offer from the king to send corn to the commander in Sardinia as a favour to Gaius, the Senate was indignant and sent them packing.

EPITOME OF LIVY, Bk. 60

The consul L. Orestes subdued a rebellion in Sardinia.

125 BC   Consuls: M. Plautius Hypsaeus, M. Fulvius Flaccus
**   Censors: Cn. Servilius Caepio, L. Cassius Longinus Ravilla**

(a) The census

EPITOME OF LIVY, Bk. 60

The count of citizens totalled 393,736.

(b) Franchise proposal of the consul Flaccus

VALERIUS MAXIMUS 9.5.1

The consul M. Fulvius Flaccus was making shocking proposals for granting citizenship, and the right of appeal to the People to anyone who did not want to take up the grant of citizenship. With difficulty he was compelled to appear before the Senate and there urged to desist from what he was doing with a mixture of threats and appeals, but he refused to answer.

APPIAN, *Civil Wars* 1.21.1–4

(*Even with Scipio dead*) the possessors none the less continued to use all manner of pretexts and excuses to delay any land-distributions. So some people came up with a proposal to grant Roman citizenship to all the allies, since it was they who were being most obstructive, the idea being that in return for a greater reward they would stop arguing about the land. For their part the Italians were very happy to fall in with this offer, for they put a higher value on the citizenship than on their lands. Their chief collaborator was above all others Fulvius Flaccus, consul that year and also one of the agrarian commissioners. The Senate was unhappy about what would happen if they gave political equality to their subjects. And this project came to nothing.

APPIAN, *Civil Wars* 1.34.4

As consul Fulvius Flaccus had been the very first man above all others to bring right into the open an Italian agitation for Roman citizenship, holding out the prospect of their being partners in empire instead of subjects. He introduced the bill, and pressed for it strongly, but the Senate on this account sent him off to a military command.

EPITOME OF LIVY, Bk. 60

M. Fulvius Flaccus was the first man to conquer the Ligurians north of the Alps, when he was sent to help Marseilles against the Gallic Salluvii, who were ravaging Massilian territory.

(c) Orestes' command in Sardinia extended

PLUTARCH, *C. Gracchus* 2

The Senate decreed that the troops in Sardinia should be relieved and replaced, but that Orestes should stay on, so that Gaius would have also to stay on there as his quaestor.

(d) Revolt and destruction of Fregellae, a Latin colony situated some 100 kilometres S.E. of Rome

EPITOME OF LIVY, Bk. 60

The praetor L. Opimius accepted the capitulation of the Fregellans, who had revolted. He destroyed Fregellae itself.

ASCONIUS p. 17 (Clark)

It is well known that Opimius in his praetorship captured Fregellae, and as a

result was seen to have repressed all the other allies of the Latin Name, who
were ill-disposed.

124 BC   Consuls: C. Cassius Longinus, C. Sextius Calvinus

(a) Fabrateria founded to replace Fregellae

VELLEIUS PATERCULUS 1.15

In the consulship of Cassius Longinus and Sextius Calvinus Fabrateria was
founded.

*(Fabrateria was pretty certainly not a Latin colony, as Fregellae had been, but a
Roman citizen colony.)*

(b) Gaius Gracchus comes back from Sardinia and is elected tribune for 123 BC

APPIAN, *Civil Wars* 1.21.4–5

(Flaccus' franchise proposal of 125 BC had come to nothing), and the people, who
had still been hopeful about the land, were dispirited. While in this mood they
were delighted when Gaius Gracchus, one of the agrarian commissioners and
the younger brother of the author of the agrarian law, came forward for the
tribunate, though he had lain low for a long time after his brother's disaster.
Held in low esteem by many in the Senate, he stood for election as tribune and
won a resounding success.

PLUTARCH, *C. Gracchus* 2.3–3.2

*(The Senate had extended Orestes' command in Sardinia, hoping that Gaius would
be forced to stay on with him.)* Finding himself in this predicament, Gaius was
angry and at once took ship for Rome. His arrival there was a surprise: not only
was it criticised by his enemies, the masses too were startled at a quaestor's
leaving his province before his governor. Nevertheless, when he was arraigned
before the censors, Gaius asked leave to speak, and so converted his audience
that when he left the hearing he left behind the impression that he had been very
badly treated. He had, he declared, completed twelve years of military service,
while others had served only the prescribed ten; he had served his governor as
quaestor for two years, though so far as the law was concerned he could have
come home after only one. Unlike others who had gone out, he alone had taken
with him a full money-belt and brought it home empty; the rest had drunk away
the wine they had taken in their baggage and come back with the empty jars
filled with gold and silver.

Subsequently other charges and accusations were pressed against him,
alleging that he had encouraged the allies to secede and had had a hand in the
reported secret plans behind the Fregellan revolt. He cleared himself of
suspicion and proved his innocence, and then at once set out to win a tribunate.
The 'establishment' was united in opposing him, but such huge crowds poured
into Rome from Italy that large numbers could not find accommodation, the
Campus Martius could not hold them all, and their shouts rang out from attics
and rooftops round about. But so great was the pressure the notables exerted on

the commons that Gaius' hopes of coming first were disappointed, and he came only fourth (*out of ten*).

AULUS GELLIUS, *Attic Nights* 15.12

When Gaius Gracchus got back to Rome from Sardinia, he delivered a public address to the people. Here is some of what he said:

"I so conducted myself in my province as I thought would be to your advantage, not as I supposed would prove best for my personal advancement. I kept no cook-house, no slave-boys of remarkable beauty waiting on me; at my entertainments your sons behaved more properly than even at general headquarters."

Later on he continues:

"I so conducted myself in my province that nobody could truthfully say that I received as much as a penny as a present or that anyone was out of pocket on my account. I spent two years in Sardinia. If ever a prostitute crossed my threshold, if ever anyone's slave-boy was solicited on my account, you may reckon me the lowest and basest man on earth. When I held myself back so decently from their slaves, you can make up your own minds how you suppose I lived with your sons."

Then, somewhat later:

"So it was, citizens, that when I set out back to Rome I brought back empty from Sardinia the money-belts which had been full when I arrived there. Others took out full jars of wine, and brought the jars back stuffed with silver."

(c) Gaius' speech against Aufeius' proposal

AULUS GELLIUS, *Attic Nights* 11.10

The story which I said in the preceding chapter was told by Critolaus of Demosthenes was applied to Demades when Gaius Gracchus had this to say in his speech against the Aufeian law:

"If, men of Rome, you are prepared to use your intelligence and common sense, you will realise that there is not one of us politicians who comes here without having his price. All of us who address you are looking for something, no one comes before you on any matter except to take something away with him. As for myself, who advocate that you should increase your revenues in order that you may the more easily meet your own needs and those of our country, I am not here for nothing. But what I seek from you is not money but your good esteem, and honour. Those who come here to persuade you to reject this bill are not after honour from you, but money from Nicomedes. And those who seek to persuade you to accept this bill are not after your good esteem, but a rich reward from Mithridates to put in their pockets. As for those from our same place and our same order who hold their peace, they are the most cunning of all: they take their price from everyone, and cheat everyone. You suppose that they are far above such things, you give them your confidence as being high-minded men. But the agents of King Nicomedes and King Mithridates think that it is in their rulers' interests that they maintain silence, and so they shower them with gifts and money. There is a story that once upon a time in Greece a dramatist was preening himself on being paid a whole talent for a single play he had written; but Demades, the finest public speaker in the land replied: 'So you think it wonderful that your words have earned you a talent? Let me tell you that I have been paid ten talents by a king just to keep my mouth shut.' It is just the same now: these gentlemen are being very highly paid for their silence."

The date of this speech is not given, but most probably it was delivered in 124 BC in opposition to some proposed arrangements in the new province of Asia.

(d) Plague of locusts in North Africa

EPITOME OF LIVY, Bk. 60

It is recorded that Africa was infested by huge swarms of locusts, and suffered great damage from their rotting dead bodies.

123 BC   Consuls: Q. Caecilius Metellus, T. Quinctius Flamininus

The assignment of the various enactments and proposals of Gaius Gracchus and his associates as between 123 and 122 BC is often arguable. The chronology followed here is that argued for in D. L. Stockton, The Gracchi (Oxford 1979), Appendix 3. The surviving continuous accounts of 123 BC are set out in extenso, *rather than chopped up under sub-headings, so as to give the reader a better sense of the overall character and 'flavour' of the individual authors.*

(a) The continuous accounts

APPIAN, *Civil Wars* 1. 21.5–23.1

Having been elected tribune with resounding success, Gaius at once set about plotting against the Senate, fixing a monthly allowance of corn for every citizen, to be paid for from public funds, although it had not beeen the practice to make such distributions before. And by this single measure he briskly won over the people to his support, with the collaboration of Fulvius Flaccus. And straight-away after that he was elected to hold a second tribunate for the following year; for by this time a law had been passed to the effect that, should an insufficient number of candidates present themselves for the tribunate, the people might elect a man to make up the full number from the whole citizen body without any restrictions.

Thus Gaius Gracchus got a second tribunate. With the people in his pay, so to speak, he set about courting the so-called knights as well, who rank halfway between senators and commons, with another political ploy of the following nature. He proposed to take the law-courts, which were discredited because of bribery, away from the senators and give them to the knights. He especially sought to discredit the senators by bringing up against them recent cases like those of Aurelius Cotta and Salinator and, third on his list, Manius Aquillius, the conqueror of Asia: all three had owed their acquittals to flagrant bribery of the court, and the official provincial delegates who had come to Rome to accuse them were still in the capital and going around full of loud and bitter recriminations. The Senate's keen sense of shame about all this weakened its resistance to the bill, and the people ratified it.

So it was that the law-courts were transferred from the Senate to the knights, and there is a story that just after the law had been carried Gracchus declared that he had completely destroyed the Senate; and the passage of time and actual experience underlined the truth of his words. For the right to sit in judgement over all Romans and Italians, including the senators themselves, to any extent, and impose financial penalties and loss of civil rights and sentences of exile, elevated the knights to be, so to say, their masters and turned the senators into their virtual subjects. Taking their stand alongside the tribunes when it came to voting on anything and in return securing from them whatever they wanted, they made the senators more and more frightened of them. So the whole balance of political power was quickly turned upside-down, with the Senate retaining only the appearance of power while in practice the knights possessed the reality. For the knights went so far as not merely to exercise control but even to persecute the senators openly in violation of the legal proprieties. They took to accepting bribes and acquired a taste for the enormous profits involved, and indulged it more shamelessly and with less restraint. They suborned men to accuse the rich by collusion and force, and entirely did away with prosecutions for bribery, with the result that this sort of investigation became totally obsolete and the judiciary law gave birth to a new faction struggle which lasted a long time and was no less bitter than those that had gone before.

Gracchus also constructed long stretches of roads throughout Italy, which brought a host of contractors and artisans under his control, ready to do his bidding; and he proposed the founding of many colonies.

PLUTARCH, *C. Gracchus* 3.2–8.2

On assuming office as tribune Gaius at once became the leading figure, overshadowing everyone else; his power as a public speaker was unrivalled, and his personal family tragedy added eloquence to his words when he mourned the fate of his dead brother. He would bring the people round to this subject on any pretext....'Before you very own eyes these men clubbed Tiberius to the ground and dragged his dead body down through the heart of the city from the Capitol and threw it into the river. Those of his friends who were taken were killed without trial. Yet it is our traditional Roman practice, if a man is arraigned on a capital charge and does not appear to answer it, to send a trumpeter to his door at daybreak to sound a summons, and forbid the court to decide his case until that has first been done. So meticulous were the safeguards once insisted on in criminal trials.'

Having prepared the ground by exciting the people with such words (as a speaker he had a very powerful voice and very strong lungs), he introduced two bills: the one banned any magistrate who had been deprived of his public office by the People from ever again holding any other public office, the second provided that any magistrate who had outlawed any citizen without trial should himself stand trial before the People. The first of these bills was aimed straight at degrading Marcus Octavius, the man who had been stripped of his tribunate by Tiberius, the other at catching Popillius who as praetor (*Plutarch is wrong here;*

Popillius was consul at the time: see under 132 BC) had outlawed Tiberius'
friends. Popillius did not wait to stand trial, but fled from Italy. The former bill
Gaius himself withdrew, announcing that he was sparing Octavius in deference
to the entreaties of his own mother, Cornelia. The people admired his conduct
and went along with him in this, for they held Cornelia in high honour no less
on account of her sons than of her father (*Scipio Africanus Major*); they later set
up a bronze statue of her with the inscription 'Cornelia, the Mother of the
Gracchi'. We also have reports of many things said by Gaius against one of his
enemies in defence of his mother in the rough and downright style of the
popular orator: 'Do you dare to speak ill of Cornelia, the woman who bore
Tiberius?'. The man he was attacking had a reputation for effeminacy: 'How can
you have the effrontery to compare yourself to Cornelia? Have you, like her,
given birth to a child? Yet every Roman knows that she has been without a man
for longer than you have ever been one'. Such was the tartness of his verbal
attacks, and many similar examples can be found in his published speeches.

Of the proposals which he introduced by way of gratifying the people and
putting down the Senate there were: a land-allotment law distributing the public
land among the poor; a military law requiring clothing to be provided at public
expense without any deductions from the soldiers' pay, and forbidding the
recruiting of boys who had not reached their seventeenth year; a law about the
allies giving the Italians equal voting-rights with Roman citizens; a corn law
lowering the price of provisions for the poor; and a judiciary law whereby he did
most to trim the power of the Senate. For senators had a monopoly of
jurisdiction, and on this account were formidable to both the people and the
knights; but Gaius enrolled three hundred of the knights in addition to the
senators, themselves numbering three hundred, and made all six hundred jointly
responsible for trying court-cases. In proposing this law he is said to have shown
remarkable earnestness, and especially in this respect: whereas all previous
popular leaders had faced towards the Senate-House and the Comitium, as it
was called, he was the first to turn and deliver his speeches facing outwards
towards the open area of the Forum, and he continued this practice thereafter,
thus by a small change in physical posture beginning a great innovation,
somehow turning Rome itself from aristocracy to democracy, signifying that it
was to the mass of the people and not the Senate that speakers should address
themselves.

When the people not only accepted this law but even granted Gaius the
discretion to choose the judges from among the knights, a sort of monarchical
power settled on him, so that even the Senate had to put up with it when he was
offering suggestions. But his suggestions always involved some proposal fitting
to that body – as for example the very just and honourable senatorial decree
about the corn which the pro-praetor Fabius had sent from Spain: Gaius
persuaded the Senate to distribute the corn but repay the Spanish communities
the cost of it, and in addition to censure Fabius for making his governorship
burdensome and intolerable to the provincials; as a result Gaius won a great
reputation and affection in the provinces. He also introduced proposals for
planting colonies and building roads and constructing storehouses for corn. For
the execution of all these projects he had himself appointed supreme controller
and director, and despite the number and magnitude of these tasks he showed

no signs of being fatigued by anything. On the contrary, his quickness and energy were so amazing that it was as if he had each time only one single thing to attend to, so that even those who detested him and feared him were astonished by the dispatch and thoroughness which he displayed in everything he set his hand to. The mere sight of him filled the people with wonder, when they observed him surrounded by a crowd of contractors, technicians, ambassadors, magistrates, soldiers, and literary men. All of them he treated with graciousness, showing to everyone affability without loss of dignity, giving to each man a personal attention appropriate to his character and standing. He thus demonstrated how overharsh were the criticisms of those who sought to label him as a frightening or arrogant or bullying individual. For he was an even more accomplished winner of popularity in conversation and business than he was in his speeches from the rostrum.

He took especial pains over the roads he built, having regard to their beauty and attractiveness as well as their utility. They ran straight and unswerving through the countryside; they were paved with hewn stone, and built up with firm-rammed sand. Depressions were filled in; and where they were intersected by torrent-beds or ravines, bridges were built to carry the roads over. With the height thus levelled on each side and perfect alignment attained, a regular and elegant appearance was achieved throughout the whole work. In addition, the whole road was measured off in miles and stone milestones set up to mark the distances. Other stones were set up on both sides at lesser intervals to help travellers to mount their horses without the need for other assistance.

As a result of all this, the people made much of Gaius and stood ready to do anything and everything possible to show their gratitude. There was an occasion when he was addressing them when he said he was going to ask a favour of them which if granted would pay for everything, but that he would not hold it against them if they refused it. These words led people to believe that he was going to ask to be elected consul, and aroused a universal expectation that he was aiming to hold a consulship and tribunate at the same time. But, when the consular elections were at hand and everybody was on tiptoe with expectations, Gaius was observed escorting Gaius Fannius to the Campus and along with his friends soliciting support for Fannius' candidature. That did a great deal to turn the scales in Fannius' favour; and Fannius was elected consul and Gaius elected tribune for a second year, though he had not announced himself as a candidate nor conducted a canvass but simply because of the enthusiastic support of the people. When he saw that the Senate was totally hostile to him, and Fannius' goodwill only lukewarm, he once again set about winning popular support with further measures, proposing colonies at Tarentum and Capua and offering political partnership to the Latins.

EPITOME OF LIVY, Bk. 60

Gaius Gracchus, brother of Tiberius, but a better orator than his brother, as tribune of the plebs passed a number of pernicious laws, including (i) a corn law providing for distributions of corn to the commons at six and one third *asses*; (ii) an agrarian law – his brother had also carried one; (iii) a law whereby he sought to corrupt the equestrian order, at that time in agreement with the

Senate, to the effect that six hundred members of the equestrian order should be additionally enrolled in the Senate, and, since in those days there were only three hundred senators, that six hundred equestrians were to be combined with three hundred senators, that is that the equestrian order should have twice as much influence in the Senate. His tribunate having beeen extended for a second year, by carrying agrarian laws he brought it about that several colonies should be planted in Italy and one on the site of destroyed Carthage, where he himself went out and planted the colony having been elected a triumvir.

DIODORUS SICULUS 34/35.25–27; 37.9

By his public advocacy of the suppression of aristocracy and the establishment of democracy Gaius Gracchus was able to draw on the willing support of all classes. Indeed they became not just willing supporters but virtually the prime movers in his bold plans. Each and every one of them, inspired by his own selfish hopes, was ready to face any risk to defend the laws which began to be introduced as if he were defending his own private advantage. By stripping the senators of their right to sit in judgement and appointing the knights to serve as judges, he made the inferior element in the senate master over the superior; and, by shattering the harmony which had existed hitherto between Senate and knights, he exposed both of them to the pressures of the mob. He split the state into two, thus paving the way for personal supremacy. He squandered the public treasury on disgraceful and ill-judged expenditures and bribes, so ensuring that he became the focus of all eyes. By sacrificing the provinces to the reckless greed of the public contractors, he wrung from the subject-peoples a justified hatred for the dominion of Rome. By currying favour with the soldiery through laws to relax the strictness of the old discipline, he opened the gates to anarchy and mutiny. For a man who comes to lose respect for those set in authority over him comes to lose respect for the laws as well; and such patterns of behaviour breed fatal disorder and national destruction....

Gracchus became so far gone in overbearing arrogance that when the commons voted that Octavius be exiled from Rome he let Octavius off, telling the people that he was granting Octavius this favour at the entreaty of his mother (*viz., Cornelia*)....

When Popilius was leaving Rome to go into exile he was given a tearful farewell by the crowds. For the commons were not unaware of the injustice involved in exiling him, that his conviction had been secured by bribery, and that they were being deprived of a tongue that was the scourge of miscreants....

Seventeen tribes voted against the bill (*which bill is in question is not specified in this excerpt*) and seventeen in favour; the count of the eighteenth tribe produced one last single vote in favour. While the decision of the people rested on such a fine knife-edge Gracchus was in as much agony of mind as if his very life were at risk, and when he learned that the casting of this one vote had given him victory he cried out: 'The sword hangs suspended over the heads of my enemies; for the rest, we shall be content with whatever fortune may decide!'....

When the Senate threatened Gracchus with war because of the change in the judges in the courts, Gaius boldly declared: 'Even if I should die, I shall not loose my grip on the sword that has been plunged into the Senate's side.' His words turned out to be as prophetic as an oracle's: their fulfilment came when Gracchus, having revealed himself as a tyrant, was killed without trial....

VELLEIUS PATERCULUS 2.6.1–3

Ten years later Gaius Gracchus fell victim to the same madness as had gripped his brother Tiberius....Whether wanting to avenge his brother's death or to build for himself a position of kingly power, he followed his brother's example and became a tribune. But his aims were far larger and wilder: he was for giving Roman citizenship to all the Italians and extending it almost as far as the Alps; for distributing land and forbidding any citizen to hold more than 500 *iugera*, as had long ago been laid down by the Licinian law; for establishing new customs-dues; for filling the provinces with new colonies; for transferring the courts from the Senate to the knights; and he had instituted the practice of giving corn to the commons. He wanted to allow no peace or reast anywhere, nothing was to be left where it was. Indeed, he even held a second tribunate.

(b) Gaius Gracchus' oratorical powers

CICERO, *Brutus* 125–6 (46 BC)

But see, here we have to hand (*the speeches of*) Gaius Gracchus, a man of truly outstanding intellectual power and burning energy who had had the benefit of a splendid education from childhood. Don't entertain the idea, Brutus, that any speaker has ever been fuller or richer....His early death has been a sad loss to Rome and to Latin literature. If only he had been prepared to put his country before his brother in his scale of loyalties! How easily, with that fine intellect, and had he lived longer, might he have equalled his father or his grandfather in glory! I think he would have had no match for eloquence. His style was elevated, his arguments wise, his whole manner full of weight. His speeches lack the final finished touch: much is excellently well roughed out, but not brought to full perfection. But this, I say, this orator, Brutus, if any other, is the orator for young men to read; he has the power not only to sharpen men's minds but also to bring them to maturity.

Excerpts cited from Gaius' speech 'On the laws which have been promulgated'

(i) If I were to come before you to ask a favour of you, that you suffer me to lead a quiet life in these times, for my family is among the noblest, for I have lost a brother in your cause and no one now remains of the blood of Publius Africanus and Tiberius Gracchus save myself and one young boy, so that our line may not perish root and branch, so that some shoot may remain and bear fruit in the future, I fear that if I ask such a favour you would be loth to grant it me.

(ii) Recently a (? *the*) consul visited Teanum Sidicinum. His wife announced that she wanted to take a bath in the men's bath-house there. Marcus Marius, the quaestor (*roughly, 'mayor'*) of Sidicinum was charged with clearing the bath-house of those who were using it. The consul's wife told her husband that the bath-house had not been made available to her quickly enough, and was not clean enough. Accordingly, a stake was set up in the market-place and to it was led the leader of the local nobility of the town, Marcus Marius. His clothes were stripped from him and he was flogged. When the news of this incident reached Cales, the town of Cales issued an edict forbidding the use of its public baths whenever a Roman magistrate should be there. At Ferentinum, and for the same reason, a Roman praetor ordered the quaestors to be arrested: one threw himself off the wall, the other was seized and flogged.

(iii) I shall give you just one example to show you the extent of the self-indulgence and viciousness of some younger men. Within these last few years a young man was sent on a mission back from Asia, a man who had not then held any magistracy but was serving as an acting-legate. He was being carried along in a litter. A simple countryman from Venusia met the party, and jokingly – not knowing who was inside the litter – asked them if they had a dead body in there. Hearing this, the young officer ordered his litter to be put down and had the poor fellow flogged with the litter straps so savagely that he died.

(iv) They say these things are being provided for luxury's sake.

(v) Those things are not luxuries which are needed to keep a man alive.

(vi) This alone is brought in as an extravagance for us, but for them as a necessity.

These excerpts, cited by various sources, may be found, with full references as to their source, either in ORF² pp. 190–2, or in D.L. Stockton, The Gracchi, Appendix 2. The speech may have been delivered either early in the first tribunate of Gaius or early in the second; certainty is impossible to attain, but the earlier date is here taken to be marginally preferable (see Stockton, l.c.).

(c) The law on officers deposed by the People *(de abactis)*

See Plutarch and Diodorus, above, under (a).

(d) The law that capital sentences might be imposed on Roman citizens only on the authority of the People *(ne de capite civium Romanorum iniussu populi iudicetur)*

CICERO, *pro C. Rabirio perduellionis reo* **12** (63 BC)

Gaius Gracchus carried a law forbidding capital sentence to be passed on a Roman citizen without your (*viz. the Roman People's*) ordering it.

CICERO, *In Catilinam* **4.10** (63 BC)

Gaius Caesar knows that the Sempronian law was designed to protect Roman citizens, but that the man who is an enemy of the Roman state can in no way be a citizen; indeed, the very man who carried the Sempronian Law himself paid the penalty for his crimes against the state without any authorisation from the people.

CICERO, *pro Sestio* **61** (56 BC)

When I was consul, and he (*Cato*) was tribune-elect, Cato put his own life at hazard: the speech he made in the Senate he could see might arouse such hostility that he would have to run the risk of paying for it with his own head.

CICERO, *de domo* 82: (57 BC)

Where had you (*Clodius*) carried a bill of outlawry against me, as Gaius Gracchus did against Publius Popillius?

CICERO, *de legibus* 3.26 (52–44 BC)

If I had been driven from Rome by the inflamed hatred of an enraged multitude, such as Gracchus had stirred up against (*Popillius*) Laenas...

See also Plutarch and Diodorus, cited above under (a). Aulus Gellius and others (ORF² 183–5) cites scattered words from a speech of Gaius against Popillius delivered in the small towns and villages (conciliabula) of the region around Rome, but they are little help, and so are not given here. They may contain a reference to the savagery of Popillius' actions in 132 BC.

(e) The law against judicial corruption (*ne quis iudicio circumveniatur*)

Note: all references to this law come from Cicero's speech pro Cluentio *delivered in 66 BC. Cluentius was not being tried under this law (he could not be), but the prosecution had dragged in allegations that he had bribed a (then wholly senatorial) court in 74 BC to secure the conviction of an innocent defendant. Cicero was at pains to deny this allegation, and insisted that his client would gladly have stood trial under the* lex ne quis *if only this had been possible, so as to clear his name.*

CICERO, *pro Cluentio* 104

What was the allegation against Fidiculanius (*one of the senatorial members of the court in 74 BC*)? That he had accepted a bribe of 400,000 sesterces from Cluentius. To which order did he belong? He was a senator. The customary law under which senators are called to account in such matters is the law on extortion (*repetundae*). Fidiculanius was charged under that law and acquitted without a stain on his character.

CICERO, *pro Cluentio* 144

As soon as this brief was offered to me as an expert in our legal system I at once told Cluentius that the provision concerning 'whosoever forms a combination to secure a condemnation' did not apply to him, although it did apply to senators.

CICERO, *pro Cluentio* 148

The law goes on to state: 'A capital trial shall be instituted' – against whom? Against anyone who forms a combination or association? Not so. What then? Read on – 'against any military tribune of the first four legions, quaestor, tribune of the plebs' – it goes on to name every magistracy – 'or any member of the Senate' – what then? – 'against any of the aforementioned who has or shall have combined or associated to secure the condemnation of anyone in a public court of law'.

CICERO, *pro Cluentio* 151

But, leaving on one side all the other laws which apply to us senators but not to all the other orders, this very law 'That no one shall be circumvented (*'framed' would be a good modern equivalent*) in a court of law' was carried by Gaius Gracchus; and he carried it not against the plebeians but to protect the plebeians.

CICERO, *pro Cluentio* 154

....under this law, which was then Sempronian but is now Cornelian (*viz. part of Sulla's legislation*) – for they knew that this law does not apply to the equestrian order.

CICERO, *pro Cluentio* 157

The law contains the following provisions: 'Whosoever combines' – see how wide its range is – 'associates' – that is equally unspecific and unlimited – 'agrees' – that indeed is not only unlimited but even vague and obscure – 'or gives false testimony'...

(f) The corn law (*lex frumentaria*)

CICERO, *de officiis* 2.72 (44 BC)

Gaius Gracchus' corn law was an enormous extravagance, and so it threatened to drain the treasury dry.

CICERO, *pro Sestio* 103 (56 BC)

Gaius Gracchus introduced a corn law. The commons were delighted, it made generous provision for the means of subsistence without their having to work for it. The *boni* found it repugnant, because they thought the commons were being encouraged to give up hard work and take to idleness, and they could see that the treasury was being drained dry.

CICERO, *Tusculan Disputations* 3.48 (45 BC)

....so too Gaius Gracchus. Although he had granted extravagant doles and poured out money from the treasury like water, he nevertheless spoke as if he were the watch-dog of the treasury. Why should I pay attention to words when the facts are in front of my eyes? The famous Lucius Piso Frugi had consistently opposed the corn law. But once the law had been ratified, for all that he was an ex-consul, he came along to collect his corn ration. Gracchus noticed Piso standing there in the crowd, and with the Roman people listening asked him how he could reconcile his applying for his corn ration with his opposition to the law which made it possible. 'I do not care for this fancy of yours, Gracchus, to divide my goods among every Tom Dick and Harry', replied Piso; 'but, since that is what you are doing, I shall claim my share.' Does not the conduct of that worthy and wise stateman make it plain that Rome's public wealth was being squandered by Gracchus' law? Yet read Gracchus' speeches and you will declare him to be the jealous guardian of the public purse.

See too the continuous accounts of Plutarch, Appian, Epitome of Livy, and Velleius Paterculus cited above under (a). The following fragment of Festus may possibly refer to the corn law, but it has also been taken to refer to an otherwise unknown proposal by Gaius on the subject of interest rates on loans.

FESTUS, cited by NONIUS MARCELLUS p. 728 L

He led the people to hope that they would not have to pay more than they themselves should decide.

Sections (iv) and (vi) from Gaius' speech de legibus promulgatis *cited above may well also allude to his corn law.*

(g) The law on the consular provinces (*de provinciis consularibus*)

CICERO, *de domo* 24 (57 BC)

Gaius Gracchus, who was far and away the greatest of all popular politicians, not only did not take the allocation of the consular provinces away from the Senate, he even passed a law that required them to be decided annually by the Senate. Yet you (*Clodius*) annulled the provincial allocations which the Senate had decreed under the Sempronian law.

SALLUST, *Jugurthine War* 27.3–4

Numidia and Italy were decreed under the Sempronian law as the two provinces for the consuls of the following year (*111 BC*). The two men elected as consuls were P. Scipio Nasica and L. Calpurnius Bestia, and the lot gave Numidia to Calpurnius and Italy to Scipio.

CICERO, *ad familiares* 1.7.10 (56 BC)

A decree was passed giving Caesar a grant of money and ten legates; as for preventing a new governor being assigned for his province under the Sempronian law, that was easily effected.

CICERO, *de provinciis consularibus* 17 (56 BC)

'I shall propose', he says, 'that Syria and Macedonia be designated as praetorian provinces, so that Piso and Gabinius (*the present governors of these two provinces*) can be replaced at once.' If that is allowed, yes. But (*if they are to be praetorian provinces*) a tribune will be able to veto that proposal, whereas (*if they are to be consular*) a veto is not possible.

(h) The agrarian and colony laws

CICERO, *de lege agraria* 2.81 (63 BC)

Neither the two Gracchi....nor Lucius Sulla ventured to touch the Campanian Land.

PLUTARCH, *C. Gracchus* 9.2; 10.1

Gaius had proposed two colonies and wanted to enrol the most respectable citizens as members of them....

Rubrius, one of his fellow-tribunes, having passed a law for a colony on the site of Carthage, the lot fell on Gaius to sail out to Africa (*in 122 BC*) to see to the foundation.

VELLEIUS PATERCULUS 1.15.4

In the consulship of Cassius Longinus and Sextius Calvinus (*124 BC*) Fabrateria was founded. The following year saw the foundation of Scolacium/Minervia, Tarentum/Neptunia, and the first colony outside Italy, at Carthage in Africa.

OROSIUS 5.12

In the consulship of L. Caecilius Metellus and Q. Titius (*sic*) Flamininus (*123 BC*) orders were give for the refounding of African Carthage....It was refounded, and Roman families were settled there to inhabit the place.

EUTROPIUS 4.12

In the consulship of L. Caecilius Metellus and T. Quinctius Flamininus, African Carthage was rebuilt by order of the Senate....and Roman citizens were sent there as colonists.

Two fragments from the Agrarian Law of 111 BC: Bruns *FIR* 11 lines 6 and 22

....by the law or plebiscite which the tribune C. Sempronius son of Tiberius carried, was excepted or barred from being distributed....

....which land or place was excepted by the law or plebiscite which the tribune C. Sempronius son of Tiberius carried....

The Liber Coloniarum *refers in various sections to 'Sempronian' or 'Gracchan' foundations at Ferentinum and Tarquinii in Tuscany and at Abellinum, Cadatia, Suessa Aurunca and Vellitrae in Latium and Campania; but the authority of this source is questionable, and some or all of these towns may later have laid claim to a Gracchan origin when they grew up or developed as centres for individual Gracchan settlement in those areas.*

See also the continuous excerpts from Plutarch, Appian, Epitome of Livy, and Velleius Paterculus cited earlier under (a).

(i) Road-building

See the continuous extracts from Plutarch and Appian cited earlier under (a).

(j) Military reforms

For changes in recruitment and conditions of service, and perhaps also in some rules governing military discipline, see the continuous excerpts from Plutarch and Diodorus cited above under (a). A scrap cited by the grammarian Charisius from an otherwise unknown and undated speech of Gaius suggests that he may have insisted that military tribunes, or at least the tribunes of the first four legions, must be elected and not merely appointed:

CHARISIUS in *ORF²* p.196

'Granted that those young men had met with your approval, all the same you ought still to be insisting that military tribunates of the old style should be created....'

(k) The judiciary laws

CICERO, *Brutus* 106 (46 BC)

Standing courts (*quaestiones perpetuae*) were established when he (*viz. Papirius Carbo, consul 120 BC*) was still a young man, although there had been none before then; for the tribune L. Piso was the first to carry an extortion law (*lex de pecuniis repetundis*) in the consulship of Censorinus and Manilius (*149 BC*).

CICERO, *Brutus* 128

(*The Mamilian court in 110 BC*) saw the condemnation of the priest C. Galba and four ex-consuls, L. Bestia, C. Cato, Sp. Albinus, and that outstanding Roman L. Opimius, the man who had killed Gaius Gracchus and been acquitted by the People....all were now got rid of by Gracchan judges (*iudices Gracchani*).

PLINY, *Natural History* 33.34

It was the Gracchi who first began to mark off that order (*the equestrian*) by the title of 'judges' (*iudices*) against the Senate's interests in a period of popular discontent. (*Then the name 'equestrian' came to be especially applied to the* publicani *or public contractors.*) Finally Marcus Cicero in his consulship (*63 BC*) established the designation 'equestrian' on a firm footing.

TACITUS, *Annals* 12.60

The emperor Claudius handed over (*sc. to the equestrian order*) all the legal power which had so often in the past been the cause of civil or military violence, as when laws like the Sempronian were for entrenching the equestrian order in possession of the law-courts, or again when laws like the Servilian were for giving the courts back to the Senate, or when this was almost the principal issue in the war once fought between Sulla and Marius.

CICERO, *Verrines* 1.38 (70 BC)

I shall not only mention, I shall give chapter and verse for all the crimes and scandals of which the courts have been guilty during these past ten years since the courts were tranferred (*by Sulla*) to the Senate. The Roman People will learn from me why it was that, as long as the equestrian order was furnishing judges for the courts, for a period of nearly half a century on end not even the slightest ground for suspicion of accepting a bribe to deliver a corrupt verdict was ever established against a single Roman knight (*eques*) in his capacity as a judge (*iudex*).

VELLEIUS PATERCULUS 2.13.2: 2.32.3

(*M. Livius Drusus in 91 BC*) was anxious to transfer the courts from the knights to the Senate. This power which had been vested in the knights by the Gracchan laws had enabled them to vent their savage spite on many distinguished and quite innocent men....

The duties of sitting as a judge, which Gaius Gracchus had stolen from the Senate and given to the knights....

PLUTARCH, *Comparison of Agis & Cleomenes and the two Gracchi* 2.1

The boldest of Gaius Gracchus' enterprises was his mixing of the law-courts by adding three hundred of the knights.

FLORUS 2.1: *on the Gracchan Laws*

What could seem more effective as a means of equalising freedom that that, while the Senate controlled the provinces, the authority of the equestrian order should rest at least on its control (*regnum*) of the law-courts?

*Fragments survive of a bronze tablet, often known as the 'Tabula Bembina' after its sometime owner Petro Bembo, which are unquestionably the fragments of a law establishing the full apparatus and procedure of a standard court on extortion (*quaestio perpetua de repetundis*). It is also often somewhat misleadingly termed the* Lex Acilia Repetundarum. *For argument showing that it is in fact the law on extortion carried in 123* BC *by Gaius Gracchus (whether or not its formal title was* Lex Acilia) *see D. L. Stockton,* The Gracchi *Appendix 3. The positive qualifications of those eligible to sit as judges under the law are lost, but it does specifically exclude all senators and their close relations. However, the law is fragmentary, and there seems nothing to be gained by citing odd snippets here. For a full discussion, see Stockton,* The Gracchi *Chapter 6 and Appendix 3.*

See also on the judiciary legislation the continuous passages from Appian, Plutarch, Epitome of Livy, Velleius Paterculus, and Diodorus Siculus cited earlier under (a).

(l) The Asian law (*lex de provincia Asia*)

CICERO, *Verrines,* 2.2.12 (70 BC)

There is this difference between Sicily and all the other provinces so far as concerns their liability to pay tax (*to Rome*) on their land: all the others either have to pay a fixed sum or, as is the case with Asia under the terms of the Sempronian Law, the taxes are leased out by the censors (*at Rome*).

CICERO, *pro lege Manilia* 19 (66 BC)

Believe me – you know it yourselves – the Roman money-market, the Roman credit-market, are inextricably interlocked with those Asian funds. If they collapse, they cannot but bring the Roman market down in the same ruin.

CICERO, *pro lege Manilia* 14

For the revenues raised from all the other provinces are so small that they scarcely suffice to cover the cost of their administration and security. But Asia is so rich and fertile that in the productivity of its farms and the variety of its fruits and the wide extent of its pasturelands and the multitude of its exports it easily surpasses all other countries.

Bobbiensis Scholiast on CICERO, *pro Plancio*, p. 157 St.

When Cn. Plancius' father was the president of the *publicani* (*the public contractors*) and that corporation (*societas*) seemed to have suffered a very heavy loss in the tax-collecting contract, a request was made in the Senate on behalf of the *publicani* that a reassessment should be made in accordance with the terms of the Sempronian law, and that a remission should be made in the sum due from the *publicani* to the extent that equity demanded, in proportion to the losses they had suffered through enemy invasions.

CICERO, *ad Atticum* 1.17.9 (61 BC)

The farmers who bought the Asian taxes from the censors complained in the Senate that they had been led by over-eagerness into making too high an offer and asked for the cancellation of their contract.

See also the continuous excerpts from Diodorus Siculus and Velleius Paterculus cited above under (a) and also 124 BC section (c) (see p. 37).

122 BC   Consuls: Cn. Domitius Ahenobarbus, C. Fannius

(a) The continuous accounts

APPIAN, *Civil Wars* 1.23.2–24.3

Gaius held out to the Latins the offer of a full share in the rights of Romans, reckoning that the Senate could not decently oppose such an offer to men who were Rome's kindred. To those of the other allies who could not cast a vote in Rome's assemblies he proposed to allow this right in future, hoping to have them too as favourable supporters when it came to voting on legislative proposals. The Senate was particularly upset by this and instructed the consuls to issue a proclamation forbidding any persons who lacked the right to vote to stay in Rome or come closer than within 5 miles of Rome until a vote had been taken on these proposals of Gaius. And the Senate prevailed on Livius Drusus, another of the tribunes (*for 122 BC*) to block Gracchus' proposals without publicly revealing his true reasons a tribune was not obliged to give reasons for interposing his veto. So that he might win the goodwill of the people they allowed him to propose the founding of twelve colonies; this so delighted the masses that they thought little of Gaius' proposals.

Having lost popular favour, Gaius sailed out to Africa in company with Fulvius Flaccus, who although a former consul had also been elected a tribune for this reason, a colony having been authorised in Africa on a reputedly fertile site and these two having been specially chosen as foundation commissioners so that in their absence the Senate might have a brief respite from demagoguery. They laid out the new colony on the former site of Carthage, caring nothing for the curse that Scipio had laid on it when he destroyed the city, that it should remain for ever bare pastureland. They proposed to enrol about 6,000 colonists instead of the lesser number laid down in the law, thinking by this to recover popular support; and when they got back to Rome they set about recruiting these six thousand from all over Italy.

PLUTARCH, *C. Gracchus* 8.2–12.3

One of Gaius' colleagues in the tribunate was Livius Drusus....To him the nobles turned and appealed to him to join with them in resisting Gaius and attacking them, yet not by violent means or involving himself in a conflict with the commons but by suiting his programme to please them, even making concessions which he would normally have scorned to make.

So Drusus agreed to put his tribunate at the service of the Senate, and drafted proposals which had no regard for what was right or advantageous but had one single object, to outbid Gaius for popular favour and gratitude in an almost comic rivalry. Thus the Senate made it as plain as could be that it was not taking issue with Gaius' policies but was out to destroy or humble him by any means. When Gaius had proposed two colonies to be recruited from the most respectable elements of the citizen body they had called him a rabble-rouser; but they backed Drusus when he proposed twelve and the settling in each of 3,000 paupers. Gaius had proposed making land-grants to the poor subject to a yearly rent to the state, and they had opposed him as truckling to the masses; but they were pleased with Drusus when he proposed abolishing this charge on the land he allotted. Gaius upset them by his offer of franchise-equality to the Latins; but when Drusus proposed to exempt Latins from flogging even when on military service they backed his bill. And Drusus always took care in his public pronouncements to stress that his proposals had the approval of the Senate, and that the Senate cared for the masses...

The greatest demonstration of Drusus' goodwill towards the people and of his honesty was that he was never seen to be getting any personal advantage from his proposals: others were to be foundation-commissioners for his colonies, he refused to handle the moneys involved, whereas Gaius had kept most – and the most important – of such business in his own hands. When the lot fell on Gaius to sail to Africa to oversee the foundation of the colony at Carthage which one of his colleagues named Rubrius had passed a law to found, Drusus took advantage of his absence to make even deeper inroads into Gaius' popular following and win it over to himself, above all by his attacks on Fulvius Flaccus. This Fulvius was a friend of Gaius and his colleague as a land-commissioner. He was a turbulent character and bitterly hated by the Senate, and distrusted in particular as a man who was upsetting the allies and secretly inciting the Italians to secession. Such unsupported and unproven charges Fulvius' own insane and revolutionary line made more plausible, and the hatred he incurred rubbed off onto Gaius and helped destroy him....

Meanwhile in Africa Gaius was encountering many difficulties with the founding of Carthage/Junonia: the standard at the head of the procession was seized by the wind and smashed out of its bearer's grasp, a sudden whirlwind took hold of the offerings lying on the altars and scattered them beyond the boundary markers of the colony, while the markers themselves were snatched up and carried a long way off by ravaging wolves. None the less Gaius settled and arranged everything within seventy days in all, and returned to Rome, having heard that Fulvius Flaccus was being hard pressed by Drusus and that affairs there called for his personal attention. For Lucius Opimius, one of the oligarchic faction and a powerful senator, who had previously been an unsuccessful candidate for the consulship when he was beaten by Gaius Fannius with Gaius' backing, was now enjoying widespread support and was expected to be elected consul (*for 121 BC*) because Gaius' influence was now on the wane....

As soon as he was back Gaius moved house from the Palatine to the poorer district near the Forum... and then published the rest of his proposals, meaning to put them to the vote. With large crowds flocking to him from all sides, the Senate persuaded the consul Fannius to banish all non-Romans from the capital....Gaius riposted by publishing an edict denouncing the consul and promising to protect any allies who stayed in Rome. But he did not protect them in fact, and when he saw one of his personal friends being dragged away by Fannius' attendants he passed by and did nothing to help him, either because he was afraid to demonstrate how far his power was on the wane or because, as he said, he was unwilling to give his opponents the excuse they were seeking to provoke a violent confrontation. He also chanced to come into collision with his fellow-tribunes for the following reason: a public gladiatorial show was due to be held in the Forum, and most of the magistrates had had temporary stands built which they intended to hire out. Gaius ordered them to take them down, so that the poor might have a free and unobstructed view. When none of them paid him any heed, he waited till the night before the show, collected the workmen whom he had working on his various projects, pulled the stands down, and at daybreak presented the people with a clear space to watch the show from. The masses thought this a manly action, but his reckless and violent action upset his colleagues. It was thought that he was robbed of a third tribunate because of this: though a majority of the votes were cast for him, his colleagues acted unjustly and fraudulently in their announcement and declaration of the returns. But that is disputed. None the less he took his defeat very hard...

(b) ?Proposal to alter the voting procedure in the centuriate assembly

[SALLUST] *ad Caesarem senem* 2.8

In the matter of the elections of magistrates, I am rather attracted by the proposal which Gaius Gracchus put forward when he was tribune, that the votes of the centuries should be called for by random selection from among all the five classes jumbled together.

(c) Proposal about the allies and the Latins (*lex de sociis et nomine Latino*)

CICERO, *Brutus* 99–100 (46 BC)

'Gaius Fannius, who was consul with Domitius (*122 BC*) has left us a single speech "About the allies and the Latins" which is a fine and noble one.' Whereat Atticus asked: 'Really? Is that speech the work of Fannius? Opinions differed about that when we were boys. Some said that it was written by that learned man C. Persius....others that many noble gentlemen had had a hand in helping to write that speech.' 'No', said I, 'I have never been convinced of that, although I heard the same story from our elders. I think that the reason why this suspicion was aroused was that Fannius was generally reckoned to be only a moderate orator, while that particular speech was perhaps the finest of all those delivered in that period.'

IULIUS VICTOR 6.4 = *ORF²* p.144

As in this passage from Gaius Fannius' speech against Gracchus:
  'If you give citizenship to the Latins, I suppose you imagine that you will

continue as now to find somewhere to stand to listen to a public address and attend games and public festivals? Will you not stop and think that they will crowd you out of everything?'

See also the continuous extracts from Appian and Plutarch cited above in (a) and that from Velleius Paterculus under 123 BC (a).

(d) Opposition of Livius Drusus

CICERO, *de finibus* **4.66** (45 BC)

I shall compare your grandfather Drusus with his close contemporary Gaius Gracchus. The wounds which Gracchus was inflicting on Rome Drusus set himself to heal.

SUETONIUS, *Tiberius* **3**

His outstanding achievement in opposing the Gracchi won Drusus the title of 'the Senate's champion'.

See also Appian and Plutarch cited earlier under (a).

121 BC   Consuls: L. Opimius, Q. Fabius Maximus

(a) The continuous accounts

APPIAN, *Civil Wars* 1.24.2–26.8

The men who were still at work on the marking out of Junonia's boundaries reported that Gracchus' and Fulvius' markers had been torn up by wolves, and the soothsayers interpreted this as indicating that the colony was accursed; so the Senate announced a day for a meeting of the assembly at which it was intended to repeal the law for this colony. When Gracchus and Fulvius felt the ground slipping away from under them here too, they went around like madmen claiming that the Senate was lying about the wolves. The boldest of the commons joined them and went with arms in their hands to the Capitol, where the meeting about the colony was to take place. The people had already gathered and Fulvius was beginning to speak when Gracchus mounted the Capitol with a bodyguard of his partisans; but, suddenly overcome by conscience abut the extraordinary plans which were afoot, he turned aside from the assembly place and entered a portico, where he paced up and down waiting to see what would happen. While in this upset state he was seen by a commoner called Antyllus who was sacrificing in the portico; Antyllus put his hand on him, whether he had some knowledge or suspicion or was otherwise moved to address him, and begged Gaius to take pity on Rome. This upset Gaius even more, like a frightened criminal caught red-handed, and he glared at Antyllus; and one of those standing by, though no signal or order had yet been given, but guessing simply from the fierce look Gaius gave Antyllus that the hour had come, drew his short sword and killed the man. Shouting started and the dead body lay there for all to see, and everyone ran off down the hill away from the temple for fear of suffering the same fate. Gracchus went to the Forum and tried to explain what had happened, but nobody wanted to listen and they all shunned him as being accursed. Gracchus and Flaccus were at a loss, having lost the chance to put their plans into action, and hurried off to their homes, where their partisans also gathered. The rest of the commons began from midnight onwards to occupy the Forum, as if expecting something terrible to happen. The one consul who was present in Rome, Opimius, ordered some armed men to muster at the Capitol at dawn, and sent heralds to summon a meeting of the Senate, while he himself took up his station right in the centre of things, in the temple of Castor and Pollux, and waited on events.

So things stood thus when the Senate summoned Gracchus and Flaccus to leave home and appear before them and explain their actions; but they armed themselves and hurried off to the Aventine Hill, hoping that if they could seize it the Senate would make some concessions to them about a reasonable settlement. As they ran they called out to the slaves with a promise of freedom, but none paid them any heed. With such supporters as they had they seized and strengthened the temple of Diana, and sent Flaccus' son Quintus to the Senate with a request for a settlement of differences and some way to live in harmony. But the Senate ordered them to lay down their weapons and come to the Senate House and say what they had to say, or else send no more intermediaries. When they again sent Quintus, Opimius was no longer prepared to treat him as an envoy, because of the warning that had been given, and put him under arrest, and then sent his armed men against the Gracchans. Gracchus escaped over the wooden bridge across the Tiber to a grove of trees where, to avoid been taken, he ordered the one servant who had accompanied him to cut his master's throat. Flaccus hid in the workshop of a man whom he knew; his pursuers, not knowing which building he was in, threatened to burn down the whole row, whereat the man who was hiding him, unwilling himself to betray someone who had flung himself on his mercy, told someone else to betray Flaccus' hiding-place, and he was seized and killed. The heads of Gracchus and Flaccus were brought to Opimius, who paid for them with their weight in gold. The people plundered their houses, and the Gracchan sympathisers were arrested by Opimius and jailed and then garrotted. Flaccus' son Quintus was allowed to commit suicide, and the city was then purified. The Senate also instructed Opimius to erect a temple to Concord in the Forum.

PLUTARCH, *C. Gracchus* 13.1–17.5

Having got Opimius elected consul, Gaius' enemies set about repealing many of his measures and in particular they tried to upset the Carthage settlement by way of irritating him, to see how he might provide some cause for resentment and so be got rid of. To begin with he held firm and was active in gathering a fresh set of adherents to oppose the consul. At this point his mother is said to have become an active partisan, hiring men from outside Roman territory and sending them into the city disguised as harvesters – this was allegedly mentioned in cipher in her letters to her son, but others say that she totally disapproved of what he was up to.

On the day that Opimius' collaborators were planning to move for the repeal of Gaius' laws, both sides occupied the Capitol as soon as day broke. While the consul was sacrificing and Quintus Antullius, one of his attendants, was transferring the victim's entrails, Antullius said to those standing around Fulvius: 'Make way for good men and true, you scoundrels!' Some say that at the same time he bared his arm and waved it in aggressive fashion. At any rate he was killed on the spot, stabbed with large metal styluses said to have been designed for this very purpose. The crowd was upset by this killing, and its mood changed. Gaius was angry and rounded on his supporters for giving his enemies the pretext they had long been seeking, while Opimius was delighted with the gift he had been presented with and incited the people to vengeance.

Then a storm broke and everyone scattered. Next day the consul called a meeting of the Senate and proceeded to business there, while others of set plan carried Antullius' naked corpse on a bier through the Forum past the Senate House with a great deal of noisy weeping and wailing. Opimius knew what was happening but pretended to be surprised, and so all the senators came out to watch. The bier was set down in plain view and some began to express their indignation at this allegedly terrible and monstrous crime; but most were stirred to hatred of the ruling class and to denouncing them for having killed Tiberius Gracchus on the Capitol while he was a tribune and hurling his corpse into the river, while Antullius, a mere attendant, who had perhaps been unjustly treated but who was himself chiefly responsible for what had happened to him, lay there in the Forum with the Roman Senate parading and mourning and assisting at the obsequies of a mere hired public-servant, and all this simply with the object of getting rid of the one man left who really cared for the people.

On returning to the Senate House the senators passed a decree instructing the consul Opimius to save Rome by such means as he could and to put down the tyrants. Opimius gave the senators notice to arm, and issued a proclamation for every knight to present himself at daybreak with two armed servants. Fulvius took counter-precautions and collected a crowd together, but Gaius as he left the Forum paused by the statue of his father and spent a long time looking at it in silence, and then left weeping and sobbing. This filled many of the onlookers with pity for Gaius, and they reproached themselves with deserting and betraying him, and sent to his house and kept watch at his door through the night: their behaviour was very different from those guarding Fulvius, who spent the night in fearful drunkenness and bragging, with Fulvius himself taking the lead in getting drunk and indulging in much coarse talk and behaviour quite unsuited to his time of life, while those with Gaius were quiet as in the presence of a common national calamity and kept watch for what might happen, taking it in turn to be on guard.

(*At daybreak Fulvius, the worse for wear after a night's drinking, and a glum and reluctant Gaius, proceeded to the Aventine Hill.*) When they were all assembled, Gaius prevailed on Fulvius to send his younger son to the Forum with a herald's wand....But Opimius said that negotiations could not be conducted with the Senate by intermediaries: they must come down off the hill and surrender themselves for proper trial, and then ask for clemency. He told the young man either to come back on these terms or not to return at all. Gaius, they say, wanted to go down and try to win the Senate over, but nobody else backed him up, and Fulvius sent his son back with the same request as before.

But Opimius was spoiling for a fight, and arrested the young man and put him under guard. He then set out to attack Fulvius' supporters with a large number of heavy-armed infantrymen and Cretan archers. These latter pressed their opponents very hard with their volleys, causing a lot of casualties and throwing them into disorder. As the tide of battle turned, Fulvius hid in a disused bathhouse but was soon discovered and killed along with his elder son. No one saw Gaius taking any part in the fighting, but disturbed by what was happening he took refuge in the temple of Diana....and later crossed the Tiber by the wooden bridge with a single servant, Philocrates, who killed him in the sacred grove of the Furies and then took his own life....

When the battle had begun an announcement had been made promising that anyone who brought in Gaius' or Fulvius' head would be rewarded with its weight in gold. Gaius' head had the brains removed and the cavity filled with lead....but the men who brought in Fulvius' head, being only obscure people, got nothing. Their bodies together with all the others – 3,000 were collected – were thrown into the Tiber, and their property was confiscated to the treasury. Their wives were forbidden to go into mourning, and Gaius' wife Licinia was deprived of her dowry. Most savage was the treatment of Fulvius' younger son, who had used no violence and taken no part in the fighting: arrested when he came to parley before the battle, he was killed when the battle was over. But what galled the commons even more than this and everything else was Opimius' construction of a temple of Concord ....One night unknown hands scrawled under the inscription on the temple the following line:

'Concord's temple by mad discord built'.

EPITOME OF LIVY, Bk. 61

After his seditious tribunate had come to an end, Gaius Gracchus occupied the Aventine too with an armed mob. The consul L. Opimius acting under a decree of the Senate called the People to arms. Gracchus was defeated and killed, and along with him the former consul Fulvius Flaccus, his partner in madness.

VELLEIUS PATERCULUS 2.6.4–7

The consul L. Opimius, the man who as praetor had destroyed Fregellae, made an armed attack on Gaius and Fulvius Flaccus, a former consul and a man who had celebrated a triumph, who was pursuing the same wicked plans as Gracchus and whom Gaius Gracchus had nominated to take the place of his brother Tiberius as a land commissioner – he had taken him as a partner in his bid for monarchic power. Both were killed by Opimius. The one wicked action reported of Opimius was that he announced that he would pay its weight in gold for the head of a man who was not just Gracchus but a Roman citizen. Flaccus, in armed occupation of the Aventine and responsible for starting the fighting, had his throat cut, and with him his elder son. Gracchus was trying to escape, but, when he was on the point of capture by the men Opimius had sent after him, had his slave Euporus dispatch him – Euporus at once killed himself and followed in death the master he had thus helped to death. That day saw an outstanding example of devotion to Gracchus on the part of a Roman knight named Pomponius: just like Horatius Cocles he held the bridge against Gracchus' enemies before killing himself with his own sword. As had happened before with Tiberius' dead body, so too that of Gaius was thrown into the Tiber, an astonishing act of cruelty on the part of the victors.

OROSIUS 5.12

After the tribune Minucius had upset most of the legislation of Gracchus, his predecessor in office, and repealed his laws, Gaius Gracchus and Flaccus mounted the Capitol, where a public meeting was being held, with a huge band of followers. A great tumult arose and the murder of a public herald by the Gracchans served as the signal for war. Flaccus, escorted by his two fully-armed sons, and accompanied too by Gracchus dressed only in his toga and with a short sword concealed at his side, having in vain sent ahead a herald to offer freedom to the slaves, fortified the temple of Diana like a strongpoint. He was attacked by the former consul Decimus Brutus who came at him from the Publician slope with a huge force. For a long time Flaccus put up a stubborn resistance. Gracchus had withdrawn to the temple of Minerva, and wanted to fall on his sword, but Laetorius intervened and stopped him. For a long time the issue hung in the balance until at last Opimius sent in archers who broke up the close ranks of the opposition. Flaccus and one of his sons slipped away through the temple of Luna into a private house and barred the doors, but were buried under a party-wall that was brought down on top of them. Gracchus just managed to reach the Sublician Bridge, where he got his slave to kill him so as not to be taken alive. His head was carried to the consul, his body was conveyed to his mother Cornelia at the town of Misenum.

   The consul Opimius' courage in warfare was matched by his cruelty in sitting in judgement. For he had more than 3,000 persons executed, most of whom were innocent and were killed without having a chance to defend themselves against his charges.

DIODORUS SICULUS 34/35.28a

Gaius called a meeting of his fellow-conspirators in his private house with Flaccus as his adviser, and decided that they must overcome their opponents by open force and lay violent hands on magistrates and Senate. They were all bidden to conceal weapons under their clothes and follow him and be ready to obey his orders. Opimius convened a meeting on the Capitol to discuss the situation, so Gaius set off there with his revolutionary following. But, finding the Capitoline temple already occupied and a crowd of nobles gathered there, he withdrew to the portico behind the temple in a disturbed and apprehensive state. While he was in this distracted mood, a man called Quintus who knew him fell to his knees and begged him to do no act of violence or sacrilege against his country. Gaius pushed him aside in a peremptory fashion and sent him sprawling to the ground, and bade his followers to finish him off and make this the first move of revenge against his opponents. The consul was horror-struck and reported the murder to the Senate along with the plan to attack them as well...

(b) The passing of the 'ultimate decree' (*senatus consultum ultimum*)

CICERO, *in Catilinam* 1.4 (63 BC)

The Senate once decreed that L. Opimius the consul was to see to it that the state took no harm.

CICERO, *Philippics* 8.14 (43 BC)

L. Opimius the consul having introduced the question of national security, the Senate in this matter decreed that L. Opimius the consul was to defend the state.

(c) Fighting in Gaul

EPITOME OF LIVY, Bk. 61

The proconsul Cn. Domitius (*consul 122 BC*) fought a successful battle against the Allobroges near the town of Vindalium. The reason for his attack was that they had given refuge and every assistance to Toutomotulus, the fugitive king of the Salluvii, and because they had ravaged the territory of Rome's allies the Aedui.

SUETONIUS, *Nero* 2

Having defeated the Allobroges and the Arverni, Domitius paraded through the province on an elephant with a crowd of soldiers in attendance as if he were celebrating a formal triumph.

EPITOME OF LIVY, Bk. 61

The consul Q. Fabius Maximus fought a successful battle against the Allobroges and King Bituitus of the Arverni....The surrender of the Allobroges was accepted.

Appian gives the number of Gauls killed by Fabius, who took over command in Gaul from Domitius, as 120,000; the figure given by Pliny the Elder is 130,000. The result of these operations was the effective creation of the province of Transalpine Gaul.

120 BC   Consuls: P. Manilius, C. Papirius Carbo
Censors: Q. Caecilius Metellus Balearicus, L. Calpurnius Piso Frugi
(No census figures have survived)

(a) Trial and acquittal of L. Opimius

EPITOME OF LIVY, Bk. 61

L. Opimius was indicted before the People by the tribune P. Decius on the ground of having imprisoned Roman citizens without trial, and was acquitted.

CICERO, *pro Sestio* 140 (56 BC)

Although Gaius Gracchus' death had earned him lively resentment, the Roman People itself freed Opimius from condemnation.

CICERO, *de oratore* 2.132; 106; 165; 170 (55 BC)

Opimius killed Gracchus, What justification did he have? His country gave him justification when the Senate decreed a call of arms. Take that away, no justification will remain....

   When the consul C. Carbo was defending L. Opimius at his trial before the People....he did not seek to deny the fact of Gaius Gracchus' killing, but asserted that the killing had been justified....

   As Carbo put it. 'If a consul is a man who takes counsel for his country, what else had Opimius done?'....

   Just because you defended Opimius, Carbo, that does not make these people reckon you a good citizen....

(b) Popillius Laenas recalled

CICERO, *Brutus* 128 (46 BC)

L. Bestia passed a bill recalling P. Popillius, who had been driven into exile by the violence of Gaius Gracchus.

(c) ?The Agrarian Commission

A marble fragment from Carthage has been found bearing the names (in lettering of the imperial period): Galba, Papirius Carbo, L. Calpurnius Bestia. This **may** *represent the composition of the Gracchan triumviral land commission as it stood after the dead C. Gracchus and Fulvius Flaccus had been replaced by Bestia and Galba. (See Stockton, The Gracchi p. 204, note 69). Carbo himself died in 119 BC.*

(d) The fate of the Gracchan agrarian legislation

APPIAN, *Civil Wars* 1.27

Not long after the death of Gaius Gracchus, a law was passed allowing the holders of the land, which was the source of the controversy, to sell their holdings. That had been explicitly forbidden by Tiberius Gracchus. And straight away the rich began to buy it back from the poor or brought pressure on them to sell by various pretexts. Things went from bad to worse for the poor, and in due course a tribune Spurius Thorius introduced a bill (*?119 or 118 BC*) terminating land-distribution and confirming the possessors in their holdings on payment of a rent to the state, these moneys to be spent on corn-distributions: this was some consolation to the poor, on account of the corn-distributions, but no help at all to increasing the population. Once such manoeuvres had destroyed the Gracchan Law – an excellent and most useful piece of legislation if it could have been made to work – the rents too were abolished not long afterwards (*presumably Appian is referring to the agrarian law of 111 BC*) by another tribune, and the people were left with absolutely nothing at all. In consequence Rome began to suffer an even more acute shortage of citizens who could serve in her legions....(*Appian's text at this point seems to have become garbled in transmission, and so no secure arguments can be based on it. But there may be a reference to a period of fifteen years as the duration of the Gracchan agrarian legislation, and if that is so it would point to 133 – 119/118 BC, viz. from the passage of Tiberius' original law to the passage of the second law here mentioned by Appian which brought the distribution of public land to smallholders to an end.*)

119 BC   Consuls: L. Caecilius Metellus Delmaticus, L. Aurelius Cotta

(a) Prosecution and death of Papirius Carbo (consul 120 BC)

CICERO, *ad familiares* **9.21.3** (46 BC)

Accused by L. Crassus, Carbo is said to have taken poison.

CICERO, *Brutus* **159** (46 BC)

When Crassus prosecuted C. Carbo....he was himself still only a young man.

CICERO, *Verrines* **2.2.3** (70 BC)

L. Crassus was often heard to say that there was nothing he regretted more than that he had ever brought his prosecution against C. Carbo.

(b) Tribunician activity of Gaius Marius

PLUTARCH, *Marius* **4**

Marius was inspired with the hope of pursuing a career in politics, and he won election as a tribune of the plebs with the enthusiastic support of Caecilius Metellus (*consul 109 BC, later known as Metellus Numidicus*) with whose family he had inherited ties of obligation and dependence which he had fostered from the start. But when as tribune he introduced a bill on voting-procedure which apparently weakened the nobility's control of judicial decisions*, he was opposed by the consul Cotta who persuaded the Senate to fight the bill and to

---

* The Greek word used here by Plutarch is *kriseis*, which – though it can have a general sense of 'decisions' – most naturally refers to decisions in legal matters, court-decisions. Thus it may be that Marius' law was concerned solely with voting in trials before the People (*iudicia apud populum*). But it would be hazardous to conclude that this was the sole concern of Marius' law, and it could well have been wider in its scope. Unfortunately all we know about it comes from the two passages set out above.

summon Marius to give an account of himself....Marius threatened Cotta with imprisonment...and Cotta then invited Metellus to speak; and when Metellus sided with the consul Marius summoned one of his staff and ordered him to hale Metellus himself off to prison. Though Metellus appealed for assistance to the other tribunes, none of them came to his rescue, and so the Senate gave in.

Elated with his success, Marius put his bill to the vote and it became law, and he thereby won a reputation as a fearless man who was not to be overawed by respect for rank, and as a true popular champion of the masses against the Senate. However, this impression was quickly corrected by another political action of his. When a bill was introduced to provide for corn-distributions to the citizens he opposed it vigorously and won the day, thus revealing himself as somebody who was neutral as between both sides and unwilling to truckle for the favour of either in defiance of what was expedient and proper.

CICERO, de legibus 3.38 (52–44 BC)

The Marian law stipulated that the gangways (*the* pontes *which led from the assembly-areas to the voting-platforms where votes were cast*) must be narrow.

118 BC   Consuls: M. Porcius Cato, Q. Marcius Rex

(a) Foundation of Narbo Martius (*Narbonne*) in Transalpine Gaul

VELLEIUS PATERCULUS 2.7

The colony of Narbo Martius was founded in the consulship of Porcius and Marcius.

CICERO, *Brutus* 160 (46 BC)

When Crassus (*consul 95 BC, the prosecutor of Carbo in 119 BC*) was a young man, he decided to win something of a reputation as a popular politician with a colony at Narbonne, which he did in fact found himself, as he set out to do. There survives a speech he made in support of the project, which reads like that, if I may say so, of a man of much more mature years.

CICERO, *pro Cluentio* 140 (66 BC)

When Crassus spoke against the proposal not to found a colony at Narbonne, he did all he could to diminish the authority of the Senate.

CICERO, *pro Fonteio* 13 (69 BC)

There is in that same province the Roman citizen colony of Narbo Martius, a watch-post for the Roman People, a bastion firmly planted to bar the path of the Gallic tribes.

(b) Death of King Micipsa of Numidia

EPITOME OF LIVY, Bk. 62

King Micipsa of Numidia (*he had been on the throne since 148* BC*, and had been an ally of Rome and given valuable assistance to Scipio Aemilianus in the campaign that led to the destruction of Carthage in 146* BC) died, leaving his kingdom to three sons: Adherbal, Hiempsal, and Jugurtha, who was his brother's natural son but had been adopted by the king.

SALLUST, *Jugurthine War* 11–12

A few days later Micipsa was dead. After giving him a magnificent royal funeral, the princes met to discuss the overall situation....After a long discussion about the government of the kingdom (*they failed to find common ground and*) therefore decided to divide the royal treasures and Numidia itself between the three of them. (*Not long afterwards Hiempsal was murdered treacherously by some of Jugurtha's soldiers.*)

117 BC Consuls: L. Caecilius Metellus Diadematus, Q. Mucius Scaevola (commonly known as 'Scaevola the Augur')

Marius fails to be elected an Aedile

PLUTARCH, *Marius* 5

After his tribunate, Marius announced his candidature for the curule aedileship ....As soon as it became clear that he was not going to be elected, he quickly shifted his ground and entered his name as a candidate for the plebeian aedileship....and failed there too.

Cicero, pro Plancio *51 also refers to this double defeat.*

116 BC   Consuls: C. Licinius Geta, Q. Fabius Maximus

(a) Marius elected Praetor for 115 BC and acquitted on a charge of electoral corruption (*ambitus*)

PLUTARCH, *Marius* 5

Not long afterwards, Marius tood for the praetorship and came close to defeat, being elected at the bottom of the list. He was charged with electoral malpractice...The early days of the trial went badly for him and he was faced with a difficult court, but unexpectedly the last day saw him acquitted when the votes were evenly divided between condemnation and acquittal.

VALERIUS MAXIMUS 6.9.14

When he stood for the praetorship, Marius could manage no better than bottom place among those elected. Even that success was fraught with danger, for he was charged with electoral corruption and only just managed to win a narrow acquittal from the judges (*iudices*).

(b) The dynastic struggle in Numidia

SALLUST, *Jugurthine War* 13–16

When the news of Hiempsal's murder spread quickly through Africa, Adherbal and all Micipsa's former subjects were seized with fear. The Numidians split into two factions, with Adherbal enjoying more numerous support but Jugurtha backed by the best fighters. So Jugurtha armed the largest forces he could muster, won over the cities partly by force and partly by persuasion, and set out to make himself ruler of all Numidia. Though Adherbal had sent envoys to Rome with news of his brother's murder and the threat to his own position, he nevertheless prepared to make a fight of it, relying on his numerical superiority. But as soon as the fighting began he was beaten and forced to take refuge in the Roman province of Africa, whence in due course he proceeded to Rome. Whereupon Jugurtha became apprehensive about what Rome might do, and could see no hope of avoiding an angry response unless he could use his own great wealth to work on the greed of the Roman nobility. So he sent envoys of his own to Rome with a great deal of gold and silver; they were instructed to load his old friends there with presents and then go on and buy new friends...

(*Jugurtha's agents succeeded in effecting a dramatic swing in favour of their master among the nobility. At the meeting of the Senate called to discuss the Numidian business, Adherbal based his appeal on the traditional loyalty and friendship of his house to Rome; Jugurtha's men confined themselves to claiming that Hiempsal had been a cruel ruler and had been killed by his outraged subjects, that Adherbal had been the aggressor, and that Jugurtha should be judged by the quality he had shown when serving with the Roman army under Scipio Aemilianus at Numantia.*)

The Senate then began its debate. The partisans of (*Jugurtha's*) envoys and a great many other senators who had been corrupted by their influence were extravagant in their praises of Jugurtha's fine qualities....A handful of senators who cared more for honour and justice than for money argued that Rome should come to Adherbal's rescue and that the murder of Hiempsal should be sternly punished. Conspicuous among the latter was Aemilius Scaurus, a man of noble family, energetic, partisan, greedy for power and fame and riches, but very clever in concealing the bad side of his character. Once he appreciated that Jugurtha's flagrant and scandalous bribery would inflame popular resentment, he curbed his natural cupidity....The Senate decreed that ten commissioners (*legati*) should be sent to divide Micipsa's former kingdom between Jugurtha and Adherbal. The chief commissioner was L. Opimius, a distinguished man who was a powerful force in the Senate at the time because as consul, after

Gaius Gracchus and M. Fulvius Flaccus had been killed, he had savagely exploited the nobility's victory over the commons. Though he had been one of Jugurtha's opponents at Rome, Jugurtha received him with the greatest consideration and plied him with gifts and promises... He applied the same tactics to the other commissioners and won over most of them, with only a few preferring honour to hard cash. When the division was effected, the more fertile and populous part of Numidia, that adjoining Mauretania, was assigned to Jugurtha, the remainder – it seemed preferable in appearance but was not in practice superior – which had more harbours and more developed urban centres was given to Adherbal to hold.

115 BC   Consuls: M. Aemilius Scaurus, M. Caecilius Metellus
Censors: L. Caecilius Metellus Diadematus, Cn. Domitius Ahenobarbus

(a) The census

EPITOME OF LIVY, Bks. 62 & 63

The censors L. Caecilius Metellus and Cn. Domitius Ahenobarbus expelled thirty-two members from the Senate....The count of citizens totalled 394,336.

The censors appointed the consul Aemilius Scaurus as Princeps Senatus: see Sallust, Jug. War 25.4; Pliny, Nat. Hist. 8.223.

(b) Marius' Praetorship

PLUTARCH, *Marius* 6

Marius gave a reasonably praiseworthy performance as praetor.

(c) Activities of the consul Aemilius Scaurus

de viris illustribus 72

When the praetor P. Decius remained seated as Scaurus was passing, Scaurus ordered him to stand up, ripped his clothing, and smashed his official chair to pieces. He also issued an edict forbidding any litigants to bring a case before Decius....As consul, Scaurus passed a sumptuary law and a law concerning the voting-rights of freedmen...He subdued the Ligurians and the Gantisci, and celebrated a triumph for this victory.

Gellius (Attic Nights 2.24.12) and Pliny (Nat. Hist. 8.223) also refer to the sumptuary law and note that it aimed to restrict the extravagance of dinner parties.

STRABO 5.1.11

Much of the Po valley was marshy. Scaurus drained the level ground by constructing navigable canals from the Po as far as Parma. This was the same Scaurus who built the Via Aemilia through Pisa and Luna to the Sabatian region and then on to Dertona.

114 BC   Consuls: Manius Acilius Balbus, C. Porcius Cato

(a) Marius as pro-praetor in Spain

PLUTARCH, *Marius* **6**

After his praetorship, the lot fell to Marius to be governor of Further Spain, where he is said to have cleared the province of brigandage.

(b) Numidia

SALLUST, *Jugurthine War* **20**

After their division of the kingdom, the Roman commissioners left Africa....Jugurtha, now convinced....that money would buy anything at Rome....set his mind to winning Adherbal's kingdom. Adherbal sent envoys to Jugurtha to complain of his misdoings....but they brought back only insults....Amassing a large army, Jugurtha started a war, and was clearly aiming at winning all Numidia to his rule.

(c) First trial of the Vestal Virgins

OROSIUS 5.15

A Roman knight, L. Veturius, seduced and dishonoured the Vestal Virgin Aemilia. Aemilia in turn involved two other Vestal Virgins in intercourse with drinking-companions of her own seducer. All were punished after information had been laid by a slave.

PLUTARCH, *Roman Questions* **83**

The Romans buried alive two men and two women, Greeks and Gauls, in the Forum Boarium....Information had been laid against three Vestal Virgins, Aemilia and Licinia and Marcia, by the servant of a certain knight called Barrus. They had for some time been having affairs with men, one of whom was Vetutius Barrus, the master of the informant.

CASSIUS DIO *fragment* **87.5 Boissier**

A man named Manius, who was perhaps responsible for setting up and assisting the whole deplorable affair, laid information about it because he had not been granted his freedom or any of the other rewards he had hoped for.

113 BC   Consuls: C. Caecilius Metellus Caprarius, Cn. Papirius Carbo

(a) Second trial of the Vestals

ASCONIUS, *in Milonianam* **p. 45C**

Sextus Peducaeus, tribune of the plebs, charged the Chief Pontiff L. Metellus and the whole College of Pontiffs with having given a faulty judgement in the matter of the indecent conduct of the Vestal Virgins, in that they had found only one Virgin – Aemilia – guilty, and acquitted two others – Marcia and Licinia. The People appointed Cassius to inquire into the case of these Virgins....Cassius condemned both Marcia and Licinia and with them several other Virgins: he was, some thought, over-harsh.

CICERO, *Brutus* 159 (46 BC)

The Virgin Licinia was defended by Crassus (*consul 95 BC*) when he was 27 years old.

CICERO, *de inventione* 1.43 (86–85 BC)

Curio had this to say when he defended Servius Fulvius (*on a charge of incest (viz. fornication with a Vestal Virgin)*): 'It is impossible to fall in love at first sight'.

OBSEQUENS 37

Three Vestal Virgins of most noble families and a number of Roman knights were all at the same time punished for incest.

(b) C. Porcius Cato tried for extortion (*repetundae*)

VELLEIUS PATERCULUS 2.8

The ex-consul C. Cato was condemned for extortion committed while governor of Macedonia, although judgement was found against him for a mere 4,000 sesterces.

CICERO, *Verrines* 2.2.184 (70 BC)

The distinguished C. Cato, a man of consular rank, had judgement found against him in the sum of a mere 8,000 sesterces.

(c) The looming danger of the Cimbri and Teutones

EPITOME OF LIVY, Bk. 63

The Cimbri, a nomadic people, arrived in Illyricum (*Northern Yugoslavia*) bent on rapine. They routed the consul Papirius Carbo and his army.

APPIAN, *Celtica* 13

A large plundering band of Teutones invaded the territory of Noricum. Fearing that they might break into Italy, the consul Papirius Carbo lay in wait for them in the Alps, where the crossing was narrowest. When they made no move against Italy, he took the offensive, charging them with having attacked Rome's friends, the people of Noricum. As he drew near, the Teutones sent to tell him that they had been unaware of the friendship between Rome and Noricum, and would not touch them again. Carbo commended the envoys and gave them guides for their return journey, but secretly ordered the guides to go by a roundabout route. He himself hurried along the direct route and fell on the Teutones, who were resting all unsuspecting. But he paid the penalty for his perfidy and lost many of his troops, and was nearly killed himself....The Romans escaped in small and scattered detachments and took cover in woodland, and managed with difficulty to regroup over two days later. The Teutones meanwhile moved on towards Gaul.

The ancient writers say that the Cimbri originated in the Crimea, and from there moved in their numerous and warlike bands westwards across Europe to France, picking up other nomadic or semi-nomadic tribes like the Teutones and Tigurini as they went.

112 BC   Consuls: M. Livius Drusus, L. Calpurnius Piso Caesoninus

Numidia

SALLUST, *Jugurthine War* 21–27

(*Jugurtha defeated Adherbal in battle near Cirta, the modern Constantine.*) Adherbal took refuge in Cirta with a small force of cavalry, and had it not been for the large numbers of Romans in the town, who turned the pursuing Numidians back from the walls, the war between the two kings would have been over the same day it had begun. So Jugurtha settled down to a siege....and made all haste to capture the town before the envoys whom he had heard had been sent to Rome by Adherbal could effect anything.

⋅   When the Senate learned that war had broken out in Numidia, they sent three young men to Africa with instructions to see both the kings and deliver a message from the Roman Senate and People: the kings were requested and directed to lay down their arms and settle their disagreements by legal means rather than by war....(*They managed only to see Jugurtha, who fobbed them off with a promise to send representatives to state his side of the case. When the young men were judged to have gone home, he intensified his siege. Meanwhile, Adherbal managed to slip two of his men out to go to Rome to appeal for Roman help for him*).

There were some in the Senate prepared to propose that an army be sent to Africa to rescue Adherbal as quickly as possible, and that meanwhile the Senate should take note of Jugurtha's failure to obey Rome's envoys. But those who favoured Jugurtha stuck to their guns and used every effort to prevent such a decree being passed. Nevertheless fresh envoys were selected to go to Numidia, senior men from among the nobility who had held high office, among them Marcus Scaurus, an ex-consul and at this time president of the Senate (*princeps senatus*).

(*Once more, however, the envoys went back to Rome with nothing settled. But the Italians in Cirta, hopeful that Rome would protect them, brought pressure to bear on Adherbal to surrender the town.*) Whereupon Jugurtha first had Adherbal tortured to death, then carried out an indiscriminate massacre of all the adult Numidians and the traders.

(*When news of this outrage reached Rome, Jugurtha's supporters still tried to protect him. But the tribune Gaius Memmius aroused widespread indignation, and in consequence*) Numidia and Italy were named as provinces under the Sempronian law for the consuls (*of 111 BC*). The two men elected for that year were P. Scipio Nasica and L. Calpurnius Bestia: the lot gave Numidia to Bestia, Italy to

Nasica. An army was then levied to be transported to Africa and money and supplies for it were voted.

111 BC   Consuls: P. Cornelius Scipio Nasica, L. Calpurnius Bestia

(a) Numidia

SALLUST, *Jugurthine War* 28–35

(*Jugurtha tried to send new envoys to Rome, but was told they would not be received unless they brought his surrender. Calpurnius, with Aemilius Scaurus among his legates, proceeded to North Africa. Although Scaurus had been against Jugurtha from the start, he now finally succumbed to Jugurtha's bribery, and this encouraged Jugurtha to seek peace after Calpurnius had won several initial successes, and terms were agreed.*) Thirty elephants, a large number of cattle and horses, and a small amount of silver were surrendered to Calpurnius' quaestor. Calpurnius set out for Rome to conduct the elections there. In Numidia and the Roman army there peace reigned.

(*Popular and widespread disquiet arose at Rome over these terms. The Senate was restrained by Scaurus' influence and delayed taking any action, but the tribune Memmius again roused the people. He made a speech in which he attacked the cruelty, inefficiency, and savage repression of opponents which the ruling oligarchy had displayed over the past fifteen years, with particular reference to the suppression of the two Gracchi and their supporters. He also attacked the deep corruption of the ruling class, and urged the people to stand up for themselves.*) By hammering away at these themes Memmius asked the people to pass a law to send the praetor L. Cassius to Jugurtha and bring him back to Rome under pledge of safe conduct. The object was that his testimony would more readily reveal the offences of Scaurus and all the others who were accused of having taken bribes from Jugurtha....

When Memmius' proposal had been carried, to the consternation of all the nobles, Cassius met Jugurtha and persuaded the fearful king, whose guilty conscience made him feel insecure, to trust in Rome's mercy rather than oppose Rome's force. He also added his own personal guarantee of Jugurtha's safety, which the king valued as highly as the public pledge: so great was Cassius' reputation at that time as a man of integrity. So Jugurtha returned to Rome with Cassius. (*But, once there, he managed to bribe another tribune, C. Baebius, to use his veto to block Memmius' inquiry. Meanwhile, Spurius Albinus, one of the two consuls-elect for 110 BC, anxious to renew the Numidian War – he had drawn Numidia as his province for 110 BC – pressed the claims of Massiva, a grandson of King Masinissa, to the throne of Numidia. Jugurtha arranged Massiva's assassination. He was ordered by the Senate to quit Italy.*) Leaving the city, he is said to have often looked back at it without saying a word, until at last he declared: 'A city for sale, and doomed soon to perish, once she finds a buyer!'

EPITOME OF LIVY, Bk 64

Jugurtha arrived in Rome, having been summoned there under a public guarantee of safe-conduct to give evidence against his backers, because he was alleged to have corrupted many senators with bribes.

(There follows the same story about his parting remark as in Sallust.)

(b) The agrarian law of 111 BC

This law survives in a fragmentary state, incised on the reverse face of the same sheet of bronze which carries on its obverse the repetundae *law of Gaius Gracchus. It marks the final stage in the winding-up of the Gracchan reforms. It is too long, too fragmentary, and too detailed to translate here. See E.G. Hardy,* Roman Laws and Charters.

110 BC   Consuls: M. Minucius Rufus, Sp. Postumius Albinus

(a) Numidia

EPITOME OF LIVY, Bk. 64

The legate Aulus Postumius, after having got the worst of a battle against Jugurtha, proceeded to conclude an ignominious peace, which the Senate ruled should not be ratified.

SALLUST, *Jugurthan War* 36

The consul Spurius Albinus set out for Africa at once, anxious to finish the war off before the elections, which were due to be held before very long. (*But Jugurtha eluded him,*) so with the approach of the elections Albinus returned to Rome, leaving his brother Aulus in charge of the Roman forces as his deputy....(*But the elections were delayed (see below), and eventually Aulus was lured into a trap by Jugurtha, and with his army in a desperate situation was forced to come to terms.*) Jugurtha said that he had Aulus and his army at the mercy of starvation or the sword, but nevertheless he was ready to let them go free after they had passed under the yoke if Aulus would make a treaty with him and agree to leave Numidia within ten days. These terms were harsh and disgraceful, but since the only alternative was death, peace was concluded on the king's terms.

(b) Elections delayed by tribunician wrangling

SALLUST, *Jugurthine War* 37

At that time quarrels among the tribunes caused a terrible disturbance in affairs at Rome. Two of the tribunes, P. Lucullus and L. Annius, kept trying to be elected for a second year running, in the teeth of the opposition of their colleagues, and this dispute had the effect of blocking the elections for the whole year....

(c) The Mamilian Enquiry (*Quaestio Mamilia*)

SALLUST, *Jugurthine War* 40

The tribune C. Mamilius Limetanus introduced a bill to the popular assembly to institute a court of inquiry against those men who had encouraged Jugurtha to disregard decrees of the Senate, or who had accepted money from him while serving as legates or commanders, who had handed elephants and deserters back to him, or who had made compacts of peace or war with the enemies of Rome. Those who were conscious of their own guilt or who were fearful of the dangers of factional strife made preparations to obstruct the bill; since they could not oppose it openly without admitting their approval of these and other similar acts, they went about it secretly through their friends and above all through certain Latins and Italian allies. But the plebs ratified the bill with quite incredible keenness and enthusiasm, but rather out of hatred for the nobility who were threatened by the bill than out of genuine concern for Rome's well-being. Such was the height which sectional passion reached.

With everybody else panic-stricken, with an exultant commons on the one side and his own class in full flight, Marcus Scaurus, whom I have already noted had been a legate under Calpurnius Bestia, took advantage of the general consternation to have himself elected as one of the three commissioners of enquiry authorised by Mamilius' law. All the same, the investigation was conducted in a harsh and forceful manner....

CICERO, *Brutus* 128 (46 BC)

Under this invidious law of Mamilius, Gracchan judges (*iudices Gracchani*) got rid of the priest (*sacerdos*) C. Galba and four former consuls, L. Bestia, C. Cato, Sp. Albinus, and that outstanding gentleman L. Opimius, the man who had killed Gracchus. Opimius had been acquitted when he stood trial before the People (*in 120 BC*) but now paid the price for having made a stand against an excited people.

109 BC   Consuls: Q. Caecilius Metellus (Numidicus), M. Junius Silanus
Censors: M. Aemilius Scaurus, M. Livius Drusus

(a) The Censorship

PLUTARCH, *Roman Questions* 50

When his colleague Livius Drusus (*the former tribune of 122 BC*) died in office, Aemilius Scaurus refused to resign his own censorship until threatened with imprisonment by some of the tribunes.

The Capitoline Fasti record Drusus' death in office and the fact that Scaurus had to be compelled to resign. No population figures survive for this census: indeed, we have no further figures after 115 until we come to 86 BC.

(b) Changes in the regulations about length of military service

CICERO, *pro Cornelio*, cited by Asconius p.68 C

There are, gentlemen, altogether four categories of traditional senatorial decisions concerning laws. One is that the Senate decides that a law be abrogated: as in the consulship of Q. Caecilius and Marcus Junius, that the laws which impeded military action should be abrogated.

Asconius goes on to speak of the 'abrogation of several laws which had been passed reducing the period of liability to military service'. Thus we may have here a reference to the repeal of (inter alia) Gaius Gracchus' legislation on this topic in 122 BC.

(c) Numidia: Metellus and Marius

SALLUST, *Jugurthine War* 43–69

Numidia was allotted to Metellus, an energetic man who, for all that he was an opponent of the popular party, had a reputation for fairness and honesty....As soon as he entered office, he devoted his attention to the war he was going to wage. Lacking confidence in the old army, he levied new legionaries, summoned auxiliary troops from all quarters, built up stocks of arms, weapons, horses, etc., and an abundance of supplies. In short he made ready whatever commonly is needed for a war of varied character demanding large resources. Further, in making these preparations the Senate backed him with its authority, and the allies, Latins, and foreign kings volunteered to contribute auxiliary forces – indeed, the whole state showed the greatest enthusiasm.

(Finding the army already in Africa demoralised, Metellus refrained from taking the field and concentrated on training and rehabilitation, himself setting a vigorous personal example. He brushed aside Jugurtha's overtures for peace, mistrusting them. Later he advanced cautiously into Numidia, with his legate Gaius Marius with the cavalry in command of the rearguard, and occupied Vaga. After rejecting further approaches from Jugurtha, he just managed to win a confused and hard-fought and expensive victory. Jugurtha got away, and thereafter Metellus, wary of heavy losses in pitched battles against the mobile enemy, settled down to a piecemeal conquest.)

At Vaga, where Metellus had first established a garrison at the time when Jugurtha was suing for peace, the leading citizens, overborne by the entreaties of the king towards whom they had always been loyal, entered into a plot....and invited the centurions and military tribunes and the garrison commander Titus Turpilius Silanus to their homes, where all of them were killed while dining, with the exception of Turpilius himself. They then fell upon the troops who were strolling about unarmed....In the midst of this indiscriminate slaughter, with the Numidians in a frenzy and the town quite cut off, the commander Turpilius was the only Italian to escape unharmed ....After the recapture of Vaga Turpilius was court-martialled by Metellus, and after failing to clear himself was condemned and scourged and put to death – for he was a Latin citizen*.

---

* The meaning of Sallust's Latin here – *civis ex Latio* – is ambiguous and disputed. It has been taken to mean that Turpilius was a citizen of a Latin community and not a Roman citizen (and hence protected from such punishment by his commander), or alternatively, that he was a man who had acquired Roman citizenship, though formerly only of Latin status, perhaps through holding a local magistracy in a Latin community, and hence Metellus thought he could punish him in a manner he would have hesitated to use against an established Roman citizen. However, since the true reading of Sallust is here in grave doubt, and *civis ex Latio* is little better than a conjectural restoration, it is wise not to press the issue too hard.

Plutarch *Marius* 8 reports that it was Marius who prevailed on a reluctant Metellus to impose the death penalty on Turpilius.

(d) The Cimbri

EPITOME OF LIVY, Bk. 65

The consul M. Junius Silanus was defeated in a battle against the Cimbri. When representatives of the Cimbri requested a grant of territory in which to settle, the Senate refused the request.

FLORUS 1.38 *(3.3)*

The Cimbri, Teutoni, and Tigurini....sent representatives to Silanus' camp (*in Gaul*) and then to the Senate requesting that Rome grant them some land as it were as payment for military service, so that Rome might then employ the military manpower of their tribes for any purpose she might wish....They were rebuffed, and so set about winning by fighting what they had failed to secure by petition. Silanus was unable to check their first onslaught, nor Manilius their second, nor Caepio their third: all were routed and driven from their camps.

**108 BC   Consuls: Ser. Sulpicius Galba, L. (*or* Q.) Hortensius
Suffect consul: M. Aurelius Scaurus***

Marius elected consul for 107 BC

VELLEIUS PATERCULUS 2.11

Working through the public contractors (*publicani*) and the other men engaged in business in Africa, Marius accused Metellus of being too slow and allowing the war to drag on into now its third year,....and so contrived to get elected consul and have transferred to himself the supreme command in a war which had almost been finished off by Metellus, who had twice defeated Jugurtha in pitched battle.

PLUTARCH, *Marius 8–9*

(*Metellus was angry with Marius over the business of Turpilius Silanus – see above, 109 BC (c)*) and he is said on one occasion to have insulted Marius to his face: "So, my fine fellow, you are planning to leave us and sail home to stand for the consulship. Will you not settle for waiting to hold a consulship with my son?" Metellus' son was at the time a mere youth....Marius back in Rome based his campaign for election on a widespread attack on Metellus, promising that he himself would either kill Jugurtha or capture him alive. He was brilliantly successful.

SALLUST, *Jugurthine War 64–73*

Marius asked Metellus for leave so that he might be a candidate for the consulship. But, although Metellus was outstanding in valour and renown and all other desirable qualities, yet he had an inborn disdain and arrogance, the common failing of the Roman nobility. His first reaction was one of astonishment at so unusual a request, accompanied by a purportedly friendly word of

---

* The Fasti reveal that Hortensius was removed from office after a condemnation, but on what charge we do not know. It may have been for electoral irregularities (*de ambitu*), but that is only a guess. He was replaced by Aurelius Scaurus.

warning: 'Do not embark on so insane a course, do not entertain ambitions beyond your station. All things are not for all men to aspire to, you must rest content with what you have. And, finally, take care not to ask the Roman People for something they will not give you, and will be right not to give you.'...And later, "Do not be in a hurry to go to Rome, it will be time enough for you to be a candidate when you can be one along with my son". That young man was at the time serving on his father's staff, and was about twenty....Marius was overcome by ambition and resentment, those worst of counsellors, and refrained from no word or act provided that it won him popularity. He relaxed his former strict discipline over the troops under his command in winter quarters, and talked about the war in a mixture of criticism and boastfulness to the men of business, a large number of whom were present in Utica. "With only half the army under his own command he would have Jugurtha in chains in a few days; Metellus was deliberately allowing the war to drag on...." All this talk appealed the more strongly to the men of business because they had suffered severe financial loss because of the long duration of the war, and for greedy spirits nothing ever moves fast enough....

In these ways Marius won over the Roman knights, both those serving with the army and those engaged in business, some by his personal influence but most by their hopes of an end to the war, and got them to write to their friends at Rome attacking Metellus' conduct of the war and demanding that Marius be appointed commander-in-chief. So he won powerful support for his candidature from many voters as a candidate of real worth. Coincidentally, with the nobility in retreat after the recent Mamilian law, the plebs were now looking for 'new men' (*non-nobles*) whom they could raise to high office. Thus the whole tide of events was in full flood for Marius....The upshot was that the nobility were routed, and for the first time for many years a consulship went to a 'new man'. And when subsequently the tribune T. Manlius Mancinus asked the people whom they wanted as commander in the war against Jugurtha, their overwhelming choice fell on Marius. Although shortly before the Senate had extended Metellus' command, its decision was thus frustrated.

Meanwhile Jugurtha had forced an alliance with Bocchus, King of the Gaetulians.

107 BC   Consuls: L. Cassius Longinus, C. Marius

(a) Marius' speech in Sallust

The speech put in Marius' mouth by Sallust in chapter 85 (a very long chapter) of his Jugurthine War *is a superb piece of Latin. In it Marius is depicted as delivering a vigorous attack on a broad front against the corruption, exclusiveness, and incapacity of the ruling nobility as a whole. Only in the final section does Numidia at last get a brief mention:*

'My concluding remarks will be brief. First of all, as to Numidia, let your hopes be high. For all that has so far protected Jugurtha and kept him safe – greed, incompetence, arrogance – all these defences you have yourselves demolished. Secondly, there is an army in Numidia which knows the terrain, but an army which, as Heaven is my witness, is more valiant than it has been fortunate; for the great part of it has been frittered away by the greed and rash stupidity of its commanders. And so I appeal to those of you who are of military age to join your efforts with mine to save our country. Let none of you feel fear because of the disasters that have befallen others or the arrogance of generals. I shall be there with you myself in march and in battle, to give you counsel and share in the danger with you. In everything I shall treat myself and you exactly alike. And surely with the help of the gods all waits ready for us to pluck: victory, booty, glory....'

(b) The enlistment of the poorest citizens

SALLUST, *Jugurthine War* 86

Marius enlisted recruits not in the traditional manner nor on the basis of property-qualification, but taking any citizen who chose to volunteer, property-less men (*capite censi*) for the most part.

AULUS GELLIUS, *Attic Nights* 16.10.10

The humblest and poorest of the Roman commons who reported property worth less than 1500 *asses* at the census were called 'proletarians' (*proletarii*), while those who were registered as owning no property at all or next to none were called 'head-counts' (*capite censi*)....Gaius Marius was the first man recorded as having enlisted the *capite censi*, a hitherto unheard-of act, according to some authorities in the crisis of the war against the Cimbri, but it is better to follow Sallust who says that it was during the war against Jugurtha.

(c) Numidia

SALLUST, *Jugurthine War* 86

Marius landed at Utica, and there the army was formally handed over to his command by Metellus' legate, P. Rutilius. Metellus himself had left so as to avoid meeting Marius face to face, having no taste to see what he had found it intolerable to hear about.

PLUTARCH, *Sulla* 3

On his election as quaestor, Sulla was assigned to serve under Marius in his first consulship, and with Marius he sailed to Africa to the war against Jugurtha.

VALERIUS MAXIMUS 6.9.6

Up until the time of his election as quaestor Sulla had led a dissolute life of debauchery and drinking and addiction to the theatre. So it was that the consul Marius is said to have been put out when the lot assigned to him as his quaestor for the very tough war in Africa such a dandified man-about-town.

(d) Gaul

EPITOME OF LIVY, Bk. 65

The consul L. Cassius was cut down at the head of his army by the Gallic Tigurini, a sub-division of the Helvetii who had broken away from the main body of that people, in the territory of the Nitiobriges (*roughly, an area on either side of the central stretch of the River Garonne, S.E. of Bordeaux).* The soldiers who survived the slaughter bought their safety by giving hostages and half of all their property.

CAESAR, *Gallic War* 1.7

Caesar could remember that the consul L. Cassius had been killed, and his army defeated by the Helvetii and forced to pass under the yoke.

ad Herennium 1.25

When C. Popilius (*one of Cassius' subordinate commanders*) was surrounded by the Gauls and left with no way of escape, he parleyed with the enemy commanders. The upshot was that he might lead his army away provided that he left its equipment and supplies behind. He judged it better to lose *matériel than to lose an army. He was subsequently charged with treason (maiestas).*

106 BC   Consuls: Q. Servilius Caepio, C. Atilius Serranus

(a) Ballot law of C. Coelius and condemnation of C. Popillius Laenas

CICERO, *de legibus* 3.36 (52–44 BC)

It seemed that the oral vote survived only in one class of trial, where Cassius himself (*see above, 131 BC (a)*) had made it an exception, namely trials for high treason (*perduellio*). The written ballot was extended to these trials too by C. Coelius, who as long as he lived expressed his sorrow that in order to get C. Popillius condemned (*see also 107 BC (d)*) he had injured the state.

(b) Q. Servilius Caepio's Judiciary Law

CASSIODORUS, *Chronicle*

The consul Servilius Caepio caused the courts to be shared between the knights and the senators.

The same report in virtually identical words is found in **Obsequens** *41.*

TACITUS, *Annals* 12.60

Claudius handed over all the legal power which had so often in the past been the focus of violent, even armed, dissension, as when the equestrian order was being settled in possession of the courts by bills like the Sempronian or when once again the courts were being restored to the Senate by laws like the Servilian.

CICERO, *de inventione* 1.92 (86/85 BC)

We say that something 'causes offence' if it is something that people do not like to hear said: as, for instance, if someone were to speak highly of Caepio's judiciary law in the company of Roman knights eager to serve as judges (*iudices*).

CICERO, *pro Cluentio* 140 (66 BC)

When L. Crassus (*later consul 95 BC)* spoke in support of the Servilian law he heaped praise on the Senate, and he attacked the Roman knights very roughly during the course of that speech.

Excerpt from Crassus' speech cited by CICERO, *de oratore* 1.255 (55 BC)

"Rescue us from our wretchednesses, rescue us from the jaws of those men whose cruelty cannot be satiated save by our blood. Do not suffer us to be the servants of anyone save you, the Roman people, all of you – for that we both can and should be."

CICERO, de oratore 2.199

....The Roman knights, who at that time (*sc. 95 BC*) were serving as judges in that case, entertained a hatred for Q. Caepio, who had earned their hostility because of his judiciary law.

CICERO, *Brutus* 164 (46 BC)

As for me, ever since I was a boy that speech of Crassus' in support of Caepio's law has been my guide. In it there is much fine praise for the authority of the Senate, in whose support he delivered his speech; and it also seeks to excite resentment against the clique of judges and accusers (*iudicum et accusatorum factio*), in attacking whose power it was then essential to speak in a manner which would have a popular appeal.

(c) Trial of Metellus Numidicus for extortion*

CICERO, *pro Balbo* 11 (56 BC)

I heard this story from my father when I was a boy, about the trial of Q. Metellus on a charge of extortion (*de pecuniis repetundis*)....When Metellus' account-books were being circulated for inspection by the court, there was not a single man among those worthy Roman knights who were sitting as judges in the case who did not avert his gaze and turn away from them, so as to avoid risking giving the impression that he doubted the honesty and accuracy of the entries which Metellus had made.

(d) Gaul: the Tolosa scandal

OROSIUS 5.15

After capturing a Gallic town called Tolosa (*Toulouse*) the proconsul Caepio removed 100,000 pounds of gold and 110,000 of silver from the temple of Apollo. After it had been sent off under guard to Marseilles, all of it is said to have been criminally made away with. This led in due course to a large-scale enquiry at Rome (*see below, 104 BC*).

JUSTIN 32.3.10

All the gold and silver from Tolosa was stolen by the Roman consul Caepio.

---

* This date is uncertain, but it seems probable that Metellus' trial may have followed on his command in Africa, and preceded Caepio's jury law, and hence dates from late 107 or early 106 BC.

(e) Numidia

Sallust, Jugurthine War *92–100 records Marius' relentless pressure on Jugurtha, which finally led his ally King Bocchus to go over to the Romans. Sulla, whose conduct is specially praised, was sent to negotiate with Bocchus.*

(f) Catulus' three successive electoral defeats

CICERO, *pro Plancio* 12 (54 BC)

Quintus Catulus, born into a great and distinguished family and a man of great wisdom and integrity, was defeated in the consular elections by, I will not stress Gaius Serranus (*consul 106 BC*), a thoroughly stupid man but a man at any rate of noble birth, nor Gaius Fimbria (*consul 104 BC*), a "new man" but a man of great spirit and high intelligence, but by of all people Gnaeus Mallius (*consul 105 BC*), not merely a non-noble but a worthless, unintelligent fellow and a despicable and sordid character.

105 BC   Consuls: P. Rutilius Rufus, Cn. Mallius Maximus

(a) New training methods of Rutilius Rufus

VALERIUS MAXIMUS 2.3.2

The consul P. Rutilius broke new ground not covered by any previous commander by calling in instructors from the gladiatorial school of C. Aurelius Scaurus to train his legionaries in a more skilful technique of weaponry, both in attack and in defence.

FRONTINUS, *Stratagems* 4.2.2

When (*in 104 BC*) C. Marius had a choice between two armies, that which had served under Rutilius and that which had served under Metellus and subsequently under himself, he opted for Rutilius' army because although it was smaller it was better trained and disciplined.

(b) Gaul: the Battle of Arausio (*Orange*)

SALLUST, *Jugurthine War* 114

At about this time our generals Q. Caepio and Cn. Manlius were defeated in a battle against the Gauls. The news of this defeat filled all Italy with dread.

EPITOME OF LIVY, Bk. 67

M. Aurelius Scaurus, legate of the consul, was captured by the Cimbri after the army had been routed. Interrogated by the enemy, he warned them not to cross the Alps to attack Italy, assuring them that the Romans were invincible. He was cut down on the spot by a wild young man called Boiorix. The same enemy defeated the consul Cn. Manlius and the proconsul Q. Servilius Caepio, and both their camps were taken and looted. Eighty thousand soldiers were killed in the neighbourhood of Arausio.

LICINIANUS p. 11 F

They also captured the former consul, M. Aurelius Scaurus (*consul suffect 108 BC*), after he had been thrown from his horse. Interrogated by his captors, he neither did nor said anything unworthy of a Roman gentleman who had held the highest offices. So he was executed, though he could have escaped....Terrified by this victory of the Cimbri the consul Mallius wrote to Caepio entreating him to effect a junction of their two armies so that they might make a stand against the Gauls with their combined forces. But Caepio refused, and crossed the Rhone, boasting to his own men that he would help the cowardly consul; but he declined even to inform Mallius of his plan of campaign, and refused to listen to the envoys sent by the Senate urging Caepio and Mallius to put aside their personal feud and join together to save the state. And even when envoys came from the Cimbri to ask for peace and territory to settle in and seed-corn for planting he rejected their advances so high-handedly that, despairing of peace, they attacked the next day. His camp was not very far from that of Mallius, but despite the short distance he could not be prevailed on to effect a junction of the two armies. Most of his army was destroyed....The battle was fought on the sixth of October.

(c) Numidia: Jugurtha captured

Sulla negotiated with Bocchus on Marius' behalf, and Bocchus duly handed Jugurtha – who had taken refuge with that king – over to Sulla to deliver to Marius.

PLUTARCH, *Marius* 10

Sulla had a signet-ring specially made with a seal depicting Jugurtha being handed over to him by Bocchus.

PLINY, *Natural History* 37.1.9

As dictator Sulla always sealed documents with the scene of Jugurtha being handed over to him.

See E. A. Sydenham, The Roman Republican Coinage *p. 145 and plate 24 no. 879, for silver denarii issued by Faustus Cornelius Sulla, the dictator's son, about 63/62 BC, the reverse of which depicts Sulla seated with Bocchus kneeling and offering an olive-branch, and behind him Jugurtha also on his knees and with his hands bound. This presumably was a reproduction of Sulla's famous seal.*

(d) Excitement following Arausio; election of Marius to a second consulship

SALLUST, *Jugurthine War* 104

When news arrived that the war in Numidia had been won and that Jugurtha was being brought to Rome as a prisoner, Marius was elected consul in his absence and allocated Gaul as his province. On the first day of the new year he entered on his office as consul and celebrated a magnificient triumph. At that crisis in Rome's affairs, all his country's hopes and wealth rested in his hands.

CICERO, *de provinciis consularibus* 19 (56 BC)

Who had more personal enemies than Gaius Marius? L. Crassus and M. Scaurus disliked him, all the Metelli hated him. Yet, so far from voting against the grant of the province of Gaul to their enemy, these men supported the extraordinary assignment of that province to him so that he might command in the war against the Gauls.

EPITOME OF LIVY, Bk. 67

Marius' tenure of the consulship was continued for several years because of the fear aroused by the war with the Cimbri.

LICINIANUS p. 14 F

Mallius' fellow-consul Rutilius, with fear of the advancing Cimbri shaking the whole country, made all men of military age take an oath not to leave Italy; and all the coastal regions and ports of Italy were forbidden to allow any man aged less than 35 to take passage on any ship.

104 BC   Consuls: C. Marius II, C. Flavius Fimbria

(a) Disgrace of Caepio

ASCONIUS 78 C

L. Cassius Longinus, who was tribune of the plebs in the consulship of C. Marius and C. Flavius, carried a number of laws aimed at diminishing the power of the nobility, including this one, namely that anyone who had been condemned by the People or stripped of his *imperium* by the People was barred from membership of the Senate. His chief motive was his quarrels with Q. Servilius (*Caepio*), who had been consul two years earlier and had been stripped of his *imperium* by the People after his failure against the Cimbri.

EPITOME OF LIVY, Bk. 67

Caepio, whose rashness was the cause of the disaster, was condemned and his property was confiscated by the state – the first man this had happened to since King Tarquin – and his *imperium* was abrogated.*

(b) Toulouse Gold Scandal

*This is referred to under **106 BC** (d), above. The case was apparently heard in a special court in 104 BC: so Broughton,* Magistrates of the Roman Republic, *1.566, note 8.*

---

* This had happened late in 105 BC, it seems. The defeat at Arausio had occurred on 6 October, 105 BC.

(c) Trial and acquittal of M. Junius Silanus

ASCONIUS 80 C

Silanus had been worsted by the Cimbrians (*see above, 109 BC*), on which ground Domitius brought him to trial before the People. It was charged against him that in this business with the Cimbri he had acted without the instructions of the People, and that this had been the prime cause of the disasters which the People had suffered in the war against them....But Silanus was acquitted by a large majority. Cn. Domitius (*Ahenobarbus*) was tribune in the consulship of C. Marius (*for a second time*) and C. Fimbria.

CICERO, *divinatio in Caecilium* 67 (70 BC)

Not so very long ago we know that Cn. Domitius brought M. Silanus to trial just on account of the injuries suffered by a single member of the Gallic tribe of the Aegritomari, a friend of his father's (*consul 122 BC*).

(d) Trial of Scaurus and *Lex Domitia de Sacerdotiis*

ASCONIUS 21 C

When Domitius was tribune of the plebs he became angry with Scaurus because Scaurus had not co-opted him as a member of the College of Augurs, and so he indicted him before the People and requested that he be fined...., the allegation being that through Scaurus' fault the holy public rites of the Dei Penates which took place at Lavinium were not being conducted with sufficient correctness and proper ritual observance. Scaurus was acquitted, but three tribes voted for condemnation and in the thirty-two which voted for his acquittal only a few votes in each tribe tilted the tribal vote in his favour.

VELLEIUS PATERCULUS 2.12

In that year (*103 BC – Velleius misdates*) the tribune of the plebs Cn. Domitius carried a law that the priests, who had hitherto been co-opted by the members of the Colleges, should be elected by the People.

SUETONIUS, *Nero* 2

Cn. Domitius, when he was tribune, hostile to the pontiffs because they had co-opted someone else into the place left vacant by his own father, transferred the right of filling vacancies in the priestly colleges from the Colleges themselves to the People.

(e) Agrarian bill of L. Marcius Philippus

CICERO, *de officiis* 2.73 (44 BC)

Philippus made a pernicious remark when he was tribune and trying to pass an agrarian bill – he cheerfully put up with its defeat and in that showed himself decidedly a man of moderation – but in working for its passage he said a lot of things of a rabble-rousing nature and in particular this, that 'there were not two thousand men in the state of any real substance',....a remark tending towards equalisation of property, and what could be a greater pestilence than that?

(f) Saturninus Quaestor

CICERO, *de haruspicum responsis* **43** (56 BC)

We know that Saturninus became a *popularis* out of indignation at the action of the Senate: at a time of shortage of corn, when Saturninus was quaestor in charge of the corn-supply, the Senate dismissed him and appointed M. Scaurus to take charge.

(g) Marius elected to a third consulship

Inscriptiones Latinae Selectae **59**

C. Marius was elected to his third consulship in absence.

(h) Judicial Legislation of Servilius Glaucia

The year of Glaucia's tribunate and of the lex Servilia Glauciae *which he carried and which repealed the* lex Servilia Caepionis *passed by the consul Servilius Caepio in 106 BC cannot be determined with any real assurance. It must fall between 106 and 100 BC. The two dates most favoured are either 104 or 101 BC. The former is here preferred, but with no great confidence. See also under* **101** *BC.*

CICERO, *Verrines* **2.1.26** (70BC)

Indeed, as I believe, it was Glaucia who first provided that the defendant's hearing should be completed in a double session: previously either a decision could be given after the first session of the court, or further complete rehearings could take place.

Valerius Maximus (8.1.11) tells how under the earlier system a case had once gone through seven hearings, each of which failed to produce a verdict either way, until the eighth and last produced a verdict of acquittal.

CICERO, *Brutus* **224** (46 BC)

C. Servilius Glaucia was a terrible scoundrel, but a very acute and clever and witty man. He had the support of the commons, and had bound the equestrian order to him by the benefit his law gave them.

CICERO, *pro Rabirio Postumo* **8** (54 BC)

The Julian Law (*of 59 BC*) directs that recovery should be sought from those persons who have come into possession of those moneys which were appropriated by the condemned man (*in other words, Julius Caesar's recovery law – the* lex Julia de repetundis *– made it possible to recover not merely from the convicted person but also from third parties*)....This section of the Julian Law is taken over verbatim not only from the Cornelian Law (*of Sulla*) but from the even earlier Servilian Law.

ASCONIUS 21 C, commenting on a passage from Cicero's speech *pro Scauro*

"He was indicted by Q. Servilius Caepio (*son of the consul of 106 BC*) under the Servilian Law, at a time when the courts were in the hands of the equestrian order and, after the condemnation of P. Rutilius (*92 BC*), nobody however innocent did not go in fear of those courts."

Q. Servilius Caepio indicted Aemilius Scaurus on a charge of extortion in the province of Asia under the *repetundae* law of Servilius Glaucia.

(i) Marius in Gaul

PLUTARCH, *Marius* 14

Marius had a great stroke of luck. The barbarian Cimbri's tide turned and carried them into Spain, thus giving him time to train his soldiers and get them fit and restore their morale.

Cf. Plutarch, Marius *25 for innovations in weaponry*

PLINY, *Natural History* 10.16

In his second consulship Marius made the eagle the special standard of the Roman legions. It had previously been the chief standard, but there were also four others: the wolf, the minotaur, the horse, and the boar were carried before the individual ranks. A few years earlier the custom had begun of leaving all these behind in camp and carrying the eagle alone into battle; Marius discarded them altogether.

FESTUS 267L, 345L

"Marius' mules" is a name that derives from a practice of Marius, who accustomed his soldiers to labour along carrying their own baggage on a kind of hod....

The soldiers had customarily fought with small targes, which Marius abolished and substituted Bruttian shields.

Strabo (4.8) records Marius' works to improve the navigability of the mouth of the River Rhone at Marseilles.

PLUTARCH, *Sulla* 4

Marius employed Sulla as a legate in his second consulship and as a military tribune in his third.

(j) Slave revolts in Attica and Sicily

ATHENAEUS 6.104, p.272e

The philosopher Posidonius reports that the many tens of thousands of slaves who worked in chain-gangs in the Attic mines rose up and killed the mine guards, seized the fortress of Sunium, and for a long time plundered Attica. This was the time when the second slave revolt was beginning in Sicily.

DIODORUS SICULUS 36.2

Just before the outbreak of the second Sicilian slave revolt a number of small and short-lived slave-revolts took place in Italy, as if heaven was giving a fore-warning of the greatness of the revolt that was about to break out in Sicily.

(k) Trouble in Asia

JUSTIN 37.4.3

After concluding an alliance with Nicomedes of Bithynia, Mithridates of Pontus invaded Paphlagonia, conquered it, and divided it with his ally. When the Senate heard the news, envoys were sent to both kings ordering them to restore the Paphlagonians to their previous independence. Not in the least perturbed by the Roman warnings, Mithridates proceeded to occupy Galatia as well. Nicomedes....said that he would restore Paphlagonia to its rightful king, changed his own son's name to Pylaemenes, the traditional name of the kings of Paphlagonia, and thus pretended that he had restored the territory to its royal line....So the envoys went back to Rome, having been made fools of.

103 BC   Consuls: C. Marius III, L. Aurelius Orestes

(a) Tribunate and legislation of L. Appuleius Saturninus

N.B. The dating of the legislation of Saturninus between his first tribunate in 103 BC and his second in 100 BC is disputed. The pattern followed here is not universally accepted.

de viris illustribus 73

The seditious tribune Lucius Appuleius Saturninus, wanting to win favour with the Marian soldiers, carried a law to assign veterans a hundred *iugera* (*about 60 acres*) of land apiece in Africa. When his colleague Baebius sought to veto the bill, he got the people to stone Baebius and drive him off.

ad Herennium 1.21

When L. Saturninus was threatening to carry a corn-bill (*?fixing the price at 6⅓ asses a modius**), Caepio, who was urban quaestor at the time, told the Senate that the treasury could not afford such a massive largesse. The Senate decreed that if Saturninus tried to move the ratification of the bill he would be judged to be acting against the state. Saturninus began to put the proposal. His colleagues interposed their veto. None the less Saturninus brought out the voting-urn. Caepio....then launched an attack at the head of the loyalists, pulled down the voting-gangways, threw down the voting-urns, and in general tried to block the law's passage. Caepio was indicted on a charge of high treason (*maiestas*).

VALERIUS MAXIMUS 4.7.3

When Caepio (*consul 106 BC*) was imprisoned because he seemed to be to blame for our army's destruction by the Cimbri and Teutoni, the tribune L. Reginus, mindful of their long and close friendship, released him from public custody;

---

* The MSS give ⅚ of an *as* as the price of a *modius* (just over one English stone) under this bill, but the Latin can very easily be amended to read instead 6⅓ *asses*, the price fixed by Gaius Gracchus. It is uncertain whether Gaius' law had by now been repealed or superseded. We know from Cicero (*Brutus* 222, *de officiis* 2.72) that a certain M. Octavius did have the Gracchan law abrogated, replacing it with what Cicero called a more moderate one. But the date is unknown, and suggestions have ranged between 121 and the late 80s BC.

indeed, he went even further in proving his friendship by accompanying Caepio into exile (*at Smyrna*).

ad Herennium 1.24

One line of defence is when the defendant maintains that his action was not deliberate, but the result of carelessness or bad luck or constraint. Caepio, for example, when facing the tribunes attributed the loss of his army to bad luck.

LICINIANUS p. 13 F

Cn. Mallius was exiled from Rome on the same charge as Caepio through the bill carried by L. Saturninus.

CICERO, *de oratore* 2.107 (51 BC)

The question is a precise one, a moot point of definition, such as gave rise to a heated dispute between myself (*M. Antonius, consul 99 BC*) and P. Sulpicius Rufus (*tribune 88 BC*) at the trial of Norbanus* (*tribune 103 BC*). I was prepared to concede that many of the charges which Sulpicius was levelling against Norbanus were true, but I denied that they constituted a case that Norbanus had been guilty of treason (*maiestas minuta*). The whole of that trial turned on the precise meaning of '*maiestas minuta*' in Saturninus' law.

CICERO, *de oratore* 2.197

Force, pursuit, stone-throwing, tribunician cruelty (*sc. on the part of Norbanus*) – they were all there in that terrible and wretched misfortune of Caepio....Finally, it was clear to everybody that M. Aemilius Scaurus, the *princeps senatus* and the first man in Rome, had been struck by a stone, and nobody could deny that L. Cotta and T. Didius had been forcibly ejected from the temple when they were trying to veto the bill.

CICERO, *de oratore* 2.124

Antonius did not hesitate to demonstrate to the court that Norbanus' violence had had its origin in the grief of the people and their hatred for Caepio and his loss of his army; it could not be repressed, it was justified.

CICERO, *de officiis* 2.49 (44 BC)

The eloquence of P. Sulpicius was demonstrated when he indicted that violent and useless fellow, C. Norbanus.

VALERIUS MAXIMUS 8.5.2.

When Norbanus was on trial for treason before a public court (*quaestio publica*), M. Aemilius Scaurus tried quite openly to destroy him.

CICERO, *pro Fonteio* 24 (69 BC)

Marcus Aemilius Scaurus, for all that almost the whole world was ruled by his casual nod, was not believed when he gave evidence under oath against C.

---

* The date of Norbanus' trial is uncertain. See also 95 BC (a).

Fimbria and C. Memmius (*in both cases the trials were for extortion (repetundae)*).

PLUTARCH, *Marius* 14

His fellow-consul having died, Marius returned to Rome for the consular elections. There were many good candidates, but Lucius Saturninus, having been courted by Marius, harangued the people with the message that they must elect Marius. Marius pretended that he did not want to be elected again, whereupon Saturninus called him a traitor for seeking to avoid command at the hour of his country's great danger.

EPITOME OF LIVY, Bk.67

Marius won a fourth consulship after hypocritically pretending that he did not seek it.

(b) A Lull in the Fighting in the North

EPITOME OF LIVY, Bk.67

Having laid waste everything between the Rhone and the Pyrenees, the Cimbri crossed over into Spain, where, after despoiling numerous places, they were put to flight by the Celtiberians. They returned to Gaul and joined up with the Teutoni in the territory of the Veliocassi (*the region round Rouen*).

Marius spent the year organising his forces, etc. Sulla was now a military tribune in his army.

JUSTIN 38.3.6

Appreciating what a great war he was setting in motion, Mithridates sent envoys to the Cimbri, and othes to the Gallograeci and Sarmatians, to seek help. All these people he had already courted with various gifts and good turns while meditating his war with Rome.

(c) Marian settlements in Africa

CAESAR, *Bellum Africanum* 56

The Gaetulians from the royal cavalry, men of high rank, and the cavalry commanders, whose fathers had in the past served with Marius and been granted estates and lands by him, had after Sulla's victory been put under the power of King Hiempsal.

Inscriptions from the imperial period refer to Uchi Maius as a 'Marian Colony' and to Thibaris as a 'Marian Municipality', and Thuburnica calls Marius 'founder of the colony'. But they were probably Gaetulian settlements which probably (in the case of Thuburnica certainly) did not acquire colonial or municipal status before imperial times. All three places were outside the bounds of the province of Asia. (See P. A. Brunt, Italian Manpower, Appendix 12).

(d) Colony at Cercina and Land Commission (both possibly 100 BC)

Inscriptiones Italiae (Degrassi) 13 nos 7, 75, 6

C. Julius Caesar, son of Gaius, grandson of Lucius, father of the Deified Julius, praetor, quaestor, military tribune, was a *Decemvir* and as such founded the colony at Cercina (*off the coast of Tunis.*).

C. Julius Caesar etc., military tribune, *Decemvir* for the granting assigning and adjudication of land, quaestor, *praetor peregrinus*, proconsul in Asia.

C. Julius Caesar Strabo, son of Lucius, curule aedile, quaestor, military tribune (*twice*), *Decemvir* for the granting assigning and adjudication of land, pontifex.

(e) Second Sicilian Slave War

A serious slave uprising took place in Sicily, and the governor's attempt to suppress it misfired. For a full account, see Diodorus Siculus 36.3–8.

102 BC   Consuls: C. Marius IV, Q. Lutatius Catulus
Censors: Q. Caecilius Metellus Numidicus, C. Caecilius Metellus
Caprarius

(a) Attempt by Q. Metellus to exclude Saturninus and Glaucia from Senate

APPIAN, *Civil Wars* 1.28

The Censor Q. Caccilius Metellus tried to strike from the roll of the Senate the senator Glaucia and the ex-tribune Appuleius Saturninus, on the grounds of personal unfitness. He did not succeed, for his fellow censor would not support him.

CICERO, *pro Sestio* 101 (56 BC)

When Q. Metellus as censor had put a black mark against the name of L. Saturninus, a man of enormous popularity, and had refused to register in the census the false Gracchus, in the face of organised rioting....

VALERIUS MAXIMUS 9.7.2

L. Equitius tried to kill the censor Q. Metellus by stoning because Metellus refused to register him as the supposed son of Gracchus.

de viris illustribus 73

Saturninus suborned a certain individual of freedman status to pretend that he was the son of Tiberius Gracchus. To counter this claim, Sempronia, sister of the two Gracchi, was produced, and neither entreaties nor threats could bring her to recognise the shameful claim.

Inscriptiones Italiae (Degrassi) 13 pp.21–2

Q. Caecilius Metellus Numidicus, son of Quintus, censor....refused to register L. Equitius....

OROSIUS 5.17

L. Appuleius Saturninus was a very bitter enemy of Q. Caecilius Metellus. When Metellus was censor he had him dragged from his house and when he escaped to the Capitol laid siege to him with an armed mob. He was driven off by the enraged Roman knights after much butchery around the Capitol.

(b) Marius elected to his fifth consulship

CASSIUS DIO fr. 94

After his victory at Aquae Sextiae (*see below*), Marius so won over the nobles who had hated him that he was praised to the sky by high-born and commoners alike. He was elected consul for the coming year to finish off the job with the willing and consenting support of the nobles.

(c) Battle of Aquae Sextiae

PLUTARCH, *Marius* 15

The barbarians divided their forces. The Cimbri went north through Noricum to attack Catulus, to force their way through into Italy by that route, the Teutones and Ambrones through Liguria along the coastal route to face Marius.

EPITOME OF LIVY, Bk. 68

The camp of the consul C. Marius was attacked in great strength by the Teutoni and Ambrones. He fought off the attack, and then in two subsequent battles near Aquae Sextiae (*Aix-en-Provence*) destroyed them – their losses are said to have been 200,000 dead and 90,000 prisoners. Marius was elected to a fifth consulship in his absence. He was voted a triumph, but chose to postpone celebrating it until he had also beaten the Cimbri.

The Cimbri at this time gave Catulus a rough handling in the extreme north of Italy, after crossing the Alpine passes.

(d) M. Antonius and the Cilician Pirates

EPITOME OF LIVY, Bk. 68

The praetor M. Antonius attacked the pirates of the Cilician coast.

OBSEQUENS 44

The pirates in Cilicia were wiped out by the Romans.

(e) The Slave War in Sicily

DIODORUS SICULUS 36.9

Gaius Servilius was sent out to command in place of Lucullus, but he too achieved nothing worth remembering. Hence subsequently he was exiled along with Lucullus. Tryphon having died, Athenion succeeded him in command of the slave forces. He set about besieging cities and ranging freely and without fear over the whole country, with Servilius doing nothing to stop him.

FLORUS 2.7

Athenion routed the praetorian armies as well, and captured the camps of both Servilius and Lucullus.

101 BC   Consuls: C. Marius V, Manius Aquillius

(a) The Cimbri defeated at Vercellae

EPITOME OF LIVY, Bk. 68

The Cimbri were defeated in battle by the combined armies of Catulus and C. Marius, with losses reported at 140,000 of the enemy killed and 60,000 captured.

PLUTARCH, *Marius* 25 ff.

The Cimbri said that they were waiting for the Teutones, and were surprised that they were so long in arriving. They either really did not know of their destruction, or they wanted to give the impression that they did not believe the report....Boiorix, the Cimbrian King, rode out with a small escort....and challenged Marius to a contest on a named day at a named place. Marius' reply was that the Romans never consulted their enemies about when to fight, but that he was none the less prepared to make an exception this time. It was agreed to fight the third day from then and that the plain around Vercellae (*about 40 miles west of Milan*) should be the place. It was good ground for the operations of the Roman cavalry, and convenient for the barbarians to deploy their great numbers....Sulla, who was present at the battle (*according to Plutarch, Sulla 4, Sulla had fallen out with Marius and got himself tranferred to Catulus' command*), gives an account of it....The battle was fought just after the summer solstice, and the Romans celebrate a festival for it at the end of July each year....The most numerous and best of the enemy troops were cut to pieces....Above 60,000 were taken prisoners, and the dead are said to have numbered twice as many....A hot dispute arose between the troops of Catulus and those of Marius over which had the best claim to have won the battle....but the whole honour of the day was ascribed to Marius....and he was called 'the third founder of Rome'.

(b) Grant of citizenship to Spanish cavalry

VALERIUS MAXIMUS 5.2.8

Two cohorts of Camertians who had held up the weight of the Cimbri with outstanding courage in the front line of the battle were granted Roman citizenship by Marius. This was contrary to the terms of the Camertian treaty with Rome. But Marius justified his action excellently and truthfully when he said that the din of battle had deafened him to the words of the civil law.

CICERO, *pro Balbo* 46 (56 BC)

Can I induce you to approve the man responsible for that exemplary action, which you reprehend, Gaius Marius? Marius gave the citizenship to whole cohorts of the Camertians, for all that he knew that their city had the most venerable and fairest of treaties with Rome.

(c) Marius' Triumph and sixth consulship

EPITOME OF LIVY, Bk. 68

Marius was welcomed back by a united populace. Offered two triumphs, he was satisfied with but one. The leading men of Rome, who had once detested him as an upstart (*novus homo*) raised to such great honours, maintained that he was the Saviour of Rome.

EPITOME OF LIVY, Bk. 69

C. Marius, who had bought his sixth consulship by massive bribery....

VELLEIUS PATERCULUS 2.12.6

His sixth consulship was given him as if in reward for his great achievements.

PLUTARCH, *Marius* 28

Marius now aspired to a sixth consulship, with more ardour than any man had ever shown for a first. He courted the people, and ingratiated himself with them....P. Rutilius Rufus (*consul 105 BC*), in other respects a truthful and decent man, but a man who had a private quarrel with Marius, tells us that he won his sixth consulship by the huge sums which he distributed among the electorate....and got them to elect also Valerius Flaccus, more of a lackey of his than a colleague. The people had never before bestowed so many consulships on one man, except Valerius Corvinus. And there was the great difference that there was 45 years between the first and sixth consulships of Corvinus....

(d) The lex Servilia Glauciae (*see also 104 BC*)

CICERO, *Verrines* 1.26 (70 BC)

Indeed, I think, it was Glaucia who first carried a law providing for *comperendinatio;* before that the case was either decided at a single hearing or there was *ampliatio.*

Briefly put, comperendinatio *limited trials to two hearings, whereas with* ampliatio *the court could produce a succession of hearings by bringing in a succession of verdicts of 'not proven' (*non liquet*). A famous case was said to have been reheard seven times, and only on the eighth occasion was the (allegedly blatantly guilty) defendant acquitted.*

CICERO, *pro Scauro* (= *Asconius 21C*) (54 BC)

(*In the year 92 or 91 BC the younger Q. Servilius Caepio, son of the consul of 106 BC*) arraigned M. Aemilius Scaurus under the Servilian Law (*of Servilius Glaucia*) at a time when the courts were in the hands of the equestrian order and when, after the condemnation of P. Rutilius, there was no one, however innocent he might be, who did not go in fear of them.

CICERO, *Brutus* 224 (46 BC)

C. Servilius Glaucia was far and away the greatest scoundrel since the world began; but he was very clever and crafty and extremely witty. He had the common people in his pocket, and had bound the equestrian order to him through the good turn his law did them.

CICERO, *pro Rabirio Postumo* 8 (54 BC)

The Julian Law (*de repetundis, 59BC*) required that damages are to be recovered from third parties, *viz.* from such persons as are now in possession of the moneys taken by the condemned defendant. If this is an innovation of the Julian

Law – which contains many provisions which are stricter and more awesome than in the old laws – then this too is certainly introducing a novel practice in this category of cases. But if this section of the Julian Law is taken over word for word from what stood previously not only in the Cornelian Law (*of Sulla*) but even before that in the Servilian, then good heavens, gentlemen, what is all the fuss about?

CICERO, *pro C. Rabirio perduellionis reo* **20** (63 BC)

The equestrian order, who at that time (*viz. 100 BC*) were a great part of the Roman state and monopolised all the prestige of the courts.

CICERO, *pro Balbo* **54** (56 BC)

Did our forefathers want the prizes of a prosecutor to exceed those of a warrior? Yet if under that very harsh law, the Servilian*, the leading men of the state, our wisest and weightiest citizens, were content that this path to Roman citizenship should by the command of the Roman People lie open to Latins, that is to allies,....can there be any doubt that the decisions of military commanders (*imperatores*) should be valid in the same area as the rewards of the courts have been validated? Are we to suppose that the Latin Peoples formally accepted as applying to them either the Servilian Law or all the other laws which proposed rewarding men of Latin status with a grant of Roman citizenship, for whatever reason?

(e) Saturninus and the Mithridatic Embassy: his second tribunate

DIODORUS SICULUS 36.15

Ambassadors arrived in Rome from King Mithridates, bringing with them a great deal of money with which to bribe the senators. Saturninus saw a chance to attack the Senate, and treated the embassy scandalously. In reply, the senators encouraged the ambassadors and promised to help them, so they brought an indictment against Saturninus for his scandalous treatment of them. The issue was public and important, because of the inviolability of embassies and the Romans' customary severity and strictness in such matters. Saturninus was summoned to appear before the Senate, where such cases were by convention decided, and could have been sentenced to death. He was in very great danger, and very much afraid. (*He appealed to the people to save him*) and the people answered his appeal: tens of thousands of them came running to the place of the hearing, and contrary to expectation he was acquitted. With the people behind him, he became tribune for the second time (*viz. for 100 BC*).

EPITOME OF LIVY, Bk. 69

L. Appuleius Saturninus, aided by C. Marius, and having had a rival candidate

---

* Some (*e.g. E. Badian in CR 1954, 101 ff*) believe that the reference here is to the *lex Servilia Caepionis* of 106 BC.

A. Nunnius murdered by soldiers, was elected tribune by forceful means, and proceeded to be as violent in his tribunate as he had been in his election to it.

de viris illustribus 73

Saturninus became tribune again after the murder of a rival candidate, Aulus Nunnus.

FLORUS 2.4

Having openly murdered his rival A. Ninnius at the hustings, (*Saturninus*) tried to get C. Gracchus elected in his place, a man without tribe or guarantor or name, who had taken the name of Gracchus and adopted himself into that family.

VALERIUS MAXIMUS 9.7.1

L. Equitius, who was pretending that he was the son of Tiberius Gracchus and trying to be elected against the law as tribune along with L. Saturninus, was imprisoned by C. Marius, now in his fifth consulship. But the people tore down the doors and carried Equitius away on their shoulders in high and cheerful excitement.

VALERIUS MAXIMUS 9.7.3

Nine of the ten tribunes had now been elected and only one place remained to be filled, with two candidates still in the field. The people drove Saturninus' rival A. Nunnius by force into a private house, from which they dragged him out and killed him, in order by the death of a truly honourable citizen to make room for a blackguard to win power.

(f) Sicilian Slave War

DIODORUS SICULUS 36.10

Manius Aquillius went off to command against the runaways, and by his personal courage won a famous victory. He engaged the king of the runaways, Athenion, in personal combat – an epic fight – and killed him, though he himself was wounded in the head. He moved against the 100,000 remaining runaways, who did not withstand his onset but fled to their strongholds. For all that Aquillius did not relax, but was everywhere active until he had besieged and defeated them.

(g) Mithridates and Nicomedes

JUSTIN 38.1.2

Nicomedes the King of Bithynia invaded Cappadocia where the king's death had left the throne vacant. When Mithridates heard the news, out of pretended family affection he sent help to his sister to drive Nicomedes out of Cappadocia. His forces expelled Nicomedes' garrisons from Cappadocia, and he restored the kingdom to his sister's son.

100 BC   Consuls: C. Marius VI, L. Valerius Flaccus

(a) Legislation of Saturninus, and exile of Metellus Numidicus

EPITOME OF LIVY, Bk. 69

After Saturninus had used violence to carry his agrarian law, he indicted Metellus Numidicus because the latter had refused to take the oath required by the law. Though the decent citizenry were for defending him, he went into voluntary exile at Rhodes so as not to be the cause of civil commotions.

APPIAN, *Civil Wars* 1. 29–31

Appuleius Saturninus introduced a bill for the distribution of the lands which the Cimbri had captured in the territory which the Romans now call Gaul. Marius had recently driven the Cimbri out and won these lands for Rome, they being considered no longer the property of the Gauls themselves.

Saturninus was also insisting that if the People ratified the proposal senators must within five days swear to abide by the law on pain of removal from the Senate and a fine of twenty talents. He planned thereby to deter other ill-affected opponents, and in particular Metellus, whose pride would not permit him to take the oath. So the law stood and Saturninus named the day for voting on it, and sent people off around the countryside to tell the men there, in whom he reposed the most confidence since they had served in Marius' army. The fact that the Italians stood to gain by the bill annoyed the people....

When it had been carried, Marius as consul brought the matter formally before the Senate, and, knowing Metellus to be a stubborn and determined character in his opinions and whatever he had committed himself to, he began by laying a trap for him and put forward the proposition that he himself would never willingly swear this oath. Metellus joined him in this declaration and everybody praised their action, and Marius terminated the session. Then on the fifth day, the limit set by the law for taking the oath, Marius summoned the Senate hurriedly in the late afternoon and told them that he was fearful about the people's enthusiasm for the law but that he saw a way out by the following device: he would swear to obey this law, insofar as it was a law....He took the oath first along with his friends, and then all the others followed suit, each worried about his own fate. Metellus alone would not swear but stuck fearlessly to his previous declaration....

Glaucia and Saturninus went rushing off to tell the people living in the country that they would not get any land and that the law would not hold good unless Metellus were banished, and they drafted a bill of banishment against him directing the consuls to outlaw him. The city-dwellers were indignant and escorted Metellus everywhere with swords in their hands. He praised them and thanked them for their good will, but said he would not bring his country into any danger on his account. So saying, he left Rome, and Marius published the notice of outlawry after Saturninus had got his bill passed.

PLUTARCH, *Marius* 29

Saturninus, now tribune, proposed his agrarian law, with an additional clause requiring the Senate to come and swear an oath to abide by whatever the people

decreed and not try to subvert it in any respect. In the Senate Marius pretended
opposition to this section of the law, saying that he would refuse to take the
oath, and thought every right-thinking man would do the same....But he was
lying about his true opinions, and setting an inescapable trap for Metellus
....hoping that by his refusal to take the oath himself he would induce Metellus
to refuse to take it either, and thus expose himself to the people's implacable
hostility. And so it turned out....A few days later Saturninus summoned the
senators to appear before his tribunal to take the oath. Marius was present, and
a silence fell, and all eyes fastened on him. Bidding farewell to all his fine words
in the Senate, he said that he was not so pig-headed as to pretend absolutely to
prejudge a matter of such importance: so he would swear to obey this law,
insofar as it was a law. He added this sophistry merely to cover his own
shame....Through their fear of the people all the other senators in turn took the
oath till it came to Metellus. But for all the entreaties and advice of his friends to
give in and not expose himself to the dire penalties which Saturninus proposed
to bring in against non-swearers, he would not swallow his pride and take the
oath, but stuck to his principles, ready to suffer any dreadful punishment rather
than defile his honour....Saturninus then carried a bill directing the consuls to
outlaw him. The most despicable members of the mob were ready to kill him,
but the best people were concerned and ranged themselves on his side; but
Metellus refused to be the cause of civil strife, and left Rome.

*The accounts of Plutarch and Appian are so close – something even more obvious
in their original Greek – that they must derive at bottom from the same source.
That source could well be the memoirs of Rutilius Rufus, referred to as a source by
Plutarch a few lines earlier and as a man who was a devoted friend of Metellus but
personally at odds with Marius. The whole story is hard to credit as it stands, and
reads like a piece of hagiology designed to glorify Metellus and revile Marius and
Saturninus.*

CICERO, *de domo* 82 (57 BC)

When and where did you ever carry a bill to have me outlawed, such as
Saturninus carried against Metellus?

CICERO, *pro Sestio* 37 (56 BC)

Metellus' action added rather more to his own glorious reputation than to the
obvious safety of Rome when he alone refused to swear to a law which had been
carried by force....He had to deal with the invincible army of C. Marius, and
had C. Marius as his private enemy, the saviour of Rome, now consul for the
sixth time; he had to deal with L. Saturninus, tribune for the second time, a
vigilant man and one who if no moderate champion of the popular cause was at
least popular and scrupulous. He left Rome to avoid the disgrace of defeat or
the heavy cost in lives of a victory.

*The Piracy Law from Delphi, dating pretty certainly from 100 BC and the work of
Saturninus or a friendly colleague (see Stuart Jones in JRS 16 (1926) 155 ff) is of
great interest in that it reveals not only a piece of legislation we would know*

nothing of but for the chance of epigraphic discovery, but also the full wording of a sanctio *or oath-clause parallel to that briefly alluded to above:*

SEG iii. no. 378 = Riccobono *FIRA* 1. 121 ff

The consul next in office shall send letters to all the peoples who are friends and allies of the Roman People bidding them to see to it that Roman citizens and their Latin and Italian allies shall be able to go about their proper business in the cities and islands of the east without danger, and sail the seas in safety, and that for the same objects Marcus Antonius (*praetor 102 BC, governor of Cilicia 101 BC*) shall see to these things so far as Cilicia is concerned. He is likewise to write to the King of Cyprus, the King of Alexandria and Egypt, the King of Cyrene, and the Kings of Syria, all of them friends and allies of the Roman People, to make it clear that it is their duty to see to it that no pirate shall make his base in their kingdoms or territories or bounds, nor permit the governors and garrison commanders they appoint to give refuge to any pirates, and to see to it that as far as it is in their power the Roman People shall find them willing partners to secure the safety of everyone....(*There follow references to Rhodes and the conduct of future Roman governors of provinces east of the Adriatic.*)

The praetor consul or proconsul governing either Asia or Macedonia shall, within ten days from learning that this law has been ratified by the People in the Assembly, swear an oath that, whatever this law ordains, he shall do it in all respects, nor do anything contrary of his own evil intent.

The magistrates at present in office, with the exception of the tribunes of the plebs and the *eparchoi*, shall within five days from the day on which the People ratifies this law, or in the case of future magistrates, with the exception of the *eparchoi*, within five days of taking office,...swear by Jupiter and our ancestral national gods that, whatsoever is specified in this law, all that they will perform, and see to it that it is effective, and do nothing in contravention of this law, or cause any other so to act, or act otherwise than is laid down in this law....(*The* sanctio *or oath then follows, providing for a fine of 200,000 sesterces for each single dereliction from the oath of complete and positive compliance with the law.*)

What is pretty certainly another copy of this same law has been unearthed on the island of Cnidos: for text, translation and commentary see Journal of Roman Studies 1974, 195–220.

de viris illustribus 73

Having been elected tribune a second time, Saturninus earmarked Sicily, Achaea and Macedonia for new colonial plantations and applied the Toulouse Gold *(see above 106 BC (d))* made off with by Caepio's crime, for the purchase of lands.

CICERO, *pro Balbo* 48 (56 BC)

But, seeing that the colonies had not been founded under Saturninus' *lex Appuleia,* in which law Saturninus had empowered C. Marius to create (*either 3 or 300: the reading is contested between* ternos *and* trecenos) Roman citizens in each colony....

(b) The electoral riots

EPITOME OF LIVY, Bk. 69

The tribune Appuleius Saturninus had the consular candidate C. Memmius killed, fearing him as hostile to his own policies. The Senate was outraged – C. Marius, a man of fickle and changeable convictions, who always bent with the wind of fortune, had changed over to the Senate's side – and Saturninus was suppressed along with the praetor Glaucia and some other partners in their madness in what was almost an operation of war.

OROSIUS 5.17

Saturninus feared that Memmius might be elected consul, and had him killed by his catspaw P. Mettius as he was trying to make his escape from a confused fracas that had suddenly blown up.

VALERIUS MAXIMUS 3.2.18

The tribune Saturninus and the praetor Glaucia and the tribune-designate Equitius (the 'false Gracchus') had stirred up a revolutionary situation, and nobody was prepared to oppose an excited people, when M. Aemilius Scaurus took the lead and urged the sixth-time consul C. Marius to defend liberty and the laws with his strong arm, and ordered that his own armour be brought to him forthwith. For all his great age and the feebleness of his body he buckled it on and took his stand leaning on his spear at the door of the Senate-House,,,,By his constancy and readiness he inspired Senate and equestrian order to exact vengeance.

CICERO, *pro C. Rabirio perduellionis reo* **20–21** (63 BC)

A decree of the Senate was passed 'that the consuls C. Marius and L. Valerius should summon to assist them those tribunes of the plebs and those praetors whom they saw fit and take steps to safeguard the might and majesty of the Roman People'. The consuls summoned all the tribunes of the plebs save Saturninus and all the praetors save Glaucia: 'Let all those who wish to see their country safe take up arms and follow our commands'. All answered the call. Arms were issued to the Roman people from public buildings and armouries, the consul C. Marius overseeing the distribution. At this point I shall pass over everything else to ask you, Labienus, a personal question. When Saturninus was in arms and holding the Capitol, there were with him C. Glaucia, C. Saufeius, even that supposed 'Gracchus' from the cells of the slave-barracks. I will add another name, since you so wish, that of Q. Labienus, your uncle. In the Forum stood the consuls C. Marius and L. Valerius Flaccus, and behind them the whole Senate....and the equestrian order....and all men of all classes who thinking that their own safety was bound up with the safety of the state had taken up arms. What then was C. Rabirius to do? Answer me, Labienus, answer me! When by decree of the Senate the consuls had issued a call to arms, when M. Aemilius, the *princeps senatus*, had armed himself and taken up his position in the Comitium....when even Q. Scaevola, worn out by age and in appalling health, stood there leaning on his spear showing at one and the same time his physical weakness and strength of spirit, when L. Metellus, Servius Galba, C. Serranus. P. Rutilius, C. Fimbria, Q. Catulus, and all the other ex-consuls of the time had taken up arms for the common safety....

APPIAN, *Civil Wars* 1.32–3

The consular elections came round. Marcus Antonius was elected to one of the consulships without any dispute, and the one remaining was contested between Glaucia and Memmius. Memmius being far and away the more distinguished of the two, Glaucia and Saturninus sent some armed men to attack him at the election itself and they cut down and killed Memmius with everybody looking on. The assembly broke up in confusion (*subsequently Saturninus along with Glaucia and a quaestor called C. Saufeius seized and occupied the Capitol*). The Senate voted to put them down, and Marius, though displeased, nevertheless began with deliberate slowness to start issuing some arms. While he was dawdling, some people cut off the water-supply to the Capitol. Dying of thirst, Saufeius said that they should fire the temple, but Glaucia and Saturninus, hoping that Marius would protect them, surrendered themselves, and Saufeius followed their lead. With everybody at once shouting for him to put them to death, Marius had them locked up in the Senate House saying that he would deal with them according to the law. People thought this just an excuse, and ripping the tiles from the roof battered Saturninus and his companions to death, a quaestor and a tribune and a praetor, still wearing the insignia of their offices. A great crowd of others died in the fighting, among them another tribune, supposedly the son of Gracchus, on that the first day of his tribunate....

Florus (2.4) tells in general the same story about the surrender and 'lynching' of Saturninus and his men.

CICERO, *Brutus* 224 (46 BC)

Glaucia, a man of the most shameful background and character, would have been consul the year after he was praetor had his candidature for the consulship been adjudged legal.

OROSIUS 5.17

When, driven by Marius, Saturninus himself and Saufeius and Labienus had taken refuge in the Senate House, some Roman knights broke down the doors and killed them. C. Glaucia was dragged out of Claudius' house and butchered. The tribune Furius decreed that the property of them all should be forfeit to the state. Saturninus' cousin Cn. Dolabella was killed along with L. Giganius while trying to escape through the Vegetable Market.

de viris illustribus 73

Armed with a decree of the Senate, to the effect that the consuls were to see to it that the state take no harm, Marius attacked Saturninus and Glaucia and besieged them in the Capitol, where they were forced to surrender after the water pipes had – very cleverly – been broken. But the pledge of safety given to the surrenderers was not kept. Glaucia had his neck broken, and Saturninus after taking refuge in the Senate House was killed by stones and roof-tiles thrown down on him. A certain senator Rabirius carted his head around celebration-parties to make a mockery of it.

Inscriptiones Latinae Selectae (Dessau) **59**

Marius, consul for the sixth time, rescued the state when it had been thrown in turmoil by the seditious activities of a tribune of the plebs and a praetor.

CICERO, *pro C. Rabirio perduellionis reo* **28** (63 BC)

But even if a guarantee of safety was given to Saturninus, as you keep on alleging, it was given not by C. Rabirius but by C. Marius. What guarantee, Labienus? How could it have been given except by the decree of the Senate?

(c) Validity of Saturninus' legislation

CICERO, *de legibus* **2.12–14:** begun 52 BC

In this dialogue Quintus Cicero has just agreed that no law can properly be called a 'law' unless it is right and sound and good. Marcus replies.

MARCUS. Many pernicious and pestiferous motions are carried by popular
    assemblies which no more merit the name of 'laws' than if they were passed
    by a compact between a band of brigands. Just as one cannot truthfully give
    the name of 'medical science' to what is prescribed by ignorant quacks who
    kill rather than cure, so one cannot give the name of 'law' to any pernicious
    proposal a popular assembly may happen to pass.... The only true laws are
    those which punish wrongdoers and protect and defend the good.
QUINTUS. I entirely agree, and I do not think that any other law can be
    considered or even called a 'law'.
MARCUS. So you do not think that the Titian and Appuleian (*viz. Saturninan*)
    laws were laws?
QUINTUS. Certainly not, nor even the Livian (*of Livius Drusus, tribune 91 BC*).
MARCUS. And quite right, too, seeing that in addition they were invalidated* by
    a single sentence of a senatorial decree in the twinkling of an eye. But that
    true law, whose force I have explained, cannot be invalidated or abrogated.

(d) Attempt to recall Metellus Numidicus

OROSIUS 5.17

Cato and Pompeius published a bill to recall Metellus Numidicus and all Rome

---

* Whether the remark about invalidation applied only to the Livian laws is not as clear as it might be. Personally, I think it probably does, and so tells us nothing about Saturninus' laws in this respect. But others disagree.

rejoiced; but it was vetoed thanks to the pressure exercised by the factions of the consul Marius and the tribune Furius.

(e) Trial of Q. Servilius Caepio the younger

ad Herennium **2.17 and 21**

A man is guilty of high treason (*maiestas minuta*) if he damages the base on which the greatness of the state rests. In what does such damage lie, Q. Caepio? Votes, magistracies. Thus clearly you deprived the people of their vote and of the advice of the magistrates when you broke up an election assembly....

Caepio was charged with *maiestas*. The point at issue fell by strict law under the definition of the charge.

(f) Birth of Julius Caesar

MACROBIUS, *Satires* **1.12.34**

The month 'Quintilis' was renamed 'Julius' (*July*) in honour of the dictator Julius Caesar, because his birthday fell on the fourth day before the Ides of that month (*12 July*).

SUETONIUS, *Divus Julius* **88**

Caesar died in his sixty-fifth year (*viz. March 44 BC*).

(g) Colonies in Liguria and Corsica

STRABO, *Geography* **4.6.7**

The Romans founded a colony at Eporedia as a bulwark against the Salassi....

PLINY, *Natural History* **3.17.123**

The town of Eporedia was founded by the Romans following the instructions of the Sibylline oracle.

PLINY, *Natural History* **3.6.80**

Corsica contains thirty-two communities, and two colonies, one Marian founded by C. Marius, and another at Aleria by the dictator Sulla.

VELLEIUS PATERCULUS 1.15

Eporedia was founded when Marius (*for the sixth time*) and Valerius Flaccus were consuls.

SENECA, *ad Helviam* **7.9**

There (*viz. in Corsica*) two Roman citizen colonies were founded, the one by Marius, the other by Sulla.

99 BC   Consuls: M. Antonius, A. Postumius Albinus

(a) Abortive attempt to recall Metellus

PLUTARCH, *Marius* **31**
When a proposal was introduced to recall Metellus from exile, Marius opposed it vigorously by both words and deeds....

APPIAN, *Civil Wars* **1.33**

When Saturninus and his associates had been killed, the Senate and the people loudly demanded the recall of Metellus, but they were boldly opposed by the tribune P. Furius, the son of a freedman, who refused to be moved even when Metellus' son made a public appeal to him and threw himself in tears at his feet.

CICERO, *post reditum ad Quirites* **11** (57 BC)

Neither C. Marius, who was his personal enemy, nor the two men who succeeded him as consuls, the most eloquent M. Antonius and his colleague A. Albinus, ever made any appeal to either Senate or people on Metellus' behalf.

CICERO, *post reditum in senatu* **25** (57 BC)

Pathetic appeals, with weeping and bedraggled clothes, were made to the Roman people on behalf of Q. Metellus by his splendid young son, by the ex-consuls Lucius and Gaius Metellus and their sons, by the consular candidate Q. Metellus Nepos, by the sons of his female relatives – Luculli and Servilii and Scipiones. Yet in this Senate House no mention was ever made of Q. Metellus. When he was recalled, he owed it to tribunician bills.

DIODORUS SICULUS 36.16

There were speeches about the exile of Metellus at assembly meetings over a period of two years....His son's outstanding filial devotion earned him the *cognomen* of 'Pius'.

(b) Agrarian proposal of the tribune Sextus Titius

OBSEQUENS 46 (*cf. 100 BC (c), above*)

When the tribune Sextus Titius was stubbornly carrying through a bill to assign lands to the people in the face of the opposition of his colleagues, two crows flying above the crowd started fighting and tearing each other with beaks and claws. The diviners (*haruspices*) announced that sacrifices should be made to Apollo and that the bill which was being discussed should be voided.

VALERIUS MAXIMUS 8 *Damnati* **3**

A similar chance was the undoing of Sextus Titius too. He was innocent of the charge against him, and the passing of his agrarian law had won the favour of the people. Nevertheless, because he had a bust of Saturninus in his house, the whole assembly voted to put him down.

(c) End of Slave War in Sicily

OBSEQUENS 45, under the year 100 BC

The runaways in Sicily were cut down in a number of engagements.

EPITOME OF LIVY, Bk. 69

The proconsul Manius Aquillius ended the slave war in Sicily.

DIODORUS SICULUS 36.10

Thus the slave war in Sicily came to a tragic end, having lasted almost four years.

CICERO, *de oratore* **2.195** (55 BC)

Aquillius celebrated an ovation on the Capitoline (*the date of which is known to have been earlier than 26 January 98 BC*).

98 BC   Consuls: Q. Caecilius Metellus Nepos; T. Didius

(a) Recall of Metellus Numidicus. Marius goes to Asia; his augurship

PLUTARCH, *Marius* **31**

When his opposition to Metellus' recall finally proved vain, Marius abandoned it. When the bill of recall was carried with enthusiasm by the people, Marius did not stay to see Metellus' return but sailed off to Cappadocia and Galatia. His pretext was that he was going there to pay some sacrifices which he had vowed to the goddess Cybele (*the Great Mother*), but he had another reason which he kept private....He hoped that if he could stir up the kings there, and especially incite Mithridates, who seemed the most likely to make a fight of it, he would himself be at once appointed to the command of such a war....

CICERO, *ad Brutum* **1.5.3** (43 BC)

While Marius was away in Asia (*98 or 97 BC*) he was elected an augur under the Domitian Law (*of 104 BC*).

EPITOME OF LIVY, Bk. 69

Q. Caecilius Metellus returned from exile to an enthusiastic welcome from the whole of Rome.

CICERO, *ad familiares* **1.9.16** (54 BC)

They say that after his return to Rome Q. Metellus was a broken and dispirited man. They keep saying it, but it is not true.

CICERO, *pro Plancio* **69** (54 BC)

It was by Calidius' law that Q. Metellus was reinstated.

VALERIUS MAXIMUS 5.2.7

Metellus Pius, who through his unswerving devotion to his exiled father won as famous a *cognomen* by his tears as others have done by their victories in war, did not hesitate when he was consul (*in 80 BC*) to appeal to the people in support of a candidate for the praetorship, Q. Calidius, because as tribune Calidius had carried the bill for his father's recall.

There are several other references to the devotion of young Metellus and the warmth of the older Metellus' reception on his return.

(b) The Lex Caecilia Didia

CICERO, *de domo* **53** (57 BC)

What, I ask you, what was the force and purpose of the *lex Caecilia Didia* if it was not this: that the People should not be compelled by voting on bills which combine a number of different items either to say Yes to what it did not want or No to what it did want?

CICERO, *Philippics* **5.8** (43 BC)

Where is the *lex Caecilia Didia,* where the requirement that a bill should be published at least three weeks before it can be voted on?

(c) Death of Publius Furius

APPIAN, *Civil Wars* **1.33**

The tribune C. Canuleius thereupon indicted Furius (*who had in 99 BC as tribune blocked Metellus' recall*), and the people without waiting to hear any speeches tore Furius to pieces.

The same story is in Cassius Dio (fr. 95.3).

(d) Trials of C. Appuleius Decianus and Sextus Titius

CICERO, *pro Rabirio perduellionis reo* **24** (63 BC)

As for C. Decianus, when he was with the enthusiastic support of all decent men prosecuting that complete scoundrel P. Furius, just because he ventured during his speech to deplore the death of Saturninus, he was himself condemned.

VALERIUS MAXIMUS 8 *Damnati* **2**

It was his own mouth that brought destruction on that most honest man C. Decianus. When he was prosecuting that terrible villain P. Furius, because in one part of his speech he had ventured to deplore the death of L. Saturninus, he failed to get Furius convicted and on top of that was hoist with his own petard.

CICERO, *de oratore* **2.48** (*Antonius, consul 99 BC, speaking*) (55 BC: see 99 BC (b), p. 100)

One often has to appear as a witness in court....For example, I was obliged to appear as a witness against Sextus Titius, that turbulent revolutionary; in giving my evidence I set forth the whole policy of my consulship, whereby I had resisted that tribune and defended my country, and all the things which he had in my opinion done against the interests of the state.

(e) Trial of Manius Aquillius *(could be a year or two later)*

CICERO, *Verrines* **2.5.3** (70 BC)

I am reminded of the great authority and impact of the impression made by M. Antonius' speech at the trial of Manius Aquillius. He was not merely a skilful speaker, but a bold one. As his speech drew to its close, he took hold of Manius Aquillius and stood him there in front of everyone and ripped his tunic from his chest so that the Roman people and the court could see the scars of the wounds he had received while facing Rome's enemies. He had much to say too about that wound which Aquillius had had dealt to his head by the enemy commander *(above, 101 BC(f))*. The result was that he so moved the men who were about to deliver the verdict as to make them terribly afraid: had this man whom fortune had rescued from the weapons of the enemy when he set his own life at naught been preserved not to have his praises sung by the Roman people but to be the victim of the cruelty of a Roman court?

CICERO, *pro Flacco* **98** (59 BC)

Our fathers acquitted Manius Aquillius, though he stood convicted by clear evidence of many charges of self-enrichment, on account of the bravery he had shown in fighting the slaves in Sicily.

CICERO, *de oratore* **2.196** (*Antonius speaking*) (55 BC)
The emotional appeal of my speech was greatly assisted by the tears of Gaius Marius, who was present in the court. I frequently addressed him by his name and begged him to help his former colleague *(as consul in 101 BC)* and appealed to him to speak up himself in defence of the common fortune of military commanders....

(f) Spain

The Fasti Triumphales *record a triumph celebrated by L. Cornelius Dolabella for victories in Lusitania.*

97 BC   **Consuls: Cn. Cornelius Lentulus, P. Licinius Crassus**
              Censors: L. Valerius Flaccus, M. Antonius

(a) Abolition of human sacrifice *(cf. 114 BC (c))*

PLINY, *Natural History* **30.3.12**

Finally, in the six hundredth and fifty-seventh year of the City, in the consulship of Cn. Cornelius Lentulus and P. Licinius Crassus, a senatorial decree was passed banning human sacrifice; and it is plain that down to that time abominable rites had been performed.

(b) The censorship (*and Marius' hopes*)

PLUTARCH, *Marius* 30

Having clashed with both the leading politicians and the people at large, when the censorial election came round Marius defied expectations by not standing for election himself. Frightened that he might not be elected, he allowed other and inferior men to be chosen.

VALERIUS MAXIMUS 2.9.5

M. Antonius and L. Flaccus as censors expelled Duronius from the Senate, because he had as tribune repealed the law limiting expenditure on private entertainments. It was a *cause célèbre*.

CICERO, *de oratore* 2.274 (55 BC)
Mancia had heard that you (*viz. Antonius*) when you were censor had been charged with electoral corruption by M. Duronius.

(c) Spain: successes of Didius, and service of Sertorius

EPITOME OF LIVY, Bk. 70

T. Didius as proconsul won successes in battle against the Celtiberi.

APPIAN, *Iberica* 99

When Titus Didius arrived in Spain, he killed about 20,000 of the Arvaci; the great town of Termesus, which had always been disobedient to Rome, he moved down from the heights and replanted in the plain and forced the inhabitants to live there without any fortifications. After over eight months' siege he took and conquered Colenda, and sold the whole population including the women and children into slavery.

AULUS GELLIUS, *Attic Nights* 2.27.2

Sallust in his *Histories* has this to say about Sertorius: 'He won a great reputation while serving as a military tribune in Spain under the command of Titus Didius'.

96 BC   Consuls: Cn. Domitius Ahenobarbus, C. Cassius Longinus

Cyrene bequeathed to Rome

EPITOME OF LIVY, Bk. 70

King Ptolemy Apion of Cyrene died bequeathing his kingdom to the Roman People, and the Senate commanded that the cities of the kingdom should become free cities.

95 BC   Consuls: L. Licinius Crassus, Q. Mucius Scaevola

(a) The affairs of Norbanus and Caepio*

CICERO, *de oratore* 2. 198–201 (*Antonius speaking*) (55 BC)

On top of that, you (*Sulpicius*) were a young man, and your championing of the public interest was thought to redound greatly to your credit, while there was I, a former censor, who it seemed could scarcely not be acting dishonourably in defending a seditious fellow (*Norbanus*) who had shown such cruelty in destroying a former consul (*Caepio, consul 106 BC*). The members of the court were all upstanding citizens, the Forum was packed with true patriots, so that my excuse for defending the accused seemed a frail thing and likely to win me little consideration – it was simply that the defendant had once been my quaestor....Then I changed tack and concentrated my attack on Caepio's defeat (*at Arausio in 105 BC*) and the deplorable loss of his army. Thus I rekindled the grief of those who had lost kinsmen in that battle, and brought back to life the hostility of the Roman knights, before whom the case was being heard, and their hatred of Q. Caepio, whom they themselves had detested because of his law about the courts....So in the end, by appealing to the emotions of the judges rather than their reason I managed to defeat your prosecution case, Sulpicius.

CICERO, *Brutus* 162 (46 BC)

We have the brief defence (defensiuncula *is an emendation of the MS reading* defensione iuncta, *which makes no sense*) of Q. Caepio which L. Crassus delivered when he was consul, not all that short for a laudation, but short for a speech.

(b) The Lex Licinia Mucia

CICERO, *de officiis* 3.47 (44 BC)

It is a wicked thing to prohibit non-citizens from entering a town that is not their own and physically to expel them from it, as Pennus (*tribune 126 BC: see above under the year*) did in our father's day, and Papius (*tribune 65 BC*) rather more recently. Of course, it is quite right and proper to forbid anyone who is not a citizen to masquerade as a citizen, as was laid down in the law which those wise consuls, Crassus and Scaevola, carried. But it is downright uncivilised to bar non-citizens from even entering a town.

CICERO, *pro Cornelio* (= *Asconius 67C*) (65 BC)

As to the *lex Licinia Mucia*, which dealt with the reduction of the number of

---

* See also the entries above under 106–103 BC. The detail is hard to sort out. All we can be sure about so far as concerns the date of the trial of C. Norbanus (*tribune 103 BC, later a 'Cinnan' consul in 83 BC*) is that it must be later than 97/96 BC, when M. Antonius was censor – he describes himself in the first passage above as an ex-censor (*homo censorius*) at the time – and earlier than 91 BC, which is the dramatic date of Cicero's dialogue *de oratore*. The reference in the second passage to Crassus' championing of Caepio as consul in 95 BC is pretty clearly not to a trial speech but rather some retrospective reflections; there is also the perfectly respectable possibility that the Caepio in question here may be the son of the consul of 106 BC, also a Q. Servilius Caepio, and not his father.

citizens, I can see that it is universally agreed that, for all that it was carried by the two consuls who were of all those we have known the wisest, it was not only ineffective but positively badly damaging to Rome.

CICERO *de oratore* **2.257** (55 BC) *citing humorous verses about the law:*

> Hush! Be quiet! Why this noise?
> You've no Roman mum and dad.
> Why were you so cocky, then?
> Off with you, or you'll be sad.

CICERO, *pro Sestio* **30** (56 BC)

There was nothing that upset the allies and the Latins more than – what happened very rarely – to be ordered out of Rome by the consuls.

CICERO, *pro Balbo* **54** (56 BC)

Even under that harshest of laws, the *lex Servilia* (*?Caepio's ?Glaucia's*), the leading men in the state, the most weighty and wisest of our citizens, allowed an avenue to the citizenship to be open by order of the People to the Latins, that is to peoples bound to us by treaty; nor was this right impugned by the *lex Licinia Mucia*.

CICERO, *pro Balbo* **48**

When that very stringent investigation had been set in hand by the *lex Licinia Mucia*, was there any man who came from a treaty-allied state and had been granted Roman citizenship who was brought to trial?

CICERO, *pro Balbo* **48**

Titus Matrinius of Spoletium, one of the men granted citizenship by C. Marius (*under Saturninus' colony law: see 100 BC (a)*), stood trial. He came from one of the most loyal and distinguished of Latin colonies....But such was the enormous prestige of C. Marius that he did not avail himself of the services of his relative, the incredibly eloquent L. Crassus, but himself in a few weighty words defended Matrinius and won the case.

SALLUST, *Histories* **1.20 M**

The *lex Licinia* was unpopular with everybody living south of the Po.

ASCONIUS 67 C, commenting on Cicero, *pro Cornelio* **(above)**

Cicero here refers to the orator L. Licinius Crassus and Q. Mucius Scaevola the *pontifex maximus*....At a time when the peoples of Italy were fired by an enormous appetite for Roman citizenship and for that reason a large number of them were passing themselves off as Roman citizens, it seemed necessary to carry a law to restore everyone to his proper legal citizenship status in his own native place. However, so alienated were the leaders of the Italian peoples by this law that it was perhaps the chief cause of the Italian War which broke out three years later.

Bobbiensis Scholiast on Cicero, *pro Sestio* **(above): p.129 Stangl**

....the sort of law which L. Licinius Crassus and Q. Mucius Scaevola passed ordering the allies and Latins to go back to their own home towns.

(c) The East

JUSTIN 38.2.3

The Senate....deprived Mithridates of Cappadocia and (*as a sop to him*) took Paphlagonia from Nicomedes. Both regions were granted freedom and independence. But the Cappadocians declined the gift of freedom and said that they were a people who could not live without a king. So Rome appointed Ariobarzanes to be their king.

STRABO, *Geography* 12.2.11

The Cappadocian royal line having become extinct, the Romans granted independence to the Cappadocians, who were their long-standing friends and allies. But the Cappadocians sent an embassy to decline this freedom – they said it was something they could not cope with – and to ask Rome to name a king for them.... The Romans instructed them to elect a king from among themselves of their own choosing, and they choose Ariobarzanes.

JUSTIN 38.3.1

The king of Armenia at that time was Tigranes. He had been sent as a hostage to the Parthians a long time before, and they had never sent him back to take over his father's kingdom. Mithridates very much wanted to enlist him as an ally in a war against Rome, something he had long been planning.

94 BC   Consuls: C. Coelius Caldus, L. Domitius Ahenobarbus

(a) Prohibition of loans to foreign embassies

ASCONIUS, *in Cornelianam* 57C

C. Cornelius had (*as tribune in 67 BC*) proposed a bill forbidding the lending of money to ambassadors from foreign peoples. The Senate turned it down, declaring that they thought the matter was already satisfactorily dealt with by the decree of the Senate which had been passed some years earlier in the consulship of L. Domitius and C. Coelius, seeing that only a few years earlier (*than 67 BC*) they had used this latter decree to ban any loan to the Cretans.

(b) Scaevola in Asia

DIODORUS SICULUS 37.5

Q. Mucius Scaevola (*consul 95 BC*) was sent to govern Asia, and chose the best adviser among his friends, Rutilius Rufus (*consul 105 BC*), to accompany him, and consulted him about all the administrative and judicial affairs of the province....By his sober and frugal conduct he managed to rescue the province from the deplorable state into which it had fallen. For the public contractors (*publicani*), working hand-in-glove with those who controlled the courts at Rome, had satiated the province with their illegal excesses....Scaevola's justice was incorruptible and stern....and he corrected the crimes of the *publicani* .....compelling them to make financial restitution to anybody they had cheated out of money and punishing capital crimes with death.

CICERO, *ad familiares* **1.9.26** (*written in 54 BC to Lentulus Spinther, then governor of Cilicia*)

I received your letter about the *publicani*, and I could not but approve its fairness....I shall not cease to defend your decrees, but you know what the *publicani* have always been like, and how bitterly hostile they were even to good old Quintus Scaevola.

CICERO, *ad Atticum* **5.17.5 and 6.1.15** (*both written in 51 BC when Cicero was himself governor of Cilicia*)

At the same time, I think that this great reputation I have won here for fair-dealing and probity will shine all the brighter if I leave quickly – like Scaevola, who governed Asia only for nine months....As to Bibulus' edict for Syria, I am aware of nothing new in it apart from the proviso which you wrote to me about to say that 'it is a serious and damaging slight against our order (*viz. the knights*).' But I myself have a clause to the same effect, though phrased more discreetly, which I borrowed from Q. Mucius Scaevola's Asiatic edict: 'provided that the transaction has not been so arranged that it ought not in good faith to be allowed to stand'. I have followed Scaevola a great deal in my own edict, including his declaration, which the provincials regard as a sort of charter of freedom, that where both parties to a suit are locals it should be settled in accordance with the local law.

The question whether Scaevola governed Asia after his consulship or a few years earlier when he was a praetor cannot be answered with any real certainty.

93 BC   Consuls: C. Valerius Flaccus, M. Herennius

(a) Sulla praetor

PLUTARCH, *Sulla* **5**

Sulla was a candidate for the praetorship, but failed. But he did get elected the following year, partly by being attentive to the popular mood and partly by bribery. Hence it was that when during his praetorship he once said angrily to Caesar, 'I will use my official authority against you', Caesar retorted, 'You do well to call it *your* authority. After all, you did buy it.'

de viris illustribus **75**

Sulla was the *praetor urbanus* in his year. He got Cilicia as his province.

PLINY, *Natural History* **8.16.53**

The first man to stage a fight involving numbers of lions at Rome was Scaevola, Publius' son, when he was a curule aedile. But the very first to stage one with a hundred maned lions was L. Sulla, the later dictator, in his praetorship.

SENECA, *de brevitate vitae* **13.6**

L. Sulla was the first to put on a show in the circus with lions that were not chained up – some had been given involving chained animals. They were killed by spearmen specially provided by King Bocchus (*of Mauretania*).

(b) The East

JUSTIN 38.3.3

At the first approach of Tigranes, Ariobarzanes upped and left for Rome. Thus, thanks to Tigranes, Cappadocia once again began to come under the control of Mithridates.

(c) Spain

FASTI TRIUMPHALES, 2 June and 4 June, 93 BC

Titus Didius son of Titus grandson of Sextus, proconsul of Spain, celebrated a triumph over the Celtiberians....

P. Licinius Crassus son of Marcus grandson of Publius, proconsul, celebrated a triumph over the Lusitanians....

92 BC Consuls: C. Claudius Pulcher, M. Perperna
Censors: Cn. Domitius Ahenobarbus, L. Licinius Crassus

(a) Censorial ban on the schools of the so-called 'Latin Orators'

SUETONIUS, *de grammaticis* 25

Cn. Domitius Ahenobarbus and L. Licinius Crassus issued the following edict when they were censors: 'We have been informed that there are certain persons who have instituted a new type of instruction, and set up schools for young men to attend. They call themselves "the Latin Orators", and young men spend whole days there. Our forefathers decided what they wanted their sons to study and which schools they should regularly attend. These new practices, which contravene the practice and principles of our forefathers, are neither suitable nor proper. Accordingly, we have decided to make known our disapproval both to those who operate these schools and to those who are in the habit of attending them'.

CICERO, *de oratore* 3.24; 93 (dramatic date 91 BC)

This large field, no longer tenanted by the Greeks, with the result that our young men had almost got out of the habit of learning, was suddenly occupied a couple of years ago by, please Heaven! some Latins who set themselves up as teachers of rhetoric. When I (*Crassus*) was censor, I abolished them by my edict, not because, as some people or other kept saying, I was opposed to the idea that young men should have their wits sharpened, but on the contrary because I refused to allow their wits to be blunted while their impudence was being nourished.... Since the schools were schools of impudence, I judged it my duty as a censor to take steps to see that this creeping cancer was stopped.

TACITUS, *dialogus de oratoribus* 35 (dramatic date, the sixties of the first century AD)

Nowadays our young men go off to the schools of those who are called 'rhetoricians'. These men it is clear emerged a little before Cicero's day and did not meet with the approval of our ancestors, for they were ordered by the censors Crassus and Domitius to close, as Cicero puts it, 'those schools of impudence'.

(b) Clash between the censors

*Domitius accused his fellow-censor Crassus of luxurious living, and Crassus replied to his charges at a public meeting notable for its noise: see Pliny (*Nat. Hist. *17.1*), and Cicero (*Brutus *164*, de orat. *2.227*).

(c) Trial and condemnation of P. Rutilius Rufus*

VELLEIUS PATERCULUS 2.13

Once the knights had gained control of the courts by the Gracchan laws, they vented their spite on many distinguished and totally innocent men, and above all they condemned P. Rutilius, the first gentleman not only of his own age but of all time, when he came before them on a charge of extortion (*repetundae*).

EPITOME OF LIVY, Bk. 70

P. Rutilius was as free from all guilt as a man can be. Yet, because when he was a legate to the proconsul Q. Mucius he had protected Asia from the crimes of the public contractors, and had become hated by the equestrian order for that, he was condemned by the knights, who then had charge of the courts, on a charge of extortion and forced into exile.

CICERO, *Brutus* 115 (46 BC)

When the completely innocent Rutilius was brought to trial – and we know that that trial shook the state to its foundations – he declined to call on the services of the two finest speakers of the time, the ex-consuls L. Crassus and M. Antonius. He conducted his own defence, with some help from his sister's son, Gaius Cotta.

CICERO, *pro Fonteio* 38 (69 BC)

Though P. Rutilius was found guilty, it is my opinion that he is to be numbered amongst the best and most innocent of men. Yet this most sober and honourable gentleman had to listen to many tales told at his trial of lust and debauchery.

QUINTILIAN, *institutio oratoria* 11.1.12

P. Rutilius failed to appreciate where his own best interests lay, both when at his trial he employed that almost Socratic type of defence, and when he chose to remain an exile though P. Sulla offered to recall him.

VALERIUS MAXIMUS 2.10.5

What can be worse than being condemned by a court, worse than exile? Yet neither could rob P. Rutilius of his high standing and prestige after he had been struck down by the plotting of the *publicani*. When he went off to Asia and to

---

* See also 104 BC (h) and 94 BC (b). Various other sources refer to Rutilius' trial and conviction, amongst them Cassius Dio (*fr. 97*), who says that Marius was said to have had a hand in it.

exile, all the cities of that province sent embassies to await and greet him. It was more like a triumph than an exile .

(d) M. Aemilius Scaurus attacked (or could be 91 BC)

ASCONIUS, commenting on a passage from Cicero's *pro Scauro* – son of the man here mentioned: 21C

'He was indicted by Q. Servilius Caepio (*son of the consul of 106 BC*) under the Servilian Law (*of Servilius Glaucia*) at a time when the courts were in the hands of the equestrian order and there was nobody, however innocent he might be, who did not go in fear of them.'

Q. Servilius Caepio indicted Scaurus under the extortion law of Servilius Glaucia because of the hostility aroused by his legateship in Asia and the allegation that he had illegally extorted moneys.* So self-controlled and confident was Scaurus that he retaliated by indicting Caepio, and by accepting a shorter period to prepare his case ensured that Caepio's trial came on earlier. Scaurus also encouraged the tribune M. Drusus to change the courts.

(e) The East

EPITOME OF LIVY, Bk. 70

Ariobarzanes was restored to his kingdom of Cappadocia by L. Sulla. King Arsaces (*of Parthia*) sent an embassy to Sulla to seek friendship with the Roman People.

PLUTARCH, *Sulla* 5

After his praetorship Sulla was appointed to Cappadocia, ostensibly to restore Ariobarzanes, but in truth to check the growing power and ambitions of Mithridates. Sulla took no large force with him, but had eager support from Rome's allies. He killed many Cappadocians, and even more of the Armenians who had come to help them, and drove out Gordius and made Ariobarzanes king. While he was in the Euphrates region, he received a visit from the Parthian Orobazus, the ambassador of King Arsaces. This was the first contact between Parthia and Rome.

91 BC   Consuls: L. Marcius Philippus, Sextus Julius Caesar

(a) M. Livius Drusus the Younger, tribune 91 BC

de viris illustribus 66

As aedile, M. Livius Drusus gave a most splendid public show. When he was quaestor in Asia, he made himself the more conspicuous by declining to wear any official insignia.

Inscriptiones Latinae Selectae 49

M. Livius Drusus son of Marcus grandson of Gaius, pontifex, military tribune,

* Valerius Maximus (*3.7.8*) says that Scaurus was said to have taken bribes from Mithridates.

decemviral commissioner for minor suits at law, tribune of the plebs, decemviral commissioner for the granting and assigning of lands under his own law and quinqueviral commissioner for the granting and assigning of lands under the Saufeian Law, was killed during his year of office.

CICERO *de officiis* **1.108** (44 BC); *de oratore* **1.24** (55 BC); *pro Milone* **16** (52 BC); *Brutus* **222** (46 BC)

As a young man, M. Drusus was remarkably austere in character....Drusus undertook his tribunate to champion the authority of the Senate....He was of the highest birth, the champion of the Senate and indeed in those times virtually its patron....

M. Drusus was a political orator of some weight....We may count him one of the chief bulwarks of the state....

DIODORUS SICULUS 37.10

He alone seemed to be the Senate's champion.

SENECA, *de brevitate vitae* 6.1–2

Livius Drusus was a forceful and energetic man. Surrounded by a huge crowd drawn from all over Italy, he had proposed new laws and Gracchan wickednesses. Failing to see any way out for his policies, which he was not allowed to carry through and which he was no longer free to abandon once he had started on them, he is said to have bitterly cursed the unquiet life he had led ever since he was a child and to have asserted that even when he was a boy he had never had a holiday. For while he was still a ward (*his father, the elder Drusus, tribune 122 BC, had died while censor in 109 BC*) and had not even yet achieved the *toga virilis* he had had the courage to make speeches of commendation for men on trial in the courts and to use his influence in the Forum, so effectively indeed that in some cases he is known to have snatched a favourable verdict. To what limits might not such premature ambition have flung itself?.... It is disputed whether he died by his own hand. He fell from a sudden wound in his groin; some wondered whether it was suicide, but no one doubted whether it was timely.

SENECA, *de beneficiis* 6.34.2

Gaius Gracchus, and after him Livius Drusus, were the first Romans to introduce the practice of classifying their companions and followers: some they received privately, some along with several others, and some *en masse*.

VELLEIUS PATERCULUS 2.14

When Drusus was having a house built on the Palatine, his architect undertook to make it totally private and free from being overlooked by anyone. But 'No', said Drusus, 'I want you to use all your skill to build me a home where everybody can see whatever I may be doing'.

PLINY, *Natural History* 25.52

Drusus was the most eminent popular tribune of them all, a man to whom above all others the plebs stood and cheered. The *optimates* blamed him for the Marsic War (*viz. the Social War*).

PLINY, *Natural History* 33.20

Caepio (*the younger*) and Drusus became enemies over the matter of a ring which was being sold at auction, whence came the beginning of the Social War and the calamity that it brought.

VELLEIUS PATERCULUS 2.13–15

M. Livius Drusus was a man of the highest nobility, of great eloquence and the most upright character. But his luck did not match his natural gifts. Though he was anxious to restore to the Senate its old glory and transfer the courts to the Senate from the knights....in seeking to implement his pro-senatorial programme he ran into opposition from the Senate itself, which did not understand that his proposals to benefit the people were no more than inducements to get the people to accept his more important proposals in return for the lesser gains they were themselves getting. In the end, such was Drusus' ill luck that the Senate much preferred the evil projects of his colleagues to his own excellent plans, spurning the honour he was offering them...Thereupon, with his excellent plans turning out badly, Drusus' mind turned to the granting of citizenship to Italy. While working for this, he had returned one day from the Forum, surrounded by his customary immense and straggling crowd of followers, when he was struck in the forecourt of his own house with a knife....

With the death of Drusus, the long-burgeoning Italian War broke out. In the consulship of L. Caesar and P. Rutilius (*90* BC) the whole of Italy took up arms against the Romans. The spark came from Asculum, where the praetor Servilius and his legate Fonteius were murdered; it caught fire among the Marsi, and then spread to every region.

FLORUS 2.5

So great was the power the Roman knights had been given that they held in their hands the fate and fortunes of the chief men in the state, and cheated and robbed the state of its revenues for their own gain. The exile of Metellus and the conviction of Rutilius had weakened the Senate and robbed it of all its glory. At this critical moment Servilius Caepio championed the knights and Livius Drusus the Senate, the two of them twins in wealth, energy and prestige – whence their rivalry. All that was lacking were eagles and battle-standards: for the rest Rome was virtually split into two military camps. Caepio opened his attack on the Senate by indicting the leading nobles Scaurus and Philippus on charges of electoral corruption (*ambitus*). To oppose him Drusus aroused the plebs to his support by proposing Gracchan laws, and similarly excited the allies by holding out the hope of the grant of Roman citizenship. A remark of his is still remembered: 'I have left nothing for anybody else to give away but mud and air'.

SENECA, *ad Marciam* **16.4**

Livius Drusus was following in the footsteps of the Gracchi.

de viris illustribus **66**

As tribune, he gave citizenship to the Latins, land to the commons, membership of the Senate to the knights, and the courts to the Senate. He was far too open-handed: he himself declared that he had left nothing for anybody else to give away but mud and air.

EPITOME OF LIVY, Bks. 70 and 71

When it was no longer able to tolerate the tyrannical way in which the equestrian order ran the courts, the Senate began to strive might and main to transfer the courts to itself, with the support of the tribune M. Livius Drusus, who in order to build up his strength excited the commons with pernicious promises of generous benefits....So as to gain greater strength to champion the cause of the Senate which he had undertaken to defend, the tribune M. Livius Drusus sought to win over the allies and the Italians by holding out the hope of Roman citizenship. Having with their help carried agrarian and corn laws by violence, he also carried a judiciary law to the effect that the courts should be shared equally between the Senate and the equestrian order. But when in the end it proved impossible to give the allies the citizenship they had been promised, the Italians were enraged and began to prepare to secede from Rome.

APPIAN, *Civil Wars* **1. 35–36**

Subsequently, the tribune Livius Drusus, a man of the most distinguished ancestry, promised at the request of the Italians once again to introduce legislation to enfranchise them. The Roman citizenship was what the Italians wanted above all else, for at one stroke they would thus become masters instead of subjects. In order to get the Roman people in a mood to accept this, Drusus sought to win them over with many colonies in Italy and Sicily, long ago promised but never realised. He also attempted to bring together by a common law the Senate and the knights, who at that time were seriously at odds with each other over the courts.

Being unable to transfer the courts openly to the Senate, he devised the following compromise: to the senators who were then because of the internal troubles scarcely three hundred in number he proposed to add an equal number of men chosen from the knights on the criterion of quality and birth (*Greek: aristindên*), so that the courts should in future be chosen from this whole six-hundred-strong body. He also proposed that the members of this new body should be liable to prosecution if any of them accepted bribes, a charge which had virtually disappeared because of the widespread practice of bribery.

That then was his compromise proposal, but it rebounded on him. The Senate resented this wholesale new enrolment and the acquisition by the knights of this the highest station in Rome, thinking it likely that once they became senators their conflict with the existing senators would become even stronger. The knights for their part suspected that the result of this manoeuvre would be that in future the courts would be transferred from the knights to the sole control of the Senate, and having had their taste of the great profits and power involved they could not view this prospect at all happily. The mass of the knights were left in the dark and full of mutual suspicions about which of them would be thought the worthier to be included among the chosen three hundred, and this led to envy felt by the lesser of them towards the greater. But above all else they resented the revival of the statutory charge of corruption, something they had come to believe by then to have been utterly got rid of so far as they were concerned.

So it came about then that, for all that they were at odds with each other, knights and senators saw eye to eye in their hatred of Drusus. Only the commons were happy with their colonies. As for the Italians – and it was in their interest above all that Drusus was following his policies – they too were apprehensive about the colony law, fearing that the Roman public land, such of it as had not been formally distributed and they themselves were continuing to cultivate either in open violation of the law or secretly, would at once be taken from them – and they thought too that they would run into a lot of trouble about their own lands as well.

The Etruscans and Umbrians, who shared the fears of the Italians, were apparently brought into Rome by the consuls to get rid of Drusus – that was the real object, but the pretext was that they meant to denounce him. Their opposition was open and vociferous, and they waited in readiness for the time of decision.* Well aware of this, Drusus did not go out much but regularly conducted his business in the poorly-lighted cloister of his house, until one evening, as he was dismissing the people there, he suddenly cried out that he had been struck, and so saying fell to the ground. A cobbler's knife was found thrust into his thigh.

CICERO, *pro Rabirio Postumo* 16 (65 BC)

When that most powerful and noble tribune M. Drusus was seeking to carry a law instituting a new charge directed against the equestrian order: 'If anyone has accepted a bribe in the judging of a case', he met with the open resistance of the Roman knights....

CICERO, *pro Cluentio* 153 (66 BC)

Those gallant gentlemen, the Roman knights, who resisted the most distinguished and powerful tribune M. Drusus, when, along with the whole of the nobility of his time, his sole object was that those who had sat in judgement should be liable to trial on such charges (*i.e., of accepting bribes*) ....

PLUTARCH, *Cato Minor* 2

The allies of Rome were trying to secure the Roman citizenship. A certain

---

* It is disputed whether Appian's word here – *dokimasia* – is meant to refer to the voting on Drusus' franchise proposal or to the decision about the validity of his laws (*on which, see below*).

Pompaedius Silo, a soldierly man of the highest standing, was a friend of Drusus, and spent many days at his house.

de viris illustribus 80

When Cato was being brought up in the house of his uncle, Drusus, neither promises nor threats could bring him to tell Q. Popedius Silo, the chief of the Marsi, that he favoured the cause of the allies.

DIODORUS SICULUS 37.13

Pompaedius, the leader of the Marsi, embarked on a great and unexpected venture. He collected ten thousand men from among those who feared the scrutiny* (*?of their claims to be citizens*) and led them to Rome with weapons concealed under their clothing. He planned to surround the Senate with armed men and demand the citizenship, or else if it were not granted he would destroy Rome's rule with fire and sword. Gaius Domitius encountered him, and asked him, 'Where are you going?' 'To Rome', was the reply, 'summoned by the tribunes to seek the citizenship.' (*Domitius managed to persuade Pompaedius to return home peacefully*)

DIODORUS SICULUS 37.11

Oath of Philippus: 'I swear by Capitoline Jupiter and by Roman Vesta and by Mars and by the Sun and by Earth, the benefactress of animals and growing things, and also by the demigod founders of Rome and by the heroes who have helped to extend Rome's dominion, that the enemy and the friend of Drusus shall be my enemy and my friend, and that I shall spare neither my life nor my children nor my parents nor my spirit if so it shall seem right to Drusus and to those who swear this oath. And if I shall become a citizen by Drusus' law, I shall consider Rome my fatherland and Drusus my chiefest benefactor. And this oath I shall exact from as many of my fellow-people as I can. May all good things come to me if I keep this oath, and the opposite if I break it.'

(b) The opposition

CICERO, *de oratore* 3.2–6 (55 BC)

When Crassus (*consul 95 BC, censor 92 BC*) got back to Rome on the very last day of the theatrical shows he was greatly upset by the speech which Philippus (*consul 91 BC*) was reported to have delivered to a public meeting: it was common ground that Philippus had declared that he was going to have to look around to find himself another advisory body (*consilium*), since he could not administer the affairs of state with the Senate as it then was.

A full quorum of senators, including Crassus, turned up at the Senate House early in the morning of 13 September, the meeting having been called by Drusus. After making many criticisms of Philippus, Drusus moved a motion of censure on this very issue, namely that the consul had made such a serious attack on the Senate at a public meeting.

(*Crassus then made what was generally agreed to have been the finest of all his*

---

* Possibly, *euthunai* here might mean the enquiry as to whether Drusus' legislation was valid.

fine speeches.) Crassus spoke with indignation of the sad plight of the Senate and its abandonment: here was a consul, whose duty it was to conduct himself like a kind father or loyal guardian, robbing the Senate of its heritage of dignity as if he were no more than a common brigand; nor was it to be wondered at that a man who had brought the state low by his policies should now be seeking to extrude the Senate from its position as the great council of state.

Philippus was a forceful character, a fine speaker and a very tough fighter; fired by what Crassus had said, he did not take it lying down but blazed up fiercely and set about compelling Crassus' obedience by way of sequestrating his property as bail for his good behaviour.

At this point Crassus is reported to have delivered himself of some inspired words, saying that a consul who did not treat Crassus as a senator was no consul in Crassus' eyes: 'As for you', he said, 'who are prepared to treat the whole authority of our whole order as something you can pawn, and cut up in ribbons in plain view of the Roman people, do you imagine that you can frighten me by these demands for bail? It will do you no good to cut away my property from me, if what you want is to constrain L. Crassus; you must cut out this tongue of mine, and even then that spirit of liberty that lives within me will still spurn your unbridled arrogance'....

This was the motion which Crassus moved in such weighty and august wording, and which that full meeting of the Senate agreed to vote for: 'that the Roman People be satisfied that the Senate had never failed in its counsel and loyalty to the State'; and Crassus' name was one of those that stood as witness to the recorded decree. This was literally Crassus' 'swan song'....for he fell sick and died a week later.

FLORUS 2.5

The day of promulgation was at hand*, when all of a sudden such a mass of men appeared from everywhere that the city seemed as if it were under siege from the approach of an enemy. Nevertheless, the consul Philippus had the courage to propose repealing legislation; but an attendant gripped him by the throat and did not let go till Philippus was bleeding from mouth and eyes. Thus the laws were carried and voted, by violence. However, the allies demanded their reward at once, but meanwhile Drusus proved unable to keep his promise, and was suffering for his rash proposals; in the circumstances, Drusus' death was timely. But the allies, nothing daunted, did not cease to demand by force of arms that the Roman people honour his promises to them.

de viris illustribus 66

When his enemy Caepio continued to oppose his policies, Drusus threatened to have him hurled from the Tarpeian rock. As for the consul Philippus, when he was opposing the agrarian laws Drusus twisted his neck so forcefully at a public meeting that a great flood of blood burst from his nostrils – alluding to his luxurious standard of living, Drusus said it was thrush soup! Subsequently, Drusus fell from the heights of popularity into disfavour: the commons were happy with their land-grants, but those who were dispossessed were indignant;

* What was being 'promulgated' is not at all clear. (*This passage follows immediately on that already cited above from Florus*).

the knights chosen to be senators were overjoyed, but those passed over were annoyed; the Senate rejoiced in its renewed control of the courts, but did not like to accept knights among its number. As a result Drusus was worried, and kept putting off the demands of the Latins, who were agitating strongly for the citizenship which had been promised them, when he suddenly collapsed in public...and was carried home in a faint. Public prayers were offered all over Italy for his recovery, and, when the Latins were planning to murder the consul at the Latin Festival on the Alban Mount, Drusus warned him to take precautions. This led to charges against him in the Senate and as he returned home he was struck by an assassin in the crowd, and fell. Hostile suspicion for the murder fell on Philippus and Caepio.

VALERIUS MAXIMUS 9.5.2

When the Senate sent to Drusus to summon him to appear in the Senate House, 'Why don't you instead', he replied, 'come to the Curia Hostilia which is just by the speakers' platform (*rostra*), that is, to me?' I am ashamed to say what the upshot was: a tribune treated the authority of the Senate with contempt, the Senate obeyed the tribune.

CICERO, *pro Plancio* 33 (54 BC)

A certain Granius....met M. Drusus, and when Drusus greeted him in the usual way with 'What are you up to these days, Granius?' Granius' response was, 'My God, Drusus, what on earth are you up to these days?'*

ASCONIUS, commenting on Cicero, *pro Cornelio*: 68–69C

'As when the Senate decrees that the People are not in its view bound by a law which has been passed, as happened with the Livian laws in the consulship of L. Marcius and Sextus Julius.'

I think you remember that these Livian laws are those which the tribune M. Livius Drusus carried that year. He had begun by championing the senatorial cause and carrying laws in favour of the *optimates*, but later on he became so wild and abandoned that he lost all sense of moderation. So the consul Philippus, his personal enemy, got the Senate to agree to abolish all his laws by a single senatorial decree. It was ruled that they had been passed in contravention of the auspices and the People were not bound by them.

CICERO, *de domo* 41 (57 BC)

The Senate adjudged that the People were not bound by the laws of M. Drusus on the grounds that they had contravened the lex Caecilia Didia.**

*For other Ciceronian references to the invalidation of the Livian laws, see Cicero, de domo 50; de legibus 2.31; and de legibus 2.14, which is cited above, **100** BC (c).*

DIODORUS SICULUS 37.10

When the Senate was invalidating his laws, Drusus announced that, although as a tribune he had absolute legislative freedom and the power to veto senatorial

---

* The Latin *'Quid agis?'* is really our 'How are you?' It has to be adapted here to bring out the wordplay.
** Which forbade 'tacking': see above, 98 BC (b).

decrees, he chose not to use that power, knowing full well that they would soon reap the just reward for their sins. The invalidation of his laws would mean the invalidation of his law about the *iudices* in the courts: allowed to stand, that would have meant that the incorruptible would never have had to fear indictment, while those who plundered the provinces would have been hauled up on charges of accepting bribes. Thus those who were enviously destroying his own repute were by their own votes voluntarily making themselves hostages to fortune.

(c) The Varian Law and Commission

APPIAN, *Civil Wars* 1.37

Thus was Drusus slain, while he was tribune. The knights sought to make his policy a springboard for legal attacks on their opponents, and persuaded the tribune Q. Varius to bring in a measure to indict all those who either openly or secretly assisted the Italians against Rome, hoping thereby to bring all the powerful men under a shameful charge and, themselves being the judges, get them out of the way and themselves become even more powerful in their control of the state. When the other tribunes refused to allow Varius' proposal to be put to the vote, the knights drew daggers and surrounded them and ensured its passage. Thereupon accusers immediately brought charges against the most illustrious senators. Of these, Bestia did not stay to answer the charge but preferred voluntary exile rather than surrender into the hands of his enemies. He was followed by Cotta, who did come before the court, where he made an impressive defence of his policies and actions and hurled open contempt at the knights, before himself also leaving Rome before a verdict could be delivered. Memmius, the conqueror of Greece, was led into a scandalous trap by the knights, who broke a promise to acquit him and condemned him to banishment; he lived out the rest of his life on Delos.

ASCONIUS, commenting on a passage from Cicero, *pro Scauro* 22C

'Servilius Caepio it was, too, who indicted this loyal defender of Rome (*M. Aemilius Scaurus*) on a charge of treachery, under the Varian Law. Scaurus was also harassed by the tribune Q. Varius.'

Not long before, when the Italian War had broken out, because the nobility was hated for the refusal of citizenship to the allies, the tribune Q. Varius passed a law to establish a court of enquiry concerning those men through whose aid and advice the allies had taken up arms against the Roman People. Thereupon Q. Caepio, an old enemy of Scaurus', hoping that he had found the opportunity to ruin him, persuaded the tribune Q. Varius to summon the seventy-two-year-old Scaurus to appear before him on a charge of having stirred up the war. He was summoned by an attendant, though he was only slowly getting over an illness; but for all that his friends tried to persuade him not to expose himself at his age and in his weak state of health to popular hostility, he went off to the Forum on the arms of young men of the highest nobility, and had this to say when invited to reply to the charge: 'The Spaniard Q. Varius alleges that M. Aemilius Scaurus, the president of the Senate, has called our allies to arms. M. Aemilius Scaurus, the president of the Senate, denies the charge. There are no witnesses. Which of us, citizens, does it please you to believe?'. His words had such an electrifying effect on everybody that the tribune himself dismissed the charge.

VALERIUS MAXIMUS 8.6.4

Q. Varius, who owed his *cognomen* 'Hybrida' to the obscurity of his title to the citizenship, as a tribune forced through a law in face of the veto of his colleagues which ordered an enquiry against those who of malice preprense had driven the allies to arms, a great disaster for Rome. It sparked off first the Social, then the Civil War. Later, when he had ceased to be tribune, his own law caught him in the trap of his own making.

CICERO, *Brutus* 304 (46 BC)

Only the court established by the Varian Law remained in session, all the others being suspended because of the war.

CICERO, *Brutus* 205

The speech of Cotta entitled 'In his own defence under the Varian Law' was written for Cotta by L. Aelius, at Cotta's request.

(d) Drusus and the coinage

PLINY, *Natural History* 33.3.46

In his tribunate Livius Drusus debased the silver coinage by the admixture of copper in the ratio of one to eight. (*But this could be a reference to the elder Drusus, tribune 122 BC*)

(e) The Social War

DIODORUS SICULUS 37.2

With the commons and the Senate fighting each other, and the Senate calling in the Italians to help with the promise of a law granting the Roman citizenship they longed for so much, and none of the promises to the Italians being fulfilled, the war of the Italians against Rome broke out, in the consulship of Lucius Marcius Philippus and Sextus Julius.

CICERO, *de officiis* 2.75 (44 BC)

It is less than a hundred and ten years since L. Calpurnius Piso passed the very first law on extortion (*149 BC*). Since then, so many laws, each harsher than the last, so many defendants, so many condemned men, so great an Italian war started because of the fear the courts inspired, such terrible plundering and despoiling of our allies when laws and courts had been displaced – why, we owe our survival not to our own strength but to the weakness of others.

VELLEIUS PATERCULUS 2.15

Their cause was most just: they were seeking the citizenship of a state whose dominions their own arms safeguarded; every year and in every war they furnished twice as many infantry and cavalry, and yet were not admitted to the right to be citizens of the state which through them had reached that pinnacle of power which enabled it to treat with disdain men of the same blood and the same race and spurn them like strangers and aliens.

JUSTIN 38.4.13

The whole of Italy rose up together in the Marsic War: the demand was now no longer liberty, but partnership in dominion and franchise.

FLORUS 2.6

The allies with every justice on their side were demanding the right of Roman citizenship. Their own efforts had helped to make Rome great, and Livius Drusus in his greed for power had fired these hopes in the allies. After Drusus was murdered, that same torch which kindled his funeral pyre set the allies ablaze to take up arms and defeat Rome....The first war-plan was to assassinate the consuls Julius Caesar and Marcius Philippus while they were about their sacral functions at the Latin Festival on the Alban Mount. That horrible plan miscarried because it was betrayed, but then all the passion came boiling up at Asculum where in the great concourse of the games there the Roman delegates present were butchered....This was the signal for the trumpets to sound the call to battle from every part of Italy, as the rebel leader Poppaedius sped through peoples and towns everywhere.

EPITOME OF LIVY, Bk. 72

The Italian peoples seceded from Rome: the Picenes, Vestini, Marsi, Paeligni, Marrucini, Samnites, and Lucanians. The war began in Picenum. The proconsul (*sic*) Q. Servilius (*Caepio, praetor 91 BC*) was murdered in the town of Asculum along with all the Roman citizens who were in the town. Rome declared a state of emergency.

APPIAN, *Civil Wars* 1.38–9

When the Italians heard of the murder of Drusus, and the excuse for the banishing of the victims of the Varian Law, they thought it intolerable that this should happen to the men who were working in support of their cause. Seeing no other way now left for them to acquire the citizenship, they resolved on outright defection and a full-scale war. They held secret negotiations among themselves, formed a common front, and exchanged hostages with each other as a pledge of good faith. For some considerable time the Romans remained unaware of all this, thanks to their preoccupation with the trials and political struggles at Rome. When they did learn of it, they sent out men well acquainted with the particular communities to find out quietly what was going on. One of them spied a young man being taken from Asculum to be a hostage in another town, and passed the information on to Servilius, who was proconsul in those parts. (Apparently at that time certain magistrates were governing parts of Italy as proconsuls: the Emperor Hadrian much later revived this practice, but it did not long survive him.) Servilius hurried to Asculum, where a festival was going on, and delivered a threatening harangue to the crowds, whereupon they supposed that the plot had been discovered and killed him. They also killed his legate Fonteius....and followed up these murders by sparing none of the other Romans there, who were rushed and slaughtered by the mob, which proceeded to loot their possessions.

The rebellion having started, all the other neighbouring peoples joined in: Marsi, Paeligni, Vestini and Marrucini; they were followed by Picenti, Ferentini, Hirpini, Pompeiani, Venusini, Iapyges, Lucanians, and Samnites, peoples which had become hostile to Rome before, and all the other peoples between the River Liris and the corner of the Adriatic, both maritime and inland. ...Apart from defensive garrisons, they mustered a joint force of 100,000 foot and horse. The Romans sent an equal number of men to face them, composed of Roman citizens and still-loyal allies.

DIODORUS SICULUS 37.13

Servilius treated them not as free men and allies but as slaves; his insults and frightening threats incited the allies to take vengeance on him and the others.

OBSEQUENS 114–115

Romans were butchered at Asculum at festival-time....
Romans were savagely tortured by the Picenes....

(f) The East

JUSTIN 38.3.4

On the death of Nicomedes, his son, also named Nicomedes, was driven from his kingdom of Bithynia by Mithridates.

APPIAN, *Mithridatica* 10

(*At the same time as the expulsion of Nicomedes*) Mithraas and Bagoas drove out Ariobarzanes, the Roman-nominated king of Cappadocia, and restored Ariarathes.

90 BC   Consuls: L. Julius Caesar, P. Rutilius Lupus

(a) Financial stringency

CICERO, *de lege agraria* 2.80 (63 BC)

Have you forgotten what mighty armies you sustained on the fruits of the Campanian Land in the Italian War, when all other sources of revenue had been lost?

(b) The Varian Enquiries

CICERO, *Brutus* 304 (46 BC)

Hortensius served in the ranks in the first year of the (*Social*) war, and as a military tribune in the second, when Sulpicius was a legate. Marcus Antonius was also absent from Rome. With all the other courts suspended because of the war, only that established by the Varian Law continued to function. I often attended its hearings....I was very upset when Cotta was banished....Then the following year Q. Varius had to go, condemned under his own law.

(c) The Enfranchisement of Italy

*The various stages and details of the process whereby the whole of Italy up to the line of the River Po (Padus), together with some former Latin colonies north of the Po like Cremona and Aquileia, became incorporated into the Roman state are sometimes disputable. Rather than chop the evidence up into bits and pieces under the various years, it seems better to collect it all here in one place. We may begin with the **Lex Julia**, carried at the end of 90 BC by the consul Lucius Caesar.*

CICERO, *pro Balbo* 21 (56 BC)

'The Julian Law, which gave citizenship to allies and Latins, was such that any communities which did not themselves accept it as binding on them could not have the citizenship. In this connection, a serious dispute arose at Heraclia and at Naples; in those two cities a large proportion of the population was in favour of keeping the independence of their treaty of alliance rather than accepting Roman citizenship.'

AULUS GELLIUS, *Attic Nights* 4.4.3

'All the Latins were granted citizenship by the Julian Law.'

APPIAN, *Civil Wars* 1.49

'Fearing that Rome might be encircled (*if the rebellion spread more widely*), the Senate....voted that those of the Italians who still held to their alliances with Rome should become Roman citizens, which was what almost all of them most wanted. When the news reached Etruria, the Etruscans happily accepted the citizenship. By this act of generosity the Senate made those who were loyal still more loyal, strengthened those who were wavering, and undermined the resolution of those who were at war with Rome with some hope of the same concession. But the Romans did not enrol these new citizens in the existing thirty-five tribes, for fear that their greater numbers would swamp the votes of the old citizens. They created ten new tribes for them, which were to vote last. This meant that their vote was often valueless, once the votes of the previous thirty-five had been taken and produced well over a majority already. Either this was not noticed to begin with, or else the Italians were only too pleased even with this; but, when it came to be appreciated later, it sparked off another political crisis.'

An opaque fragment of the historian Sisenna (fr. 17P) mentions: 'Lucius Calpurnius Piso (tribune 89 BC)...a decree of the Senate....two new tribes...' but how to fit that in is very dubious. Of the general process, Velleius has this to say:

VELLEIUS PATERCULUS 2. 16

'Such were the varying and cruel fortunes of the Italian War that within a period of two years two Roman consuls, Rutilius and then Porcius Cato (*consul 89 BC*) were killed in action against the enemy, and Roman armies were in many places put to flight....The insurgents had chosen Corfinium as their capital, renaming it 'Italica'. Subsequently, however, by gradually granting Roman citizenship to those who had not taken up arms or had laid them down in good time, Rome's strength was repaired, as Pompeius Strabo, Sulla, and Marius restored a reeling and sagging Republic.'

And later he has this to say:

VELLEIUS PATERCULUS 2.20

'Cinna (*in 87 BC*) was no more restrained than Marius and Sulpicius had been (*in 88 BC*). Though the citizenship had been granted to Italy in such a way that the new citizens were to be distributed among eight tribes, the intention being that their power and sheer numbers should not shatter the standing of the old citizens and that the beneficiaries should not have more power than their benefactors, Cinna promised to distribute the Italians among all the tribes.'

In 89 BC, the consul Cn. Pompeius Strabo, father of Pompey the Great, carried out the 'Latinisation' of Transpadane Gaul, that is of that part of Italy north of the Po (though existing Latin communities there had been given full Roman citizenship under the Julian Law).

ASCONIUS 3C

'Gnaeus Pompeius Strabo, the father of Cn. Pompeius Magnus, established the Transpadane colonies. This he did, not by introducing new settlers (*coloni*); the existing inhabitants of the towns simply stayed put, with Pompeius giving them the Latin Right (*ius Latii*), that is to say that they were to have the same right as any other Latin colony, namely that men there might acquire Roman citizenship by standing for local office in their own home-town.'

A law was carried by two tribunes in 89 BC. We hear of this law only from Cicero (the scholiast on this passage adds nothing save error). In his defence of Archias, Cicero was concerned only with cives adscripti, *supplementary honorary citizens of former allied cities in Italy, like Archias himself; it may be however that there was more to this law than the single section which Cicero cites as bearing on his client's claim:*

CICERO, *pro Archia* 7 (62 BC)

'Archias was granted his Roman citizenship under the law of Silvanus and Carbo (*the* lex Plautia Papiria *of M. Plautius Silvanus and C. Papirius Carbo*): "If any persons have been registered as *cives adscripti* of a state bound to Rome by treaty, and if at the time when the law was passed they had a domicile in Italy, and if they made application to a (*or 'the'*) praetor within sixty days...." '

Censors had been appointed after the usual interval in 92 BC. The election of P. Licinius Crassus and L. Julius Caesar as censors for 89 BC before the usual five-year period had elapsed suggests that their main task was to be the enrolment and registration of the new citizens created by the Julian Law of late 90 BC. But we know on the firm evidence of Cicero that under these two censors:

CICERO, *pro Archia* 11

'No registration of any part of the citizen-body took place.'

To sum up so far: what seems clear is that the Julian Law of 90 BC offered citizenship to a particular category of Italian states, those which had stayed loyal to Rome. The offer may also possibly have been open to other states which quickly ceased fighting. The offer was to communities as a whole, not to individuals; and the communities had themselves to accept or decline the offer – Rome was not trying to impose her citizenship by her own unilateral act. We happen to know *from an inscription that has chanced to survive that the Julian Law also empowered commanders in the field to grant citizenship as a reward for outstanding service: ILS 8888 records the grant by Pompeius Strabo of citizenship to a troop of Spanish auxiliary horse for such service (*virtutis causa*), and specifies that this was done 'in accordance with the Julian Law' (*ex* lege Julia*). Later the* lex Plautia Papiria *made provision for at least certain individuals (*cives adscripti*): if there was more to it than that, we cannot say. The Romans were clearly worried about the impact of a mass of new voters, and tried to cushion it by declining to distribute them evenly through all 35 existing tribes (block-voting 'constituencies' based on an individual's place of residence), instead creating new tribes for them or confining them to a limited number of the old tribes.*

So far as we can tell, no move had as yet been made to extend citizenship to rebel communities.

In 88 BC (see under year), Sulpicius Rufus was tribune, and carried a law to distribute the new citizens through all the tribes. Later in the year, Sulla marched on Rome, and repealed all Sulpicius' legislation.

In 87 BC (see under year), Cinna and his friends in turn seized power in Rome, having already promised to extend the citizenship to all the Italians, both those who had capitulated after being fought to a standstill and those still fighting. Cinna's side had owed their success to massive support from ex-rebel and rebel states, so their action is understandable.

*The Livian Epitome (Bk. 60) reports, under the year 87 BC, that: 'Citizenship was granted to the Italian peoples by decree of the Senate'; and Licinianus (p. 35 Flemisch) says, in the same context, that: 'All those who had surrendered were granted the citizenship'. There is also a puzzling entry in the Livian Epitome (Bk. 84) under the year 84 BC : 'The new citizens were granted the suffrage (*suffragium) by decree of the Senate'.*

Censors were again elected in 86 BC: but the figure of 463,000 preserved as the number of citizens then counted is far too small to reflect a proper registration of any but a very few of the new citizens. The last figure we have, that of 115 BC, is 394,336. After 86 BC censors were not elected again until 70 BC, when the number of citizens counted was 910,000. Which suggests that the 86 BC count was, for whatever reasons, woefully patchy and incomplete, and that it was not until 70 BC that all the new citizens were properly and thoroughly registered and assigned to tribes and classes and centuries.

(d) The Italian League

STRABO 5.4.2

They chose Corfinium, the chief town of the Paeligni, as the common capital for all the Italians to take the place of Rome....and renamed it 'Italica'. There all the participants in the rebellion gathered and consuls and praetors were elected. The war went on for two years until they achieved the partnership they were fighting for. The war was called the 'Marsic War' after the Marsi, who began the rebellion, and above all because of Pompaedius.

VELLEIUS PATERCULUS 2.16

The most famous of the Italian commanders were Popaedius Silo, Asinius

Herius, Insteius Cato, C. Pontidius, Pontius Telesinus, Marius Egnatius, and Papius Mutilus....They chose Corfinium as their chief seat of power and named it 'Italica'.

APPIAN, *Civil Wars* 1.40

The individual contingents from each state on the Italian side had their own commanders, but the commanders-in-chief of the whole combined army were T. Lafrenius, C. Pontilius, Marius Egnatius, Q. Popaedius, C. Papius, M. Lamponius, C. Vidacilius, Erius Asinius, and Vettius Scato, who divided the forces equally between themselves to confront the various Roman commanders.

DIODORUS SICULUS 37.2

(*At Corfinium*) the rebel states set up a common Senate with a membership of five hundred....and gave them full powers for the conduct of the war. They ruled that two consuls and twelve praetors should be chosen every year. They chose as consuls Quintus Pompaedius Silo, the Marsian....and with him the Samnite Gaius Aponius Motylus, and, dividing the whole of Italy into two parts, assigned each of the two as a consular sphere of command.

A silver denarius issued by the rebels was inscribed in Oscan lettering with the word 'Vitelliu' (= 'Italia'), and showed on its reverse side a bull trampling on a she-wolf: in general, for coinage of this period, see Sydenham: The Roman Republican Coinage, *pp. 89 ff.*

(e) The Roman Commanders

APPIAN, *Civil Wars* 1.40

The Romans were commanded by Sextus (*sic*) Julius Caesar* and Publius Rutilius Lupus, the consuls....But, realising the complicated nature of the war and how it was split up into several parts, they sent out the best men of the time to serve as lieutenant-generals under the consuls: under Rutilius were Gnaeus Pompeius, father of Pompey the Great, Quintus Caepio, Gaius Perperna, Gaius Marius, and Valerius Messala; under Sextus Caesar were Publius Lentulus, (*Quintus Catulus*) Caesar's cousin, Titus Didius, Licinius Crassus, Cornelius Sulla, and, with them, Marcellus.

CICERO, *pro Fonteio* 43 (69 BC)

Just recall to mind the lieutenant-generals (*legati*) who served recently in the Italian War with L. Julius and P. Rutilius (*consuls 90 BC*) and with L. Cato and Cn. Pompeius (*consuls 89 BC*). You will know that among them were M. Cornutus, L. Cinna, and L. Sulla, all former praetors and very experienced military men; then there were C. Marius, T. Didius, Q. Catulus, and P. Crassus, men who had learned the art of war not from books but from action and victories.

---

* Appian has evidently slipped up and confused Sextus Caesar, consul 91 BC, with Lucius Caesar, consul 90 BC.

89 BC   Consuls: Cn. Pompeius Strabo, L. Porcius Cato
                Censors: P. Licinius Crassus, L. Iulius Caesar

(a) Debt troubles; murder of the urban praetor

EPITOME OF LIVY, Bk. 74

The praetor Aulus Sempronius Asellio was killed in the Forum by the money-lenders because he was giving judgement in favour of the debtors.

VALERIUS MAXIMUS 9.7.4

The indignation of the money-lenders burst on the head of the urban praetor Sempronius Asellio, who had taken up the cause of the debtors, in a frightful fashion. He was sacrificing outside the Temple of Concord when the creditors, stirred up by the tribune L. Cassius, forced him to run for his life from the very altars, drove him from the Forum, and cut him to pieces when they found him hiding in a small tavern, still dressed in his official robes.

APPIAN, *Civil Wars* 1.54

Quarrels began at Rome between creditors and debtors. The money-lenders were charging interest on loans, though an archaic law forbade lending money at interest and prescribed a penalty for anyone who did....But the charging of interest had been hallowed by long usage, so the creditors insisted on it in accordance with custom, while for their part the debtors kept delaying their payments on the excuse of war and civil unrest, with some of them even beginning to threaten legal action against the usurers. Responsibility for such matters lay with the praetor Asellio, and failing to secure an amicable agreement he allowed them to proceed against each other at law, thereby putting the conflict between custom and law in the lap of the courts. The money-lenders, indignant at Asellio's resuscitation of an archaic law, killed him (*while he was sacrificing – a similar story to that in Valerius Maximus*).

(b) The Judiciary Law of Plautius

ASCONIUS 79C, commenting on a passage from Cicero *pro Cornelio*

"I well remember that when for the first time (*or 'as soon as'*) senators were sitting in judgement in the courts alongside knights under the Plautian Law, a man detested by heaven and the nobility, Cn. Pompeius (*which should probably be amended to Cn. Pomponius*) was prosecuted on a charge of treason (*maiestas*) under the Varian Law."

    The tribune M. Plautius Silvanus, in the consulship of Cn. Pompeius Strabo and L. Porcius Cato, the second year of the Italian War, at a time when the equestrian order dominated the courts, carried a law with the help of the nobles. This law had the effect which Cicero here points to. For under the law each tribe was to elect fifteen of its own members to act as *iudices* in the courts that year. The result was that there were senators among them, and indeed even some men from the lower classes.

(c) Q. Varius Condemned (*cf. 91* BC *(c)*)

CICERO *Brutus* **305** (46 BC); *de natura deorum* **3.81** (44 BC)

The following year (*viz. 89* BC) Q. Varius was condemned under his own law, and died...

Q. Varius, vilest of men, perished miserably and cruelly; if that was because he had killed Drusus by stabbing and Metellus by poison, it had been better that they should live than that Varius pay the penalty for his crime.

(d) For matters concerning the grant of citizenship, etc., see 90 BC (c)

(e) Sulla elected consul for 88 BC

EPITOME OF LIVY, Bk. 75

Sulla left for Rome to stand for the consulship with a record of achievements behind him scarcely matched by anybody else before who had not yet achieved that rank.

PLUTARCH, *Sulla* 6

Sulla was elected consul along with Quintus Pompeius. He was fifty years old.

(f) The war in Italy

DIODORUS SICULUS 37.2

The consul Gnaeus Pompeius and Sulla, serving as lieutenant-general under the other consul, Cato, beat the Italians not once but in many brilliant battles, and turned the scales against them.

FLORUS 2.6 (*3.18*)

The great good fortune of the Roman People, always greater in times of trouble, rose again with all its strength. Cato scattered the Etruscans, Gabinius the Marsians, Carbo the Lucanians, and Sulla the Samnites.

EPITOME OF LIVY, Bk. 74

The consul Cn. Pompeius defeated the Marsians in battle.

PLUTARCH, *Marius* 33

Marius finally resigned his command because he was no longer physically strong enough to carry on.

CASSIUS DIO fr. 100

Most of Cato's army were city-bred and unfit and it was generally not a strong force. On one occasion Cato rebuked them for laziness and insubordination, and as a reward for his boldness was very nearly buried under their missiles: he would have been killed had they been able to get hold of stones, but the area was one of damp arable land, luckily, so he took no hurt from the clods they hurled at him. The instigator of the mutiny was arrested, a certain Gaius Titius, a shameless and foul-mouthed rabble-rouser who got his living from the courts and the Forum, and he was sent to the tribunes in Rome. But he was not punished.

OROSIUS 5.18.24

The consul Porcius Cato, in command of Marius' troops, performed some strenuous actions, and then boasted that C. Marius had achieved nothing greater. Because of this, in the course of fighting against the Marsians near the Fucine Lake, he was laid low in the confusion of the battle by C. Marius' son, as if by the unknown hand of one of the enemy.

EPITOME OF LIVY, Bk. 75

The consul L. Porcius won some successes and defeated the Marsians on several occasions, but he fell while assaulting their camp. That gave the enemy victory in that engagement.

APPIAN, *Civil Wars* 1.50

During that winter Porcius Cato, Pompeius' colleague, was killed fighting the Marsians.

FLORUS 2.6 *(3.18)*

Pompeius Strabo made a universal waste by fire and sword, and set no end to the slaughter until by the destruction of Asculum he avenged the spirits of so many armies, consuls, and plundered towns.

APPIAN, *Civil Wars* 1.48

Asculum was the native-town of Vidacilius, and fearing for its safety he hurried there with eight cohorts. He sent ahead orders that the inhabitants should make a sally against the besiegers as soon as they saw him coming....But the Asculans held back. Still Vidacilius broke through the enemy and dashed into the town....Giving up any hope that the town could be saved, he murdered all his enemies, built a pyre in the temple, set a couch on the pyre, and held a feast with his friends; then, at the height of the drinking, he swallowed poison and threw himself onto the pyre, telling his friends to set it alight. So died Vidacilius, a proud patriot. (*The proconsul Sextus Caesar took Cato's place, but he too died during the siege.*)

VELLEIUS PATERCULUS 2.21

Cn. Pompeius, father of Magnus, captured Asculum. Around that town, though armies were operating in many other regions at the same time, 75,000 Roman troops and over 60,000 Italians clashed in battle on a single day.

CICERO, *Philippics* 12.27 (43 BC)

The consul Cn. Pompeius, son of Sextus, parleyed with the Marsian commander, P. Vettius Scato, between their two camps. I was there, serving as a raw recruit in Pompey's army....After Scato had greeted him, Pompey asked, 'How shall I address you?' 'As a friend at heart,' said Scato, 'but by necessity an enemy.' It was a calm parley, no fear, no mistrust, indeed very little hatred. For the allies were aiming, not to rob us of our state, but to be received as members of it.

APPIAN, *Civil Wars* 1.52

Gnaeus Pompeius subdued the Marsians, the Marrucini, and the Vestini.

EPITOME OF LIVY, Bk. 76

The proconsul Cn. Pompeius accepted the surrender of the Vestini and Paeligni. The Marsians too, broken in a number of battles by the legates L. Cinna and Caecilius Pius, began to seek peace. Asculum was taken by Cn. Pompeius.

ASCONIUS 14C

Pompey the Great's father celebrated a triumph over the Picentes in the Italian War.

VALERIUS MAXIMUS 6.9.9

After the capture of Asculum, Cn. Pompeius, father of Magnus, led the young boy P. Ventidius before the gaze of the people in his triumphal procession.

PLINY, *Natural History* 7.135

By a strange irony of Fate, Publius Ventidius, who as a boy had been led captive in Cn. Pompeius' Asculan triumph, grew up to become the only Roman general to celebrate (*38 BC*) a triumph over the Parthians.

FASTI TRIUMPHALES

Cn. Pompeius, son of Sextus, grandson of Gnaeus, Strabo, consul, in the year 664 (=*89 BC*) over the Asculans of Picenum, on 25 December.

A number of sling-pellets have been turned up at Asculum, dating from this time, with various inscriptions on them, including 'Hit Pompey!' See CIL 1². 848, 853, 858.

An inscription, ILS 8888, from Rome records the grant by Pompeius Strabo of Roman citizenship to thirty Spanish cavalrymen, for bravery. The grant was made 'in the camp at Asculum on the last day of November under the Julian Law.' Pompey is styled 'Imperator.' *Over fifty men are named as serving on his advisory council (*in consilio*), among them his own son, the future Pompey the Great, then aged 17, and a 'Lucius Sergius son of Lucius of the* tribus *Tro(mentina)', who is pretty certainly the famous Catiline.*

PLINY, *Natural History* 3.70

The town of Stabiae in Campania existed right down to the last day of April in the consulship of Cn. Pompeius and L. Cato, when it was destroyed in the Social War by the legate L. Sulla. All that remains of it now is a farm.

OROSIUS 6.18.22

When a Roman army had set out to besiege Pompeii, Postumius Albinus, a former consul serving as a legate under L. Sulla, aroused the hatred of all the soldiers by his intolerable arrogance, and was stoned to death.

EPITOME OF LIVY, Bk. 75

When the legate A. Postumius Albinus was in charge of the fleet he was suspected of treachery and killed by his own troops.

APPIAN, *Civil Wars* 1.50–52, *abridged*

In the Pompeian hills Sulla beat Cluentius and drove him into Nola, killing him and some 23,000 Italian troops. Sulla then proceeded against the Hirpini and their town of Aeculanum, which he took and plundered, arguing that its surrender had not been freely made; the other Hirpine towns surrendered and were spared, and thus all the Hirpini were subdued. Next he moved against the Samnites by an indirect route, took Mutilus and his army by surprise, and broke them with heavy losses. Mutilus took refuge with a small force in Aesernia. Sulla attacked Bovianum seat of the common council of the rebels, and took it after a stiff fight. With the onset of winter, he went back to Rome to stand for the consulship. The praetor C. Cosconius burned Salapia, took Cannae, and laid siege to Conusium; forced to retreat to Cannae by a Samnite relieving army, he turned and beat the Samnites, killing 15,000. He then overran the territory of Larinum, Venusia, and Asculum, and compelled the surrender of the Poediculi.

VELLEIUS PATERCULUS 2.16

Minatius Magius of Aeculanum showed such loyalty to Rome in this war that with a legion he had raised himself among the Hirpini he helped T. Didius to capture Herculaneum, and L. Sulla to attack Pompeii and seize Compsa.

CICERO, *de divinatione* 1.72 (44 BC)

In the history written by Sulla we read that when he was in the Nola region he was sacrificing in front of his headquarters when a snake suddenly emerged from underneath the altar, whereupon the soothsayer (*haruspex*) C. Postumius begged him to lead his army out on a sally. Sulla did so and captured the great camp of the Samnites outside Nola.

EPITOME OF LIVY, Bks. 75 and 76

The legate L. Cornelius Sulla beat the Samnites in battle and took two of their camps by storm. He conquered the Hirpini. He put the Samnites to flight in several engagements, and won back several peoples. Cosconius and Lucceius won a battle against the Samnites, killed Marius Egnatius, noblest of the rebel generals, and compelled numerous Samnite towns to surrender....

The legate A. Gabinius was successful against the Lucanians and captured many towns, but fell while besieging the enemy camp.

(g) Changes in the rebel organisation

DIODORUS SICULUS 37.2

The rebels moved their headquarters to Samnite Aesernia, and chose five military commanders, to one of whom, Quintus Pompaedius Silo, they gave overall command because of his reputation as a fine general. In collaboration with the general council he organised a powerful force, bringing the total numbers old and new up to 30,000 men. On top of that, he freed slaves and armed them as opportunity arose, thus amassing not far short of 20,000, and a thousand cavalry.

(h) Thrace and Macedonia

EPITOME OF LIVY, Bk. 74

There were plundering Thracian incursions into Macedonia.

OROSIUS 5.18.30

At this time King Sothimus invaded Greece with large numbers of Thracian auxiliaries and plundered all the limits of Macedonia. He was finally beaten by the praetor C. Sentius and forced to retreat to his own kingdom.

(i) The East

APPIAN, *Mithridatica* 11

Under pressure from the Roman envoys (*who had restored Nicomedes to the throne of Bithynia and Ariobarzanes to that of Cappadocia*), Nicomedes, who had undertaken to pay a lot of money to the generals and envoys for their help, money which he had not yet paid to them, and had borrowed a great deal too from the Romans who accompanied them and who were demanding payment, reluctantly invaded Mithridates' territory. Meeting with no opposition, he plundered it as far as the city of Amastris; for, though he had a sufficient force, Mithridates withdrew, so as to provide himself with abundant justifiable reasons for war.

FLORUS 1.40 (*3.5*)

Mithridates had told the legate Cassius that the reason for the war was that Nicomedes of Bithynia was robbing him of territory.

Letter of Mithridates, SALLUST, *Histories* 4.69.10 M

'What am I to call myself? Cut off on all sides from their dominions by kingdoms and tetrarchies, because of their belief that I was wealthy and could not survive, the Romans provoked me to make war through the agency of Nicomedes.'

(j) Publicani in Asia

ILS 8770, inscription from Ilium

Set up in honour of the censor Lucius Julius Caesar, son of Lucius, who restored the sacred estate of Athena to the people (*of Ilium*), and excluded it from liability to pay taxes.

88 BC   Consuls: L. Cornelius Sulla, Q. Pompeius Rufus

(a) Tribunate of P. Sulpicius Rufus

CICERO, *de haruspicum responsis* **41** (56 BC)
So weighty a speaker was P. Sulpicius, so agreeable, so terse, that he could make a saint a sinner or a sound man lose his judgement.

CICERO, *Brutus* **203** (46 BC)

Perhaps more than anybody else I have ever heard Sulpicius was an orator on the grand scale, a truly 'tragic' orator, so to say. His voice was at once gentle and resonant, his gestures and movements full of charm – but clearly those of a trained speaker, not a professional actor. His style was full of pace and colour, without any hint of over-ornateness or superfluity.

CICERO, *de oratore* **1.25** (55 BC)

Crassus had been accompanied by some young men who were very close friends of (*Livius*) Drusus (*tribune 91 BC*), young men in whom the elder men of the time rested great hopes; they were C. Cotta, who was a candidate for the tribunate, and P. Sulpicius who was thought likely to try for a tribunate after Cotta.

CICERO, *de haruspicum responsis* **43** (56 BC)

During his tribunate Sulpicius decided to rob of all their dignity men with whom he had lived on the most intimate terms before his election.

CICERO, *Brutus* **226** (46 BC)

P. Antistius was the same age as Sulpicius, and he won approval when he first supported the right cause in opposing that extraordinary consular candidacy of C. Julius – and all the more so because, with his fellow-tribune Sulpicius himself supporting the same cause, Antistius was more outspoken and his shafts went home better.

DIODORUS SICULUS 37.12

With the Marsic war nearly over, civil strife once again engulfed Rome in violence, with many men of repute fighting for the command against Mithridates because of the enormous spoils involved. Gaius Caesar and the six-times-consul Gaius Marius were locked in rivalry, and the commons were divided in their support.

ASCONIUS 25C

The two brothers concerned were Gaius and Lucius Caesar. Lucius had been consul and censor, but Gaius was killed while of no more than aedilician rank. But so powerful a figure was Gaius that his quarrel with the tribune Sulpicius was the cause of civil war. Caesar was ambitiously working to be elected consul without having first been a praetor. Sulpicius opposed him, by legal means at first, but later with such excessive violence that it became an open armed battle.

QUINTILIAN, *institutio oratoria* **6.3.75**

When Pomponius showed C. Caesar a wound he had received to his face in the

Sulpicius riots, boasting that he had got it while fighting for Caesar, C. Caesar told him: 'Never look behind you when you are running'.

CICERO, *de amicitia* 1.2 (44 BC)

Of course you remember, Atticus – and all the more so since you were much in the company of P. Sulpicius – how much astonishment or even indignation people felt when Sulpicius was tribune and became at daggers drawn with the then consul Q. Pompeius, with whom he had previously been on the closest and friendliest of terms.

PLUTARCH, *Marius* 35

Marius found an instrument ideally suited to him in the boldness of Sulpicius. A great admirer and imitator of Saturninus in all other respects, Sulpicius nevertheless considered him too timid and dilatory in pushing his policies. He himself did not hesitate, but surrounded himself with an armed bodyguard of 600 knights, whom he named his 'anti-Senate'.

APPIAN, *Civil Wars* 1.55

The consul Sulla was assigned the governorship of Asia and the command against Mithridates. He was still at Rome. Marius, thinking it an easy and very lucrative war, wanted the command for himself, and with many promises persuaded the tribune Publius Sulpicius to work to help him get it.

(b) The Sulpician proposals

APPIAN, *Civil Wars* 1.55–56

Marius also encouraged the new Italian citizens, who had little influence when it came to voting, to hope to be distributed among all the tribes, saying nothing openly about his own personal advantage but hoping to use them as loyal adherents in everything. Sulpicius at once introduced a bill to effect this, which if it were to be enacted would achieve everything he and Marius wanted, since the new citizens far outnumbered the old. Seeing this, the old citizens vigorously opposed the new, and they fell to fighting with clubs and stones with increasing violence until the consuls, becoming apprehensive as the day for voting on the bill drew nearer, proclaimed a prolonged suspension of all public business....

But Sulpicius was not prepared to wait, and ordered his supporters to come to the Forum with hidden daggers and do whatever needed to be done, not sparing even the consuls, if it came to that. With everything in readiness, he denounced the suspension as illegal and ordered the consuls to rescind it forthwith, so that he might put his proposals to the vote....

The consuls refused, and Sulpicius' followers drew their weapons and threatened to kill them. Pompeius managed to escape, and Sulla retired to reconsider the matter, but Pompeius' son, who was married to Sulla's daughter, was killed by the Sulpicians while he was voicing his opinions too freely. Then Sulla reappeared and rescinded the suspension and hurried off to join his army at Capua, meaning to set out from there for the war against Mithridates. For as yet he had no inkling of the designs against him personally. But once the suspension had been lifted and Sulla had left Rome, Sulpicius went on to carry his law and – what was the object of the whole operation – at once had Marius elected as commander in the war against Mithridates in place of Sulla.

EPITOME OF LIVY, Bk. 77

When the tribune P. Sulpicius, urged on by C. Marius, had promulgated pernicious laws, that the exiles should be recalled and the new citizens and those of freedman status be distributed among (*all the tribes*) and C. Marius be appointed to command against King Mithridates of Pontus, and when he had brought force to bear on the consuls Q. Pompeius and L. Sulla who were opposing him, after Q. Pompeius the son of the consul Q. Pompeius and the son-in-law of Sulla had been killed, the consul L. Sulla came to Rome with his army and fought there against the faction of Sulpicius and Marius and drove it out of Rome.

VELLEIUS PATERCULUS 2.18

Sulla was assigned the province of Asia. He had left Rome and was spending some time outside Nola – this city was holding out with great tenacity and was under siege by the Roman army – ....when the tribune P. Sulpicius, eloquent, full of energy, a man of renowned wealth, influence, connections, of great strength of character and intellect....all of a sudden despicably and precipitately abandoned his upright policies and joined up with C. Marius, now over seventy but still greedy for every command and every province, and carried a law in the popular assembly to abrogate Sulla's command and assign the Mithridatic War to Marius, and other pernicious and destructive laws not supportable by a free state. On top of that he had some of his supporters sent to kill the son of the consul Q. Pompeius who was also the son-in-law of Sulla.

ad Herennium 2.45

Sulpicius, who had used his veto to oppose a proposal to recall the exiles who had not been given a chance to defend themselves (*against the charges of the Varian Commission*), subsequently had a change of heart and proposed the same measure himself, maintaining that it was different since he was recalling men who were not true exiles but had been driven from Rome by force.

PLUTARCH, *Sulla* 3

Marius got Sulpicius to join him....Though Sulpicius passed a law that no senator might contract debts totalling more than 2,000 *drachmae* (= *8,000 HS*), when he died he turned out to owe more than 3 million himself.... (*After the rioting*) Sulla was pursued into Marius' house....

Cf. the similar account in Plutarch, Marius 35, where Sulla himself is cited as saying that he did not take refuge in Marius' house, but was taken there by force.

(c) Sulpicius' measures repealed

EPITOME OF LIVY, Bk. 77

Sulla returned to Rome with his army....Twelve members of the Senate, and among them C. Marius and his son Gaius, were adjudged enemies of the state (*hostes*). P. Sulpicius hid in a villa, but was betrayed by his slave, and killed; the slave was given his freedom to honour the promise made for information, and then thrown from the rock for the crime of betraying his master. The young C. Marius crossed to Africa. His father went into hiding in the Minturnensian marshes, but was brought out thence by the local townsmen; a Gallic slave who had been sent to kill him was so overawed by the great man that he went away again, and Marius was put on shipboard by the townspeople and conveyed to Africa.

APPIAN, *Civil Wars* 1.60–61

Thereupon Sulpicius, still a tribune, and along with him the six-times consul C. Marius, and Marius' son and Publius Cethegus and Junius Brutus and Gnaeus and Quintus Granius and Publius Albinovanus and Marcus Laetorius and others, twelve in all, were exiled from Rome as having raised revolution and attacked the consuls and incited slaves to rebel on promise of freedom; they were voted public enemies and declared wanted dead or alive. Their property was confiscated to the state. Men were sent to track them down. Sulpicius was killed (*and Marius got away via Minturnae to Africa*).

PLUTARCH, *Sulla* 10

Sulla summoned the Senate and had sentence of death passed on Marius himself and a few others, including the tribune Sulpicius.

CICERO, *Brutus* 168 (46 BC)

Q. Rubrius Varro, who was adjudged a public enemy by the Senate along with C. Marius....

(d) Sulla's legislation

EPITOME OF LIVY, Bk. 77

Lucius Sulla made regulations for the running of the state, and planted colonies.

FESTUS p. 464L

The unciary law, which was passed by L. Sulla and Q. Pompeius Rufus, which provided that debtors....(*a tenth part*)....

APPIAN, *Civil Wars* 1.59

At daybreak Sulla and Pompeius summoned an assembly of the people....and introduced these measures: that no proposal might be put to the people without previous consideration by the Senate, an ancient practice which had long been abandoned; and that voting should not be by tribes but by centuries....They reckoned that by these two measures no law would be put to the masses before the Senate had approved it, and that with the voting dominated by the better-off and sensible citizens instead of by the poor and desperate there would be no springboard for revolution. They proposed many other curtailments of the powers of the tribunes, which had become highly tyrannical, and enrolled 300 of the best citizens in the Senate, whose numbers had then fallen so low as to render it easily overlookable. All the measures which Sulpicius had carried after the suspension of public business announced by the consuls were declared illegal and invalid.

(e) The elections

PLUTARCH, *Sulla* 10

Wary of the hatred of the masses, Sulla appointed Lucius Cinna, a member of the hostile faction, consul (*for 87 BC*), binding him with threats and oaths to be loyal to his measures. Cinna mounted the Capitol with a stone in his hand, and swore the required oath; and praying that if he did not stay loyal to Sulla he should fall as the stone fell, he let the stone drop from his hand. There were not a few witnesses to this scene.

CASSIUS DIO fr. 102.2

Cinna and a certain Gnaeus Octavius were returned as consuls. Sulla reckoned Octavius reliable, and he was reluctant to provoke Cinna to open hostility, since he was a powerful man and ready for anything.

(f) Death of the consul Q. Pompeius

SALLUST, *Histories* 2.21M

When the consul Sulla was proposing a bill to recall Cn. Pompeius, the tribune C. Herennius had by arrangement interposed his veto.

Some have taken this to be a reference to 80 BC, and to Gnaeus' son, Pompey the Great.

APPIAN, *Civil Wars* 1.63

The people voted the other consul, Quintus Pompeius, command in Italy and of the other army, which was then under Gnaeus Pompeius. When Gnaeus heard the news, he was put out; he received the consul in his camp, and when Quintus was engaged in some business the next day withdrew a little way, as if no longer himself in authority, until many men who had crowded round the consul, pretending to listen, killed him.

EPITOME OF LIVY, Bk. 77

The consul Q. Pompeius, who had arrived to take over his army from the proconsul Cn. Pompeius, was murdered. The murder was planned by Gnaeus.

VALERIUS MAXIMUS 9.7. *Mil. Rom.* 2

Sulla's colleague Q. Pompeius ventured by order of the Senate to join the army of Cn. Pompeius, which the latter had been commanding for some time against the public wish. But the soldiers, corrupted by the inducements of their

ambitious general, attacked Quintus as he was starting a sacrifice and cut him
down like a sacrificial victim.

(g) The war in Italy

*The rebel leader Pompaedius Silo fell in battle, and by the end of the year only the
Samnites and some of the Lucanians were still holding out in the south in the Nola
region. Diodorus Siculus (37.3) reports negotiations between the rebels and
Mithridates, which came to nothing.*

(h) Greece and the East

*Mithridates occupied Bithynia and Cappadocia and invaded Phrygia with a large
army, defeating the Roman legate Aquillius (Ep. of Livy, 76). According to
Memnon 22 (Jac.), Mithridates ordered all Romans living in Asia to be killed, and
some 80,000 were put to the sword, in a single day. The same account is found in
Appian (*Mithridatica 22*), who specifies both Romans and Italians, but gives no
numbers. Rhodes remained loyal to Rome and opposed Mithridates at sea. In
Greece, Mithridates' general Archelaus captured Athens, and Greece was divided
in its adherence, some states and islands going over to Mithridates, some holding
to Rome (Ep. of Livy, 78). Eretria, Chalcis, and all Euboea went over to
Mithridates, and the Spartans were defeated (Memnon 22 Jac.). All the islands of
the Cyclades, save Rhodes, went over to him too (Florus 1.40 (3.5)). At Athens,
the commons were the pro-Mithridatic, anti-Roman element (Pausanias 1.20.5).
An indecisive battle was fought near Chaeroneia, lasting some three days, after
which the Roman commander Bruttius Sura withdrew (Appian,* Mithridatica 29*).
When Sulla arrived, he began by laying siege to Athens' port-town, Piraeus
(*Plutarch,* Sulla 11.*)*

87 BC   Consuls: Cn. Octavius, L. Cornelius Cinna
Suffect consul: L. Cornelius Merula

(a) Cinna driven from Rome

APPIAN, *Civil Wars* 1.64–66

Those of the (*Roman*) exiles who were friends of Sulla's successor as consul,
Cinna, took heart, and began to rouse the new citizens to support Marius,
demanding that they be enrolled in all the tribes rather than to vote last and
have no power to determine anything. This was the overture for the return of
Marius and his supporters. The old citizens forcefully opposed this proposal,
with Cinna supporting the new citizens and the other consul Octavius the old
citizens. The Cinnans occupied the Forum with concealed weapons and shouted
for distribution through all the tribes. The more reliable of the commons,
themselves armed, rallied to Octavius, who descended the Sacred Way with a
dense crowd....Without any orders they fell upon the new citizens, killing many
of them and pursuing the rest to the gates of the city. Cinna went rushing
around promising freedom to slaves, but meeting with no response fled to the
neighbouring townlets, stirring them all to rebel and levying money for

war....The Senate voted to deprive Cinna of his consulship and his citizenship, and had Lucius Merula elected to replace him....Cinna went off to Capua and the Roman army there, and paid court to its commanders and to the senators who were there....The allied cities gave him money and an army.

CICERO, *Philippics* 8.7 (43 BC)

Sulla clashed with Sulpicius over the legality of laws which Sulla held had been passed by force; Cinna with Octavius over the voting-rights of the new citizens.

Schol. Gronov. p.286 St.

Cinna began to agitate about the voting-rights of freedmen, and had Octavius and the Senate against him. Civil war began. Octavius drove out Cinna, who corrupted the soldiery and bought an army. He sent to Marius in Africa, who opened the slave-camps, formed legions and came to Italy. Octavius was killed, the orator Antonius, the Crassi, the Catuli, the great glories of Rome.

VELLEIUS PATERCULUS 2.20

Cinna promised to distribute the new citizens through all the tribes, though citizenship had been granted to them on condition that they be all registered in eight tribes, lest their power and numbers should destroy the standing of the existing citizens and the recipients of the gift have more power than the grantors. With this programme he had drawn a great mass to Rome from all over Italy. He was driven from Rome by the force deployed by his colleague and the optimates and made for Campania; meanwhile his consulship was abrogated by command of the Senate, and L. Cornelius Merula was made consul suffect in his place....Cinna then corrupted the military tribunes and centurions, and next the common soldiers by lavish promises, and was received by the army at Nola. The whole force swore loyalty to him, and still with the insignia of a consul he made war on his own country, trusting in the huge numbers of the new citizens from whom he had raised by levy over three hundred cohorts, the equivalent of thirty legions. His faction lacked prestige, and to increase this element he recalled C. Marius and his son and their companions in exile.

EPITOME OF LIVY, Bks. 79–80

When L. Cornelius Cinna tried to carry pernicious measures by force, he along with six tribunes of the plebs was driven from Rome by his fellow-consul Cn. Octavius, and his powers of office were stripped from him. He corrupted Appius Claudius' army, brought it under his own command, and made war on Rome, summoning C. Marius and other exiles from Africa....The attempt could have been nipped in the bud, but Cn. Pompeius craftily cultivated both sides, and so strengthened Cinna's hand; Pompeius did not help the optimates until they were at their last gasp, the consul Octavius lacked energy, and so Cinna and Marius surrounded Rome with four armies, two of them entrusted to Q. Sertorius and Carbo. Marius stormed and cruelly plundered the colony of Ostia.

The Italian peoples were granted citizenship by the Senate. The Samnites, the only rebels still fighting, joined Cinna and Marius, and cut up Plautius and his army. Cinna and Marius, with Carbo and Sertorius, attacked the Janiculum, but were forced to retreat when beaten by the consul Octavius. Marius stormed Antium and Aricia and Lanuvium. With no hope of further resistance remaining to the optimates thanks to the inaction and perfidy of commanders and troops, who were corrupted and either unwilling to fight or anxious to scatter, Cinna and Marius were admitted to Rome. They treated it like a captured city and laid it waste with murder and looting.

LICINIANUS pp. 16ff (F)

So Marius gathered about a thousand men and sailed to Telamon (*on the coast of Etruria*) to join Cinna. Brutus and all the other exiles from Spain came in to join him. When those who had known him in his great moments of victory saw Marius unkempt and dishevelled and begging for everybody's help against his oppressors, he soon had a legion of volunteers raised. He gave the troops to Cinna, and put Sertorius and Papirius under his command. Part of the cavalry was entrusted to Milonius, with orders to make for Rome, which was thought undefended....Delay was introduced by (*Gnaeus*) Pompeius, who was lukewarm in his reception of the Senate's instruction that he come to his country's aid, until Marius had slipped into harbour. Remaining there till nightfall, Marius got control of Ostia through Valerius and his cavalry. Pompeius did not hold off from fighting Sertorius but joined open battle with him. Envoys were sent from this side to that, but in vain, since Cinna believed he would win. Marius got control of the Janiculum in a bloody battle, and by his orders those taken prisoner by his men had their throats cut. With six cohorts sent him by Pompeius, Octavius crossed the Tiber, killed Milonius, and drove off the reinforcements Sertorius had sent to Milonius. (*An unknown number – the figure is missing from the text*) of thousands of Octavius' men were killed and one senator, Aebutius, and seven thousand of the opposing troops. The Janiculum could have been taken that day, but Pompeius would not let Octavius push forward and got him to call Crassus to pull back. Pompeius did not want the war finished off before the elections could be held; he wanted to be consul himself, and people were frightened of him. Metellus was also encamped nearby – he had been besought to come to the rescue of his country by the Senate's envoys, the two Catuli and Antonius.

PLUTARCH, *Sertorius* 5

When Marius arrived from Africa, he offered to serve under Cinna's command, as a private individual under a consul. While others were for accepting the offer, Sertorius opposed it...But Cinna sent for Marius, and their forces were divided into three divisions, one under the command of each. When the war was over, Cinna and Marius indulged in every kind of atrocity; Sertorius alone put no man to death out of revenge nor was he guilty of any outrages....

PLUTARCH, *Marius* 41

Landing at Telamon in Etruria Marius proclaimed freedom for slaves. The free farmers and herdsmen of the area came running to the shore to meet him, so great was his fame....and in a few days he had assembled a large force and filled forty ships.

APPIAN, *Civil Wars* 1.67

Marius raised 6,000 Etrurians.

VELLEIUS PATERCULUS 2.21

After bloody fighting Cinna and Marius occupied Rome, with Cinna entering the city first and carrying a bill for Marius' recall.

CASSIUS DIO fr. 102.8

Cinna renewed the law about the return of the exiles.

VELLEIUS PATERCULUS 2.21

Cn. Pompeius, balked of his hope to extend his consulship, made his position so unreliable and doubtful to both sides that he seemed to be working only to his personal advantage and waiting on events: he turned himself and his army this way and that, depending on how the fire of hope of power flared up. (*After a bitter and exhausting battle with Cinna under the walls of Rome*), Cn. Pompeius died.

APPIAN, *Civil Wars* 1.68

The frightened consuls sent orders to Caecilius Metellus, who was finishing off the last stages of the Social War against the Samnites, to reach the best agreement he could with them and come to the help of besieged Rome. When Metellus would not agree the Samnite demands, Marius seized his chance and conceded all they were asking. So the Samnites came to fight under Marius.

LICINIANUS p.20F, p.21F

Metellus sent envoys to consult the Senate about the attitude of the Samnites, who were refusing to make peace unless citizenship were granted to them and all deserters, and their property restored. The Senate refused...Heaving of this, Cinna through his agent Flavius Fimbria acceded to all their terms and enrolled them in his forces. Pompeius still persisted in confusing everything....

Citizenship was granted to all the rebels who had surrendered.

Much the same account is found in Cassius Dio, fr. 102.7

(b) Marius and Cinna in Rome

EPITOME OF LIVY, Bk. 80

The consul Cn. Octavius was killed and all the opposition nobles murdered, among them the great orator M. Antonius and the two Caesars, Gaius and

Lucius; their heads were displayed on the Rostra. (*Publius*) Crassus stabbed himself rather than suffer dishonour.

CICERO, *de oratore* 3.8 (55 BC): *See also 82 BC (a)*

So it seems to me that Lucius Crassus* was not robbed of his life by the immortal gods, but rather that they granted him the boon of death. He did not see the flight of C. Marius nor the widespread and bloody pogrom that followed his return, nor the ugliness which in every way disfigured that Rome in which at the height of its glory he had stood pre-eminent...We remember how the great Q. Catulus was forced to commit suicide. As for M. Antonius, on the very Rostra where as consul he had proved himself the most constant of Rome's defenders, which he had as censor adorned with the spoils of victory, on those very Rostra his own head was displayed – he who had saved the lives of so many Romans. Not far away was the head of C. Iulius....and that of his brother Lucius....Nor did Lucius Crassus live to see his brave kinsman P. Crassus dead by his own hand, nor the statue of Vesta stained with the blood of his colleague, the Chief Pontiff....The death that day even of his bitter enemy C. Carbo would have been loathsome for him. He did not see the horrible and wretched fates of those young men who had attached themselves to him, among them C. Cotta, who a few days after Crassus' death was expelled from the tribunate and not many months later driven into exile.

Appian (Civil Wars 1. 71–5) has a long account of the atrocities. Among those who died he names the consul Octavius, the brothers Gaius and Lucius Julius Caesar, Attilius Serranus, P. Lentulus, C. Nemetorius, M. Baebius, the two Crassi, father and son, M. Antonius, Q. Ancharius, Lutatius Catulus, and the consul suffect Cornelius Merula. Sulla himself had his property confiscated, and he was declared a public enemy.

EPITOME OF LIVY, Bk. 80

Marius and Cinna declared themselves consuls for the coming year.

(c) Greece and Asia

Appian (Mithridatica 30ff) tells how Sulla crossed to northern Greece with 5 legions and some cavalry. Gathering men and supplies he moved on to Attica to attack Archelaus. On his way most of the Boeotian cities, including Thebes, rejoined Rome. Putting Athens under siege, Sulla himself directed the attack on Piraeus, where Archelaus was shielded by the huge old Periclean walls. A long and bitterly contested siege began.

PLUTARCH, *Lucullus* 2

Sulla sent Lucullus to assemble a fleet in Egypt and Libya.

EPITOME OF LIVY, Bk. 82

Mithridates stormed cities in Asia and plundered the province with great cruelty.

---

* The consul of 95 BC, who had died in autumn 91 BC.

86 BC   Consuls: L. Cornelius Cinna II; C. Marius VII
Suffect consul: L. Valerius Flaccus
Censors: L. Marcius Philippus, M. Perperna

(a) Death of Marius

APPIAN, *Civil Wars* **1.75**

Full of many terrible plans against Sulla, Marius died in the first month of his
consulship. Cinna chose Valerius Flaccus to take his place, and despatched him
to Asia.

EPITOME OF LIVY, Bk. 80

Marius died on the Ides of January.

CICERO, *pro Roscio Amerino* **33** (80 BC)

C. Fimbria had arranged to have Q. Scaevola attacked during C. Marius'
funeral....He laid an indictment against the great and noble Scaevola after
learning that he might survive his wound. When asked what charge he meant to
lay against Scaevola, they say his furious reply was: 'On the grounds that he
didn't take the sword clean through his body.'

(b) The censors

CICERO, *de domo* **84** (57 BC)

When L. Philippus was censor, he omitted his own uncle's name from the roll of
senators.

VALERIUS MAXIMUS 8.13.4

What can one say of M. Perpenna? He outlived all those he had summoned to
the Senate when he was consul (*92 BC*) and all but seven of those he had entered
on the roll of senators when he was censor with L. Philippus.

EUSEBIUS, *Chronicle* **(***Hieronymus p. 233 Foth.***)**

463,000 citizens were counted.

(c) Debt legislation

VELLEIUS PATERCULUS 2.23

The suffect consul Valerius Flaccus was responsible for a disgraceful law
reducing debts to one quarter of what was due.

SALLUST, *Catiline* **33**

It is very recent in our memory how because of the widespread extent of
indebtedness silver was paid for with bronze, with the approval of all decent
men.

CICERO, *de officiis* **3.80** (44 BC)

Our Gratidianus did not behave like a proper gentleman when he was praetor
and the tribunes had summoned all the praetors to settle the coinage question in
common together. The coinage was in such a jumble then that nobody could

know what he was worth. Together the praetors and the tribunes drew up an edict, and accompanying legal penalties, and agreed that they would all mount the Rostra together that afternoon. The others then went their several ways, but Marius Gratidianus went straight to the Rostra, where he issued as his personal edict what had been worked out in concert by them all. That action, you may like to know, brought him great honour, with statues put up in every district of Rome, and incense and offerings too. Well then, nobody was ever dearer to the hearts of the masses...Marius thought it nothing to be ashamed of to rob his colleagues and the tribunes of popularity; he thought it very useful to his ambition to get a consulship on that account, a hope he had then formed for himself.

PLINY, *Natural History* 33.132

A method was found to assay the denarius by a law so popular with the commons that statues were put up to Marius Gratidianus all over Rome.

(d) Greece

Sulla took Athens by storm and won a great victory over Archelaus at Chaeroneia. Athens fell on 1 March. Meanwhile, L. Valerius Flaccus and C. Flavius Fimbria had been sent out to replace Sulla by the Cinnans, and traversed northern Greece and arrived at the Dardanelles. A fresh army sent to Greece by Mithridates under his general Dorylaus was beaten by Sulla at Orchomenus, with very heavy losses.

85 BC   Consuls: L. Cornelius Cinna III; Cn. Papirius Carbo

(a) Lull in domestic strife

CICERO, Brutus 308 (46 BC)

For some three years Rome was free from fighting; but with the death or retirement or flight of orators – M. Crassus and the two Lentuli among the young men were away – Hortensius was the leading figure at the bar, Antistius' reputation increased more and more every day, Piso spoke often, Pomponius not so often, Carbo only rarely, Philippus once or twice. As for myself, throughout this period I devoted night and day to the study of every subject under the sun.

(b) Cinna and Carbo extend their consulships

EPITOME OF LIVY, Bk. 83

L. Cinna and Cn. Papirius Carbo were elected consuls by their own fiat for a two-year period.

(c) The East

de viris illustribus, 70

Flavius Fimbria had gone to Asia as legate to the consul Valerius Flaccus, but quarrelled with him and was dismissed. He corrupted the troops and had the commander killed, seized the insignia of command, and invaded the province.

CASSIUS DIO fr. 104.1

Fimbria, Flaccus' deputy, quarrelled with him when he reached Byzantium. Fimbria was the bloodiest and most impetuous of men, greedy for fame of whatever kind, a belittler of anyone better than himself.

*Similar accounts and low opinions of Fimbria in Memnon, Orosius, and Strabo, the latter describing him as quaestor to Flaccus (13.1.27). See also **86 BC (a)**.*

EPITOME OF LIVY, Bk. 83: *this is the whole book, covering events of 85 and 84 BC*

After defeating a number of Mithridates' commanders in Asia, Flavius Fimbria captured the city of Pergamum and just missed capturing the king himself, who had been under siege there. He stormed the city of Ilium, which recognised Sulla's authority, and destroyed it, and recovered a large part of Asia. Sulla cut up the Thracians in numerous engagements. When Cinna and Carbo....were planning war against Sulla, L. Valerius, the President of the Senate, made a speech in the Senate and together with the others who were also anxious for concord got envoys sent to Sulla for peace talks. Cinna was killed (*84 BC*) by his own troops when he tried to make them embark to fight Sulla against their will. Carbo continued as sole consul. After crossing to Asia, Sulla concluded a peace with Mithridates, which required him to evacuate Asia, Bithynia, and Cappadocia. Fimbria killed himself with the help of his personal slave after his army had deserted him and gone over to Sulla.

For Fimbria's successful operations in Asia we have accounts in Memnon, Frontinus, Diodorus Siculus, and Appian, which underline the fact that Fimbria was chiefly responsible for worsting Mithridates' forces

PLUTARCH, *Lucullus* 3

Mithridates had abandoned Pergamum and withdrawn to Pitana, where he was shut off on the landward side and besieged by Fimbria. Despairing of facing the bold and victorious Fimbria in the field, Mithridates looked to the sea and summoned and collected his squadrons of ships from all quarters. Seeing this, and aware of his own naval weakness, Fimbria sent to Lucullus (*in command of Sulla's fleet*) and begged him to come with his fleet and help to destroy this bitterest and most warlike of Rome's enemies: 'This great prize, pursued through so many battles and hard struggles, must not elude Rome's grasp....' What he said made good sense, and it was clear to everyone that had Lucullus, who was not far away, listened to Fimbria and brought up his ships and blockaded the harbour at Pitana the war would have been over and freed everyone from countless sufferings. But whether Lucullus put his loyalty to Sulla above his own personal interest and that of the state, or whether he detested Fimbria as a scoundrel whose ambition had recently led him to murder his friend and commander, or whether Fate was reserving Mithridates to be Lucullus' own antagonist, Lucullus would not comply, and allowed Mithridates to sail away and laugh at Fimbria's army, while he himself won his first naval victory over a royal fleet off Troas.

APPIAN, *Mithridatica* 54

When Mithridates learned of the defeat at Orchomenus, reflecting on the huge number of men he had sent over to Greece since the war started and their continual and swift destruction, he sent instructions to Archelaus to make the best settlement he could.

PLUTARCH, *Sulla* 22

Sulla and Archelaus met at sea near Delos.

LICINIANUS p.26F

Talks took place between Sulla and Archelaus in Aulis, and conditions of peace were offered to the king....They were as follows: Archelaus was to surrender his fleet to Sulla; the king was to evacuate all the islands and Asia, Bithynia, and Paphlagonia, and the territory of the Gallograeci; the legates Q. Oppius and Manius Aquillius and all the other many prisoners were to be freed....The Macedonians, whose loyalty had been outstanding, were to have their wives and children returned to them; in addition 70 fully fitted-out decked ships were to be given to Rome's allies, and food, clothing, and pay provided for Sulla's own men.

Other terms given by other sources for this 'Peace of Dardanus' include payment of a war-indemnity, recognition of Mithridates as King of Pontus and friend and ally of Rome, and an amnesty for those Greek cities which had supported Mithridates: see Plutarch Sulla *22, Appian* Mithridatica *55, Memnon 25 Jac.*

PLUTARCH, *Sulla* 24

They met at Dardanus in the Troad, and Mithridates agreed the terms. Sulla summoned Ariobarzanes and Nicomedes and made them bury the hatchet. Mithridates surrendered 70 warships and 500 bowmen and sailed off to Pontus. Seeing that his soldiers were unhappy about the settlement....Sulla explained to them that he could not have fought Fimbria and Mithridates together if they had combined against him.

LICINIANUS p.26F

Mithridates at last agreed Sulla's terms. He was frightened of the approach of Fimbria....and Sulla had undertaken to introduce no new conditions varying what had been agreed. Having concluded the agreement personally with Sulla at Dardanus, Mithridates returned to Pontus with what was left of his fleet.

FLORUS 1.40 (*3.5*)

The war would have been fully ended had Sulla chosen to win a genuine triumph....Mithridates suffered only a setback; Pontus was not broken, but incensed.

de viris illustribus 76

Sulla could have captured Mithridates had he not been in such a hurry against Marius and hence ready to conclude any sort of peace.

MEMNON 25 Jac.

When Marius returned to Rome after his exile, and fearing that he in turn might be exiled too for his treatment of Marius, to whom he had been opposed, Sulla approached Mithridates for a settlement, himself delaying any settlement with Rome.

For Sulla's successful campaigns in Macedonia and Thrace, see Licinianus p.27F and Appian, Mithridatica 55.

de viris illustribus 70

Fimbria was besieged at Pergamum by Sulla. Deserted by his army, which had been corrupted, he committed suicide.

VELLEIUS PATERCULUS 2.24

I think nothing of what Sulla did is more to be admired than this: while for three years the Cinnan and Marian factions held Italy in bondage, he did not seek to hide his intention to make war on them nor did he abandon the task in hand, believing that he must first crush Rome's enemy before avenging Rome's citizens....

APPIAN, *Mithridatica* 60

Sulla instructed Curio to restore Nicomedes to Bithynia and Ariobarzanes to Cappadocia.

84 BC   Consuls: Cn. Papirius Carbo II; L. Cornelius Cinna IV

(a) The new citizens

EPITOME OF LIVY, Bk. 84

By decree of the Senate the suffrage was granted to the new citizens.

(b) Negotiations with Sulla: death of Cinna

See Epit. of Livy, 83, cited under 85 BC (c).

de viris illustribus 69

When in his fourth consulship Cinna was preparing to make war on Sulla, he was stoned to death at Ancona by his army because of his excessive harshness.

PLUTARCH, *Pompey* 5

Pompey (*the future Magnus*) came to Cinna's camp, but took fright at some slanderous charge or other and quickly took himself off into hiding. With him nowhere to be seen, a noisy rumour ran round the camp that Cinna had done away with the young man. As a result men who had long been against Cinna and hated him (*rushed Cinna and killed him*).

APPIAN, *Civil Wars* 1. 76–78

Frightened of Sulla, Carbo and Cinna sent men all over Italy to collect money, troops, and provisions. They cultivated the ruling-classes and set about stirring up the newly-enfranchised communities, saying that it was for their sakes that they stood in such great danger. They set about fitting out ships, and sending for those in Sicily, and guarding the coastline, and themselves in great fear and haste neglected no preparations....Sulla sent a proud letter about himself to the Senate....which when it was read out terrified everybody, and envoys were sent to effect a reconciliation between him and his enemies....and Cinna's people were told not to raise troops until Sulla's answer was received. Cinna and Carbo promised to comply, but once the envoys had left they once again pronounced themselves consuls for the next year....and gathered an army and began to embark part of it at Liburnia, planning to sail thence to meet Sulla....(*After Cinna's death*) Carbo recalled the men who had sailed from Liburnia. He was too frightened by events to return to Rome, though the tribunes were insisting he should return to hold elections for a colleague to replace Cinna. When they threatened to deprive him of office himself, he did come back and schedule an election meeting (*but on the excuse of bad omens no election was held and he continued as sole consul.*)

EPITOME OF LIVY, Bk. 84

Sulla's reply to the envoys sent by the Senate was that he would accept the Senate's authority if the citizens who had been driven out by Cinna and had fled to him were restored to their rights. This condition seemed a fair one to the Senate, but Carbo and his faction, who preferred war, prevented the Senate's meeting. Carbo himself was barred by decree of the Senate when he tried to take hostages from all the towns and colonies in Italy as a pledge for their support against Sulla.

(c) Crassus and Metellus Pius

PLUTARCH, *Crassus* 6

Crassus spent eight months in hiding in Spain, but re-emerged as soon as he heard of Cinna's death. Quite a few men rallied to him. From these he selected 2,500 and made a round of the cities; according to many writers, he plundered one of them, Malaga....He then assembled transports and sailed to Libya, where he joined Metellus Pius, a distinguished man, who had collected a very respectable army.

(d) Sulla's arrangements in Asia

CASSIODORUS, *Chronicle*

(*In 84 BC*) Sulla divided Asia into 44 districts.

CICERO, *ad Quintum fratrem* 1.1.33 (60/59 BC)

(*The people in Asia*) cannot turn up their noses at the mention of the *publicani* (*the Roman tax-farmers*), seeing that without the help of the *publicani* they could not themselves pay the impost which Sulla had quite reasonably imposed on them. The Greeks are no more easygoing in collection of taxes than our Roman *publicani*, as witness the Caunians not so long ago and all the islanders whom Sulla put under the control of Rhodes, who appealed to the Senate to let them pay their taxes to us rather than to the Rhodians.

CICERO, *pro Flacco* 32 (59 BC)

Sulla divided the money-burden proportionately among all the cities of Asia, a practice followed by Pompeius and Flaccus when they demanded supply-grants.

APPIAN, *Mithridatica* 61

In settling the affairs of Asia Sulla bestowed freedom on Ilium, Chios, Lycia, Rhodes, Magnesia, and some other peoples, either as a reward for their alliance or in recompense for their sufferings in his cause, and registered them as 'friends of the Roman People'. He distributed his army among the remaining communities, and issued an order that the slaves freed by Mithridates should at once return to their masters. As there was widespread disobedience and some of the cities revolted, on various pretexts there were widespread massacres of both slaves and free men. Many towns had their walls demolished, and in many parts of Asia there were lootings and enslavements....Ephesus was punished with particular severity....

PLUTARCH, *Sulla* 25; cf. *Lucullus* 4

Sulla imposed on Asia a communal fine of 20,000 talents (=*nearly 500 million HS*)....

MAMA 4.52 (*inscription from Synnada*)

From the inhabitants (*of Synnada*) to the proquaestor Lucius Licinius Lucullus, son of Lucius, their patron and benefactor.

IGRR 4.1191 (*inscription from Thyateira*)

The people (*of Thyateira*) honours the proquaestor Lucius Licinius Lucullus, son of Lucius, saviour, benefactor, and founder of the people, for his goodness and kindness to them.

PLUTARCH, *Lucullus* 4

Lucullus was commissioned to collect the 20,000 talents for Sulla and to coin the money. Amidst all Sulla's harshness, it was some consolation to the cities that Lucullus acted not only with complete justice but with all the leniency permitted by such a difficult and odious task.

LICINIANUS p.28F

Sulla heard cases at Ephesus and ordered the execution of the war leaders, imposed fines on cities, and brought the unpacified cities under his control. Curio restored the kingdom of Bithynia to Nicomedes, with the addition of Paphlagonia.

A new 'Sullan Era' was instituted in Asia, its starting date being Autumn 85 BC. Cf.IGRR 4 p.730.

(e) Sulla leaves Asia

APPIAN, *Mithridatica* **63**

Sulla sailed with the greater part of his army to Greece and then to Italy....leaving Murena with two Fimbrian legions to settle what was left to do in Asia.

APPIAN, *Civil Wars* **1.79**

With 5 Italian legions and 6,000 cavalry, and some additional troops from the Peloponnese and Macedon, altogether some 50,000 men, Sulla sailed from Piraeus to Patrae and then on to Brindisi in 1,600 ships. Brindisi opened its gates to him, in return for which he later gave the town immunity from taxation, which it still enjoys. He then got his army in motion and began his advance.

(f) Tigranes occupies Syria

JUSTIN 40, Prologue

With the royal house of the Antiochi extinct, the Armenian Tigranes seized Syria.

JUSTIN 40.1.3 (*but Appian says it was 14, not 18, years*)

Summoned to the throne of Syria, Tigranes ruled there for 18 very peaceful years; he provoked nobody to war, nor was he prepared to make war himself if provoked.

EUTROPIUS 6.14

Pompey the Great (*later*) bestowed the grant of freedom on Seleucia, which is near Antioch, because it had refused to admit Tigranes.

83 BC   Consuls: L. Cornelius Scipio Asiaticus, C. Norbanus

(a) Sulla's supporters outlawed

APPIAN, *Civil Wars* **1.86**

Carbo hurried to Rome and had Metellus and the other senators who had joined Sulla declared public enemies.

(b) The new colony at Capua

CICERO, *de lege agraria* **2.89** (63 BC)

If our ancestors had ever dreamed that our great dominion, that Rome's famous discipline, would ever have produced two men like Marcus Brutus (*tr. pl. 83 BC*) and Publius Rullus (*tr. pl. 63 BC*) – for these are so far the only two men we have known who wanted to transfer this state of ours to Capua...

Cicero refers further to Brutus' colony at Capua in sections 92 and 98 of this speech, observing that its chief magistrates were called 'praetors' and were attended each by two lictors carrying fasces, just like the urban praetor at Rome.

(c) Destruction of Capitoline Temple and Sibylline Books

CASSIODORUS, *Chronicle*

In this year (*83 BC*) the Capitoline Temple was burned to the ground through the negligence of its custodians.

*Cicero notes (*Catilinarians *3.9) that 83 BC was the year of this fire. The actual date was 6 July, so Plutarch,* Sulla *27.*

DIONYSIUS OF HALICARNASSUS, 4.62

When the temple was burned down, whether deliberately, as some think, or by accident, the Sibylline Books were destroyed in the fire. The Books which exist now were got together from many sources, some from cities in Italy, some from Erythrae in Asia, three envoys having been specially sent by the Senate to make the copies. Some were transcribed by other cities and by private individuals. Some are found to have been foisted into the true Sibylline oracles, and are checkable by the so-called 'acrostics'. I repeat here what Terentius Varro wrote in his *Study of Religious Practice.*

(d) Sulla lands in Italy

APPIAN, *Civil Wars* 1.80

Sulla was joined by Caecilius Metellus Pius, who came unbidden with the forces he had gathered, still with proconsular rank....He was followed by Gnaeus Pompeius, soon to be called Magnus. He was the son of that Pompeius (*Strabo, consul 89 BC*) who had been killed when struck by lightning and who had been reckoned no friend of Sulla's; but the son expunged any mistrust, arriving with a legion which he had raised in Picenum where his father's reputation was still very high. He soon raised two more legions, and turned out to be one of Sulla's most useful adherents, so much so that for all his extreme youth (*he was then only 23 years old*) Sulla held him in honour: he was the only man, they say, that Sulla rose to greet when he approached.

PLUTARCH, *Pompey* 8

Learning that Sulla was near, Pompeius told his commanders to get their men into full ceremonial order, so as to present the commander-in-chief with the finest and most impressive display. He hoped for great honours from Sulla. He received more than he hoped for. When Sulla saw him coming, he dismounted from his horse, and when greeted by Pompeius as 'Imperator', as might be expected, he replied by greeting Pompey too as 'Imperator'.

APPIAN, *Civil Wars* 1.80

Cethegus also joined Sulla, though along with Cinna and Marius he had been one of Sulla's bitterest opponents and had been outlawed with them. He came to beg for money, offering his services to Sulla in whatever capacity he might wish.

Sulla now had a large army and plenty of high-ranking supporters, whom he used as subordinate commanders, while the two proconsuls, Metellus and himself, led the advance....

Cf. Plutarch (Sulla 27) who says Sulla landed at Tarentum.

EPITOME OF LIVY, Bk. 85

Sulla crossed to Italy with his army and sent representatives to discuss a peace settlement. Their immunity was violated by the consul C. Norbanus. Sulla defeated Norbanus in battle. Sulla had exerted every effort to make peace with the other consul, L. Scipio, but to no avail. He was about to assault Scipio's camp when the consul's army, which had been got at by soldiers sent by Sulla, went over to Sulla to a man. He could have killed Scipio, but let him go free. Cn. Pompeius, son of the captor of Asculum, had joined Sulla with three legions, and all the nobility were betaking themselves to Sulla's camp, leaving Rome deserted.

CICERO, *Philippics* 12.27 (43 BC)

Sulla met Scipio between Cales and Teanum, the one with the flower of the nobility in his train, the other with his war-allies, to settle the questions of the authority of the Senate, the suffrages of the people, and the right of citizenship, and the relevant laws and conditions. That colloquy did not altogether maintain good faith, but it was free from force and danger.

CICERO, *Philippics* 13.2 (43 BC)

Sulla was either making or pretending to make peace with Scipio. Whichever way it was, had agreement been reached there would have been no reason to give up hope that a tolerable arrangement would have resulted for settling Rome's affairs.

APPIAN, *Civil Wars* 1.86

Unable to persuade Scipio to change his mind, Sulla let him and his son go unharmed. He sent other men to open negotiations for a settlement with Norbanus at Capua. Sulla was either worried, since the greater part of Italy still supported the consuls, or he planned to repeat the trick he had played on Scipio. But he got no response – it seems that Norbanus was afraid that he might be discredited in the eyes of his troops, as Scipio had been. So Sulla continued to advance, devastating all hostile territory, while Carbo did the same, following other roads.

(e) Renewal of war in the East

APPIAN, *Mithridatica* 64–65

The Second Mithridatic War now began. Murena, who had been left behind by Sulla with the two Fimbrian legions to tidy things up in Asia, began seeking trifling pretexts for war, being greedy to win a triumph. After sailing back to Pontus, Mithridates began fighting the rebels in Colchis and the Crimea....He also had his suspicions of Archelaus as having made too many concessions to Sulla in the peace-talks in Greece. Learning of this, Archelaus took fright and fled to Murena, and excited him and persuaded him to get his own blow in before Mithridates did. Murena moved at once through Cappadocia to attack the large town of Comana, which belonged to Mithridates...killing some of the royal cavalry. When envoys came from Mithridates to remind him of the peace-treaty, he replied that he could not see one; for Sulla had not written one but simply left after seeing what had been agreed orally carried out in practice. ...Mithridates sent to the Senate and Sulla in Rome to complain of what Murena was doing....Meanwhile Murena crossed the River Halys....and over-ran four hundred of Mithridates' villages. Mithridates did not resist, but waited for his envoys to return from Rome.

82 BC   Consuls: C. Marius (*the younger*), Cn. Papirius Carbo III

(a) Violence at Rome

EPITOME OF LIVY, Bk. 86

C. Marius, son of C. Marius, was made consul by force, though not yet twenty years old....Egged on by him, the praetor L. Damasippus...butchered all the nobles remaining in Rome. They included the Chief Pontiff Q. Mucius Scaevola, who was killed after he had taken refuge in the vestibule of the Temple of Vesta.

VELLEIUS PATERCULUS 2.26

Carbo then became consul for the third time along with C. Marius, son of the seven-times consul, who was only twenty-six years old....

APPIAN, *Civil Wars* 1.87–88

The consuls for the next year were Papirius Carbo again and Marius, nephew of the great Marius, who was twenty-seven years old...When Marius saw that the situation was hopeless, he hastened to remove all his political enemies. He instructed the urban praetor Brutus to summon a meeting of the Senate as if for other business and kill Publius Antistius, the other Papirius Carbo (*tr. pl. 90 BC*), Lucius Domitius, and Mucius Scaevola the Chief Pontiff. The first two were killed in the Senate, as Marius had ordered, by assassins introduced to do the job. Domitius tried to get away and was killed at the door, and Scaevola too not far from the Senate....

de viris illustribus 68

C. Marius' son, his father's match in cruelty, surrounded the Senate with armed men, killed his enemies, and threw their bodies into the Tiber. He wore himself out by his unremitting exertions in preparations for the war with Sulla, and was asleep near the Sacriportum on the day of the battle.* So he took no part in it, but he did join in the flight and took refuge in Praeneste.

(b) Shortage of Money

VALERIUS MAXIMUS 7.6.4

When C. Marius and Cn. Carbo were consuls and opposing Sulla in the Civil War, at a time when men were not seeking victory for Rome but Rome as the prize of victory, the gold and silver ornaments in the temples were by senatorial decree melted down to keep the troops paid.

* See further below.

(c) Sulla's victory and its consequences: the proscriptions

APPIAN, *Civil Wars* 1.89

Sulla came up at once, encamped his army in front of the gates in the Campus Martius, and himself entered Rome, from which all his opponents had fled....He made such arrangements as were immediately necessary, and putting some of his own men in charge of the city set out for Clusium, where the last stages of the war were still coming to a peak.

CICERO, *Brutus* 311 (46 BC)

There followed the confusion of the recapture of Rome, and the cruel deaths of three orators, Scaevola, Carbo, and Antistius, and the return of Cotta, Curio, Crassus, the Lentuli, and Pompeius. Laws and law-courts were established, constitutional government restored. However from among the oratorical ranks Pomponius, Censorinus, and Murena were absent.

VELLEIUS PATERCULUS 2.28

Public rewards were proclaimed for the killing of Roman citizens, and whoever could kill most was richest.

OROSIUS 5.21

Soon after the victorious Sulla had entered Rome, in defiance of religion and promise of mercy he killed 3,000 men who had surrendered, unarmed and unsuspecting as they were. Subsequently many more, I will not say innocent men, but some even of Sulla's own following, were killed, reportedly over 9,000. Butchery was unrestrained throughout Rome with assassins ranging everywhere in search of revenge or loot....At last Q. Catulus spoke up openly and asked Sulla: 'Who on earth are we going to live with if we kill armed men in war and unarmed men in time of peace?' Thereupon on the suggestion of the chief centurion (*primus pilus*) L. Fursidius, Sulla initiated the publication of the infamous proscription-list. The first list contained 80 names, among them those of four ex-consuls, Carbo, Norbanus, Marius, and Scipio, and also Sertorius, then reckoned the man most to be feared. A second followed with 500 names....But even these lists apparently provided no confidence or end of wickedness. Some were murdered after being proscribed, others proscribed after they had been murdered.

APPIAN, *Civil Wars* 1.95

Sulla (*came back to Rome and*) summoned an assembly where he had much to say about his own great achievements, with many fearful threats to cow his listeners, promising to bring beneficial changes for the people if they were obedient, but vowing that no enemy of his would escape the utmost severity. Any praetors, quaestors, military tribunes, or anybody else who had collaborated with his enemies after the day when the consul Scipio had violated his agreement with him would be firmly punished. This said, he published a death proscription list of 40 senators or so and some 1,600 knights. He was apparently the first man to draw up a public list (*proscribere*) of those to be punished with death, offering prizes to the killers and rewards to informers, and prescribing punishments for anyone who hid the outlaws. He soon added other senators to the list....Men were sent out to search everywhere for those who had escaped from Rome, killing any they found.

PLUTARCH, *Sulla* 31

One of the younger men, Gaius Metellus, plucked up his courage and asked Sulla in the Senate what end there was going to be to the terrible things going on and at what point could they hope that he would stop. 'We do not beg you to spare those you have decided to punish but to free from uncertainty those you have decided to spare.' When Sulla answered that he had not yet made up his mind whom to spare, Metellus persisted: 'At least make it clear whom you mean to punish.' Sulla said he would. Some say this last remark was made not by Metellus but by one of Sulla's toadies, Fufidius. Anyway, Sulla at once proscribed 80 men, without consulting any of the magistrates. Everybody was indignant, but the next day but one he proscribed another 220, and on the third day again no fewer. He then addressed the people and told them that he had proscribed as many men as he could remember, but that he would further proscribe later any who had slipped his mind. He also laid down the death penalty for anyone charitable enough to hide any of the proscribed or help them escape, not even excluding a brother or a son or a parent, while two talents a head was the reward for killing a proscribed man, even if a slave killed his master or a son his father...The lists were published not merely in Rome but in every town in Italy.

CICERO, *de domo* 43 (57 BC)

That terrible word 'proscription', all the ruthlessness of the Sullan period, what feature of that cruelty is most deeply etched in our memories? I believe it is the punishments which were decreed for individual Roman citizens by name without any trial.

CICERO, *pro Roscio Amerino* 130 (80 BC)

Everybody knows that the sheer magnitude of what was going on meant that many crimes were committed by many people some of which Sulla did not approve of and some of which he was not aware of....What cause is it for surprise, gentlemen, that Sulla, the sole ruler of our country and of the whole world, busy making laws to establish the majesty of our dominion which he had rescued with his arms, was not able to see everything?

CICERO, *pro (Publio) Sulla* 72 (62 BC)

When L. Sulla won his heavy and stormy victory, who showed more gentleness than P. Sulla (*his nephew*)?....How many men's lives did my client not beg for from L. Sulla! How many great and distinguished gentlemen there were of our own order and of the equestrian order for whose safety he pledged himself to Sulla!

Q. CICERO, *de petitione consulatus* 9 (65/4 BC)

Sulla had put Catilina in sole command of those infamous Gauls who went around cutting off the heads of men like Titinius and Nannius and Tanusius. Among them was the excellent Q. Caecilius, his own sister's husband, a Roman knight who took no sides in politics, a man whose advanced age reinforced his natural quietness: him Catilina killed with his own hands.

EPITOME OF LIVY, Bk. 88

Sulla had the senator Marius killed: his legs and arms were broken, his ears cut off and his eyes gouged out.

ASCONIUS p.84C

Catilina had carried the severed head of Marius Gratidianus through Rome in his own hands.

VELLEIUS PATERCULUS 2.28

On top of that, the property of the proscribed was to be confiscated and put up for sale, their children deprived not only of their inheritances but even of the right to stand for public office, and, greatest injustice of all, those who were the sons of senators had to perform senatorial obligations while losing all the rights of a senator.

PLUTARCH, *Sulla* 31

What seemed most unjust of all, Sulla deprived the sons and grandsons of the proscribed of their civil rights and confiscated all their property.

SALLUST, *Histories* 1.55.6M: *Oratio Lepidi*

Sulla is the only man in history who has ever devised punishments for the unborn.

APPIAN, *Civil Wars* 1.96

There was widespread killing and banishment and confiscation in the rest of Italy too, involving those who had accepted the authority of Carbo or Norbanus or Marius or any of their lieutenants. Harsh inquisitions were held against them throughout Italy, with all sorts of charges, of holding command or joining the army or contributing money or any other service or even simply being anti-Sullan....The rich were hit most heavily.

EPITOME OF LIVY, Bk. 88

Sulla filled Rome and all Italy with murders.

SALLUST, *Histories* 1.55.17M

Innocent men were proscribed for their wealth, distinguished men were tortured, Rome was made a desert by banishments and murders, the property of wretched citizens was sold or given away as if it were so much booty taken from the Cimbri.

CICERO, *de lege agraria* 2.81 (63 BC)

Sulla, who without any scruple gave away everything to whoever he chose, did not venture to touch the Campanian Land (*ager Campanus*).

SALLUST, *Histories* 1.55.18M (*Speech of Lepidus*)

It is objected to me that I own property confiscated from the proscribed. That was perhaps the greatest of Sulla's crimes, that neither I nor anyone else would have been safe if we had done what was right. But that property which I then purchased because I was frightened, which I have paid for and which I legally own, I none the less hand back, for I have made up my mind that any booty taken from Roman citizens is an impossibility.

PLINY, *Natural History* 36.116

C. Curio could not hope to outmatch Scaurus in wealth or display; for where was he to find himself a stepfather like Sulla, or a mother like Metella who bought up the property of the proscribed at knock-down prices, or a father like Scaurus who was for so many years a leading politician, the receiver of the goods the Marian gang stole from the provinces?

APPIAN, *Civil Wars* 1.96

Having finished with individuals, Sulla turned his attention to punishing the towns themselves, demolishing their citadels and walls, imposing communal fines, crushing them with very heavy forced contributions. In most of them he settled his own former soldiers to act as garrisons in Italy, distributing among the latter sequestrated lands and houses. Thus he cemented his soldiers' loyalty to him even after his own death, as they could not be secure in their possessions unless all his arrangements were on a secure footing.

CICERO, *Paradoxa* 6.2.46 (46 BC)

Anyone who can recall the sending out of ex-slaves to plunder provinces and drain them by usury, the expulsion of neighbours, the crimes in the countryside, the deals done with slaves, ex-slaves, and dependants (*clientes*), the abandoned possessions, the proscriptions of the wealthy, the murder of townsfolk, that bloody harvest of the Sullan period....

FLORUS 2.9 (*3.21*)

Italy's most splendid towns came under the auctioneer's hammer, Spoletium, Interamna, Praeneste, Florentia.

Degrassi *ILLRP* i. no. 364 = *ILS* 6629: inscription from Interamna

This statue was set up to Aulus Pompeius son of Aulus of the tribe Clustumina, quaestor, municipal patron of Interamnium, for saving the whole community from dangers and difficulties and preserving it, by the testamentary bequest of Lucius Licinius son of Titus.

(d) Sulla's dictatorship

APPIAN, *Civil Wars* 1.99

The Romans elected Sulla to be their autocrat for as long as he chose. There had from long ago been dictators with autocratic power, but for a limited period of time. Under Sulla this autocracy first became of unspecified duration and so complete. But they added this condition to satisfy propriety, that they elected him dictator to enact such laws as he might deem fittest and to establish a sound constitution.

VALLEIUS PATERCULUS 2.28

Sulla was elected dictator, an office in disuse for 120 years, ever since the year after Hannibal had left Italy....The authority which his predecessors had used in the past to rescue the state from the gravest dangers he used as giving him *carte blanche* for unrestrained savagery.

PLUTARCH, *Sulla* 33

Sulla appointed himself dictator, reviving the office after a lapse of 120 years. He was voted immunity for all his past actions, and for the future the power of execution, confiscation, colonial and other foundations, the right to pillage, to make and depose kings as he chose.

CICERO, *ad Atticum* 9.15.2 (49 BC)

Sulla contrived to get himself named dictator by an *interrex*.

Cicero talks of Sulla's power as 'kingly' and of the 'kingship of Sulla' in de har. resp. *54 and* ad Att. *8.11.2.*

EPITOME OF LIVY, Bk. 89

When he became dictator Sulla was attended by the unprecedented number of 24 *fasces*. By new laws he set the state on a firm basis.

CICERO, *de lege agraria* 3.5 (63 BC)

Of all the laws which have ever been carried the most outrageous and unlawlike was in my opinion the law the *interrex* L. (*Valerius*) Flaccus carried about Sulla, which validated whatever he might do...It was an atrocious piece of legislation, as I have said, but there was an excuse for it in that it was apparently the work not of a man but of the circumstances of the time....

CICERO, *de legibus* 1.42 (begun 52 BC)

It is surely the most arrant stupidity to believe that any measure is necessarily just because a community has decided or enacted it. What, even if we are dealing with the laws of an autocrat?....No more so, I believe, those conditions carried by our Roman *interrex* empowering a dictator to execute any citizen he chose even without due legal process, and with impunity.

(e) Sulla 'Felix'

VELLEIUS PATERCULUS 2.27

After the killing of the younger Marius, Sulla took the name 'Lucky' (*Felix*).

FRONTINUS, *Stratagems* 1.11.11

To make his troops the keener to fight, Sulla pretended that the gods gave him foresights of the future.

de viris illustribus 75

When Marius was killed at Praeneste, Sulla had himself called 'Felix', by edict.

See too Plutarch, Sulla *34 and Appian,* Civil Wars *1.97 for much the same story. Sulla called his twins by Metella, widow of the* princeps senatus *Aemilius Scaurus, Faustus and Fausta ('blessed', 'fortunate') Sulla.*

(f) Consuls elected for 81 BC

APPIAN, *Civil Wars* 1. 100, 101

To keep up the pretence of constitutional government Sulla allowed consuls to be elected, and they were Marcus Tullius and Cornelius Dolabella. But Sulla, as dictator, was superior to the consuls, as if he were king....

Sulla was a frightening man with a terrible temper. Q. Lucretius Ofella had captured Praeneste for him and by his siege beaten the consul Marius and put the final touch to Sulla's victory. Though still only of equestrian rank he wanted to become consul without having been quaestor and aedile, appealing by ancient precedent to the magnitude of his successes. Sulla tried to get him to change his mind, and when he failed in this he killed Ofella in the middle of the Forum. Summoning an assembly of the people he told them: 'Know and learn from me that I killed Lucretius Ofella because he disobeyed me.'

(g) The war in Italy, Sicily, and Africa

APPIAN, Civil Wars 1.87

In early spring, Metellus defeated Carbo's general, Carinas, with heavy losses, near the River Aesis, and the whole region went over to Metellus, abandoning the consuls. Carbo overtook Metellus and blockaded him, till he went back into camp at Ariminum on hearing that the other consul, Marius, had been beaten in a great battle near Praeneste. Pompey hung onto his tail and harassed him....As for Marius, his defeat at Sulla's hands had come about as follows. When Marius' left wing had begun to fold up, five of his infantry and two cavalry cohorts had despaired and thrown away their standards and gone over to Sulla....Marius' whole army had fled to Praeneste, being cut up as they ran, with Sulla in hot pursuit....Sulla took a host of prisoners, killing all the Samnites among them as inveterately hostile to Rome.

Plutarch, Sulla *28 names Pompey, Crassus, Metellus, and Servilius as the most active and successful of Sulla's generals.*

EPITOME OF LIVY, Bk. 86

Sulla concluded a treaty with the Italians to allay their fears that he planned to deprive them of their citizenship and the right of suffrage recently granted them.

APPIAN, *Civil Wars* 1.89

A tough battle raged from dawn to dusk between Sulla himself and Carbo near Clusium. They broke off at nightfall, apparently with honours even.

EPITOME OF LIVY, Bk. 88

After beating his army at Clusium, Faventia, and Fidentia, Sulla forced Carbo out of Italy.

APPIAN, *Civil Wars* 1.91

At Faventia, Carbo and Norbanus diverted their march a little before the evening and approached Metellus' camp....They drew up in battle array unwisely and under the influence of anger, hoping that their unexpected move would upset Metellus. But they were beaten....and suffered massive losses.

PLUTARCH, *Sulla* 29

The Samnite Telesinus together with the Lucanian Lamponius collected a numerous force and headed for Praeneste to raise the siege there on Marius. But when Telesinus learned that Sulla was hurrying to meet him from in front and Pompey from his rear, this warlike commander, skilled in many actions, cut off from front and rear, slipped away by night and made for Rome itself with his whole army.

APPIAN, *Civil Wars* 1.92

All the Gauls living between Ravenna and the Alps went over *en masse* to Metellus.

EPITOME OF LIVY, Bk. 88

Sulla fought a conclusive battle against the Samnites, the only Italian people still in arms. It took place outside Rome by the Colline Gate.

VELLEIUS PATERCULUS 2.27

The Samnite commander, Pontius Telesinus, a gallant man deeply imbued with hatred of the Roman Name, collected about forty thousand troops. They were stout young men determined not to surrender. With this force, on 1 November, he engaged Sulla in battle near the Colline Gate and brought him and Rome close to disaster....Telesinus was everywhere amongst his men repeatedly saying that Rome's last day had come, and shouting that they must pull down and destroy the city: 'The wolves who prey on Italian freedom will never disappear unless we wipe out the wood which is their lair.' An hour after nightfall the Roman line drew on new strength and the enemy broke. Telesinus was found next day only half-alive, his expression that of a conqueror rather than of a dying man. Sulla ordered his head to be cut off and fixed on a spear and carried round the walls of Praeneste.

VELLEIUS PATERCULUS 2.27

The younger Marius at last gave up all hope and tried to break out of Praeneste by way of subterranean tunnels which had been very cleverly constructed to lead to scattered outlets in the countryside. As he emerged from one of them he was killed by men specially posted there. Others say that he died by his own hand, and others that he and Telesinus' younger brother who had broken out with him killed each other.

EPITOME OF LIVY, Bk. 88 (*the final sentence is bracketed since it is clearly an instrusive supplement.*)

C. Marius, who had been under siege at Praeneste, was killed by the Sullan partisan Lucretius Ofella while trying to escape by way of a tunnel. [That is to say, he died in the tunnel itself, when he realised that escape was impossible: he and his companion in flight, Telesinus, drew their swords on each other: Marius killed Telesinus, and himself being only wounded ordered a slave to finish him off.]

APPIAN, *Civil Wars* 1.94

Learning of the total destruction of Carbo's army and that Carbo had now fled from Italy, and that the rest of Italy and Rome itself were firmly in Sulla's hands, the inhabitants surrendered Praeneste to Lucretius. Marius entered an underground tunnel system and soon committed suicide. Lucretius cut off his head and sent it to Sulla.

Cassius Dio (fr. 109.4) tells how the local councillors of Praeneste and the soldiers taken prisoner there were butchered by Sulla, with many non-combatants also being killed in the confusion.

APPIAN, *Civil Wars* 1.95

Pompey was sent by Sulla to North Africa to deal with Carbo and to Sicily to deal with Carbo's friends there.

EPITOME OF LIVY, Bk. 89

Cn. Papirius Carbo, who had put in at Cossura (*an island midway between Sicily and Tunisia*), sent M. Brutus in a fishing-boat to Lilybaeum to find out if Pompey was there yet. He was surrounded by ships sent by Pompey (*and killed himself*). Granted military command (*imperium*) by the Senate to go to Sicily, Cn. Pompeius captured Cn. Carbo and had him executed. Carbo died crying like a weak woman.

VALERIUS MAXIMUS 9.13.2

Carbo was executed on Pompey's orders in Sicily, in his third term as consul.

EUTROPIUS 5. 8–9

The other consul too, Cn. Carbo, was killed in Sicily on Pompey's orders after fleeing there from Ariminum. The young Pompey, only twenty-one years old,*

* In fact, Pompey was born in 106 BC.

had been put in command of armies by Sulla, who appreciated his energy, and was reckoned second to Sulla. After Carbo's death, Pompey secured Sicily.

de viris illustribus 77

Pompey recaptured Sicily from the proscribed without any fight.

PLUTARCH, *Pompey* 11

While busy in Sicily, Pompey received a senatorial decree and a letter from Sulla ordering him to sail to North Africa and fight Domitius....Quickly making all necessary preparations....he left his sister's husband Memmius in charge of Sicily, and sailed off with 120 warships and 800 transports.

APPIAN, *Civil Wars* 1.108

Sertorius had been chosen (*by the anti-Sullans*) to govern Spain, while he was co-operating with Carbo against Sulla. Having captured Suessa during the armistice, he escaped to Spain and assumed its governorship. He had an army from Italy itself, and raised another force from among the Celtiberians there. *He may have gone to Spain late in 83* BC.

STRABO 5.4.11

Sulla cut the Samnites to pieces in the battle outside Rome. His orders were to take no prisoners. Those who threw down their arms, reportedly some three or four thousand, were imprisoned....and three days later troops were sent to butcher them all. Sulla's proscriptions did not end until he had destroyed or driven from Italy all who bore the Samnite name. When asked the reason for this terrible anger he explained that experience had taught him that no Roman would ever know peace as long as they had the Samnites to deal with. So the towns of Samnium have become villages, and some have even vanished altogether: Boeanum, Aesernia, Panna, Venafrum's neighbour Telesia, and others such, not one of them worthy to be reckoned a town....But Beneventum and Venusia have survived well.

(h) The East

APPIAN, *Mithridatica* 65

Murena returned to Phrygia and Galatia loaded with plunder, where he met Calidius, who had been sent out from Rome in response to Mithridates' complaints. He brought no decree of the Senate, but publicly told Murena that the Senate ordered him not to molest the king, who had a treaty of peace with Rome....But Murena continued on his violent path, and again invaded Mithridates' realm. Reckoning that the Romans were now clearly making war on him, Mithridates ordered his general Gordius to attack the villages....Gordius at once took up a position facing Murena, with a river between them; but neither opened battle until Mithridates arrived with a superior army, and a stiff engagement at once began along the river. Mithridates forced a crossing and in general got far the better of Murena....After suffering heavy losses, Murena escaped over the mountains into Phrygia by a pathless route, severely harassed by the enemy missiles. The news of this brilliant and rapid victory spread quickly and led many to go over to Mithridates.

81 BC   **Consuls: M. Tullius Decula, Cn. Cornelius Dolabella**

(a) Sulla celebrates his Mithridatic Triumph

FASTI TRIUMPHALES

L. Cornelius Sulla Felix, son of Lucius, grandson of Publius, dictator, celebrated a triumph over King Mithridates IV on 28 January (*81 BC*).

For a full description, see Plutarch, Sulla 34.

(b) Institution of Sullan Victory Games

VELLEIUS PATERCULUS 2.27

The happy day which saw the repulse of Telesinus' Samnite army from Rome was honoured by Sulla with games in the Circus to be held ever after. The games are celebrated as the Sullan Victory Games.

Cicero, pro Roscio Amerino 136, 149, and elsewhere portrays Sulla's victory as a victory for the Roman nobility.

(c) The city-boundary enlarged

SENECA, *de brevitate vitae* 13.8

Sulla was the last Roman to extend the *Pomerium*, which by ancient custom could be done only when new territory in Italy, never in the provinces, had been acquired.

(d) The Sullan Legislation

CICERO, *pro Roscio Amerino* 125 and 128 (80 BC)

How could anyone under that very proscription law, call it Valerian or Sullan, I neither know nor care, but how could anyone under that law auction off Sextus Roscius' property? For this is how they say the law ran: 'The property of those who have been proscribed....or of those who died fighting for the other side, shall be put up for sale'....I believe the law states that the proscriptions and sales shall last until 1 June.

(i) Tribunate

VELLEIUS PATERCULUS 2.30

Sulla had left the tribunician power a shadow without any substance.

CICERO, *de legibus* 3.22 (*Quintus Cicero speaking*) (52 BC)

In that matter I very much approve of Sulla, who stripped the tribunes of the power to cause trouble by their own legislation, but left them their power of assistance (*ius auxilii*).

CICERO, *Verrines* 2.1.155 (70 BC)

Q. Opimius (*tribune 75 BC*) was haled into court, the formal charge being that when he was a tribune of the plebs he had interposed a veto contrary to the

Cornelian (*viz. Sullan*) Law, but in reality because he had as tribune said something which offended a certain noble gentleman.

CAESAR, *Civil War* 1.7

Sulla stripped the tribunate of all its power but left the veto untouched.

EPITOME OF LIVY, Bk. 89

Sulla reduced the power of the tribunes and took away all their right to carry legislation.

APPIAN, *Civil Wars* 1.100

Sulla virtually destroyed the tribunician magistracy, leaving it very weak and providing by law that nobody who had held the tribunate might subsequently hold any other office. Hence anyone of reputation or birth shunned the office thereafter.

*Cicero (*pro Cluentio *110: 66 BC) says that for some years thereafter the Rostra were deserted and* contiones *discontinued.*

(ii) Praetorship & Quaestorship
POMPONIUS, *Digest* 1.2.2.32

Cornelius Sulla added four praetors (*to the existing six*).

TACITUS, *Annals* 11.22

By a law of Sulla's twenty quaestors were appointed to keep up the number of the Senate.

(iii) The Censorship
There is no evidence that Sulla abolished this office, and no reason to suppose he did. But no censors were in fact elected again until 70 BC.

(iv) The Lex Annalis (regulating tenure of magistracies)
APPIAN, *Civil Wars* 1.100

Sulla forbade a man to be a praetor before he had been a quaestor, or a consul before he had been a praetor, or any office to be held for a second time before ten years had elapsed.

(v) Provincial commands
CICERO, *ad familiares* 1.9.25 (54 BC)

Appius Claudius keeps on saying....that since he has been assigned a province by decree of the Senate he will under the Cornelian Law hold *imperium* until such time as he re-enters Rome.

CICERO, *ad familiares* 3.6.3

Not only were you* not there, where you could have seen me at the earliest

* A letter written by Cicero when arriving in Cilicia as governor to the outgoing governor, Appius Claudius: 51 BC.

opportunity, you had gone off somewhere where I could not join you within the thirty days which I believe the Cornelian Law allows for your departure.

CICERO, *ad familiares* **3.6.6.**

So that you may know where to meet me and satisfy the Cornelian Law, I arrived on the last day of June, and am heading for Cilicia by way of Cappadocia.

CICERO, *ad familiares* **3.10.6**

I recall that I was visited by some people....who said that the local communities (*of Cilicia*) were voting over-lavish expenditure for delegations (*to go to Rome in honour of the previous governor, Appius Claudius*). I did not so much order as counsel them that such expenditure should be kept within the limits of the Cornelian Law.

(vi) Priesthoods

CASSIUS DIO 37.37

(*In 63 BC*) Labienus, with Caesar's support, got the assembly to pass a law whereby priests were once again to be elected by the people. This rescinded Sulla's law on the subject, and revived that of Domitius (*of 104 BC*)

EPITOME OF LIVY, Bk. 89

Sulla increased the size of the colleges of pontiffs and augurs to fifteen members each.

CICERO *ad familiares* **8.4.1** (51 BC)

I envy you. There are so many measures being carried every day which would astonish you....P. Dolabella has been made a member of the 15-men college in charge of the Sibylline Books (*XVviri sacris faciundis*).*

(vii) Senate

DIONYSIUS OF HALICARNASSUS 5.77

Sulla composed a Senate by recruiting anyone who happened to come along.

EPITOME OF LIVY, Bk. 89

Sulla increased the Senate's numbers from the equestrian order.

APPIAN, *Civil Wars* **1.100**

As for the Senate itself, whose numbers had been reduced to a very low level by

* The number of members of this College had been 10 in pre-Sullan times.

revolution and war, Sulla enrolled about three hundred new members from the best of the knights, allowing the tribal assembly to vote on each of them.

SALLUST, *Catiline* 37

Many remembered (*in 63 BC*) Sulla's victory, when they had seen common soldiers (*gregarii milites*) appointed to the Senate...

CICERO, *de legibus* 3.27 (52 BC)

The practice whereby the censors appointed new members to fill vacant places in the Senate was discontinued.

Cf. above, quaestors (see p. 164).

(viii) The Citizens and Italy

Licinianus (p.34F) and Sallust (Hist.1.55.11M) both imply that Sulla abolished the distributions of corn.

APPIAN, *Civil Wars* 1.100

Sulla gave their freedom to more than 10,000 of the youngest and strongest of the former slaves of the proscribed, and enrolled them in the citizen body, making them Roman citizens. They were given the name 'Cornelii' by him, so as to have 10,000 of the commons ever ready to obey his orders.

APPIAN, *Civil Wars* 1.100

In order to secure the same sort of safeguard in Italy, he assigned to the twenty-three legions* which had served under him a great deal of land in the various communities, some of it public land hitherto undistributed, some of it confiscated as a punishment from the communities concerned.

CICERO, *in Catilinam* 2.20 (63 BC)

These colonists of Sulla...building like nabobs, with choice estates and large households, wining and dining in style, have got so heavily into debt that their only hope of rescue is to raise Sulla from the dead.

CICERO, *ad Atticum* 1.19.4 (60 BC)

I was in favour of confirming the people of Volaterrae and Arretium in possession of their lands which Sulla had confiscated but not distributed.

CICERO, *pro Murena* 49 (63 BC)

They could see (*in 63 BC*) Catiline surrounded by an army of colonists from Arretium and Faesulae, and standing out among them in sharp contrast men broken in the storms of Sulla's day.

CICERO, *in Catilinam* 3.14 (63 BC)

....The colonists Sulla settled at Faesulae....

A distinction made by Pliny (Nat. Hist. 3.5.52) between 'Old Clusians' and 'New Clusians' suggests Sullan colonists at Clusium. Inscriptions attest colonists at

---

* According to 1.104, these totalled 120,000 men.

Praetuttian Interamnia and at Nola. A new colony at Pompeii was given the name 'Colonia Veneria Cornelia Pompeianorum' (CIL x.p.89).

CICERO, *de lege agraria* 2.78 (63 BC)

If they say the law does not allow this, then it is not allowed even under the Cornelian Law; but we can see...the territory of Praeneste is held by a handful of possessors.

CICERO, *In Catilinam* 1.8 (63 BC)

When you confidently planned to seize Praeneste, did you not realise that that colony was fortified?

PLINY, *Natural History* 14.6.62

....The Sullan colony at Urbana not so long ago attached to Capua....

There is evidence for other Sullan colonies at Abella, Hadria, Volaterrae, Spoletium, Suessula, and Capua.

CICERO, *de domo* 79 (57 BC)

By a law introduced by the dictator L. Sulla, the Roman people in the centuriate assembly deprived municipalities of their citizenship, and of their lands. The provision about the lands stands today; that was in the people's power. But the provision about the citizenship lasted only as long as Sulla's miltitary control lasted.

CICERO, *pro Caecina* 97 (69 BC)

When I was speaking in defence of the freedom of the lady from Arretium (*79 BC*),...and Cotta objected on the grounds that the inhabitants of Arretium had been deprived of their citizenship, and I countered most vigorously with the argument that citizenship could not be taken away....the quindecimviral court after due deliberation and investigation decided that my plea was sound. And the court reached that decision even though Cotta spoke against it and while Sulla was still alive.

SALLUST, *Histories* 1.55.12M (*Speech of Lepidus in 78 BC*)

A multitude of allies and Latins are being denied that citizenship which you gave them as a reward for their many outstanding deeds, and denied it by one man. A few hangers-on of his have seized the ancestral homes of ordinary simple guiltless people as the wages for their crimes.

(ix) Public Revenues

APPIAN, *Mithridatica* 62

(*Sulla told the Asians assembled at Ephesus:*) 'I will impose on you the taxes for five years to be paid immediately, and the costs of the war, what I have spent so far and whatever additional expenditure will be involved in settling what remains to be done.'

APPIAN, *Civil Wars* 1.102

All the allied nations and kings, and not only the tributary cities but also all those which had submitted to Rome voluntarily and had sworn agreements with

Rome, together with those which by alliance or through some other good service were self-governing and free from taxation, were all of them now compelled to pay taxes and submit to Rome's authority, some of them even losing lands and harbours which they had been granted by treaty.

See too above, 84 BC (d).

(x) The Legal System

VELLEIUS PATERCULUS 2.32

The right to sit in judgement in the courts (*viz. to serve as* iudices) which C. Gracchus had taken from the Senate and given to the knights, Sulla gave back to the Senate.

TACITUS, *Annals* **11.22**

By a law of Sulla's twenty quaestors were appointed to keep up the numbers of the Senate, to whose members Sulla had transferred the courts.

CICERO, *Verrines* **1.37** (70 BC)

I shall not merely enumerate, but prove with chapter and verse, the criminal and scandalous things which have been done in the ten years since the courts have been transferred to the Senate.

CICERO, *Verrines* **1.30**

We shall not have Q. Manlius and Q. Cornificius among the *iudices*, because by then they will be tribunes of the plebs. P. Sulpicius must enter on his magistracy on 5 December. M. Crepereius and L. Cassius and Cn. Tremellius have all three of them been elected old-style military tribunes; after 1 January (*viz. 69 BC*) they will not be among the *iudices*.

CICERO, *Verrines* **2.1.79**

Are we to have this man among the *iudices*? Is he to find a place as a *iudex* in the second senatorial decury?

Schol. Gronov. p.335 St.

The Senate was divided into decuries, and one was given to the Roman people to reject *iudices* from.

CICERO, *Verrines* **2.1.77**

....The men who are outside that category, to whom the famous Cornelian Laws do not give the right to reject more than three *iudices*....

POMPONIUS: *Digest* **1.2.2.32**

Cornelius Sulla established public courts (*quaestiones publicae*), for instance to try cases of fraud, parricide, murder (*falsum, parricidium, sicarii*).

POMPONIUS:*Digest* **48.1.1: Macer**

Not all courts are 'public' courts (*publica iudicia*) but only those set up by the laws on public courts like the Cornelian Law on murder and poisoning (*de sicariis et veneficis*).

CICERO, *pro Cluentio* **148** (66 BC)

A capital charge shall lie against....any military tribune of the first four legions, any quaestor, tribune of the plebs – all the other magistracies are listed in due order – or any member of the Senate who combines or conspires to secure anyone's condemnation in a public court.*

JUSTINIAN, *Institutes* **4.18.7**

The Cornelian Law on fraud is also known as his law on wills (*testamenta*).

CICERO, *Verrines* **2.1.108** (70 BC)

There are penalties established by law on many subjects which have no retrospective effect, for example the Cornelian laws on wills (*testamentaria*) and coinage (*nummaria*) and a great many others besides, which establish no new principle of law but simply ordain that what has always been a wicked act shall be from a defined point in time matter for a public trial.

CICERO, *pro Rabirio Postumo* **8** (54 BC)

This issue concerning recovery from any third party who has received the money in question is a kind of appendix to an issue already decided on and adjudged criminal....But if this section of the law has been taken over verbatim in the Cornelian Law from the pre-existing Servilian Law...

CICERO, *pro Cluentio* **104** (66 BC)

What was Fidiculanius (*one of the senatorial* iudices *in a case tried in 74 BC*) alleged to have done? To have received 400,000 sesterces from Cluentius. He belonged to the senatorial order. The normal law under which senators are prosecuted in such a matter is the extortion law (*lex repetundarum, de pecuniis repetundis*). He was prosecuted under that law and acquitted without a stain on his character.

CICERO, *in Pisonem* **50** (55 BC)

I pass over his crossing the boundaries of his province, leading out an army, starting a war on his own initiative, entering the king's territory without instructions from the Roman People or the Senate, all of them actions expressly forbidden....by the Cornelian Law on high treason (*maiestas*)....

CICERO, *pro Cluentio* **97** (66 BC)

But, the prosecution say, Bulbus too was found guilty. Yes, but add 'of high treason', and then you will see that that trial has no connection with this present case. But, they say, this offence (*of accepting a bribe as a* iudex) was levelled at him. Certainly, but it was also made clear that he had tampered with the loyalty

---

* Cicero is citing verbatim some provisions of Sulla's law.

of a legion in Illyricum, a charge proper to the high treason court, an action dealt with in the high treason law.

CICERO, *ad familiares* **3.11.2** (50 BC)

The concept of 'high treason' is ambiguous, for all Sulla's intention that personal slander should not go unpunished.

Schol. Bob. p.78St.

In the past men condemned under the Sullan law on electoral corruption (*ambitus*) were banned from being candidates for public office for a period of ten years.

CICERO, *de natura deorum* **3.74** (45/44 BC)

Trials under the new legislation for murder, poisoning, peculation, forgery of wills, are daily occurrences now.

In pro Cluentio *147, Cicero lists a standing-court (*quaestio perpetua*) on peculation (*peculatus*) alongside those on murder, extortion, electoral corruption, etc.*

JUSTINIAN, *Institutes* **4.4.8**

The Cornelian Law on injuries (*de iniuriis*) introduced an action for injury.

AULUS GELLIUS, *Attic Nights* **2.24.11**

A number of wealthy men were notorious *bons viveurs* and squandered their wealth and property, pouring it away in banquets and parties. So the dictator L. Sulla passed a law in the people's assembly to the following effect: on the Kalends, Ides and Nones of each month, on the days when public games were held, and on certain regular religious festivals, people might legally spend up to 300 sesterces on a dinner, but on all other days no more than 30 sesterces.

MACROBIUS, *Satires* **3.17.11.**

....The sumptuary law carried by the dictator Cornelius Sulla, which did not prohibit lavish parties or set a limit to gourmandising but established lower prices for individual items....

PLUTARCH, *Sulla* **35**

When his wife Metella died, Sulla contravened his own law limiting expenditure on funerals, and spared no extravagance.

CICERO, *ad Atticum* **12.36.1** (45 BC)

I want to build her (*his dead daughter Tullia*) a shrine. I can't be budged from this. It isn't so much that I am anxious to avoid the legal penalty but rather to try my best to make her into a goddess.

PLUTARCH, *Comparison of Lysander and Sulla* **3**

Sulla introduced laws on marriage and continence for the citizens, while himself womanising and seducing other men's wives, so Sallust alleges.

CICERO, *de lege agraria* **2.35** (63 BC)

....All those lands the sale of which was the subject of decrees of the Senate (*in 81 BC*) and subsequently....

(e) Africa

EPITOME OF LIVY, Bk. 89

In Africa Cn. Pompeius defeated and killed Cn. Domitius and the King of Numidia, who were preparing to start a war.

PLUTARCH, *Pompey* **12**

Within a total of forty days, so they say, Pompey destroyed the enemy, subdued Libya (*North Africa*), and settled the affairs of the kings there. He was only twenty-four.

PLUTARCH, *Pompey* **13**

On returning to Utica, Pompey received letters from Sulla ordering him to discharge all his troops save one legion, with which he was to stay in Africa till a successor arrived to relieve him of command. This upset Pompey and he took it hard, but he concealed his feelings; his army expressed its indignation openly, and when he entreated them to return to Italy....they declared that they would never desert him....They carried Pompey to the tribunal....and kept insisting that he should stay on in command, while he tried to persuade them to obey Sulla's orders....The first intelligence Sulla had was that Pompey was in revolt....but when he learned the truth of the matter and saw everybody flocking out to give Pompey an enthusiastic welcome home, he made haste to go one better himself. He went out to meet him and ostentatiously embraced him, addressing him in a loud voice as 'Magnus' and telling everybody else there to do the same....Others say that Pompey was first given this title by the whole army in Africa, but that it gained strength and impact when Sulla confirmed it.

(f) The East

APPIAN, *Mithridatica* **66**

Sulla thought it wrong to make war on Mithridates, since a treaty had been made with him, and sent Aulus Gabinius to tell Murena that the decision not to fight Mithridates should be observed, and also to effect a reconciliation between Mithridates and Ariobarzanes.

CICERO, *pro lege Manilia* **8** (66 BC)

Sulla recalled Murena from the war against Mithridates.

(g) Pompey celebrates a triumph*

PLUTARCH, *Pompey* 14

Pompey demanded a triumph, and was opposed by Sulla....Nothing daunted, Pompey told Sulla to reflect that more men worshipped the rising than the setting sun....Struck by Pompey's boldness, Sulla shouted out twice over, 'Let him have his triumph!'....His soldiers, disappointed in their expectations of reward, were inclined to be undisciplined in the procession, but Pompey did not put himself out to conciliate them, saying that he would rather abandon his triumph than truckle to his troops. At that, Servilius, a distinguished man who had vigorously opposed the grant of a triumph, now declared that he could see that Pompey was in truth 'the Great', and worthy of a triumph.

EPITOME OF LIVY, Bk. 89

At the age of 24, and still a Roman knight, Pompey celebrated an unprecedented triumph for his successes in Africa.

de viris illustribus 77

Pompey was 26 when he celebrated his triumph.

LICINIANUS p.31F

At the age of 25, and still a Roman knight, something quite without precedent, Pompey triumphed from Africa as propraetor on 12 March.

Murena and Valerius Flaccus also celebrated triumphs over, respectively, Mithridates in Asia and the Celtiberians in Spain.

(h) Spain

PLUTARCH, *Sertorius* 7

Learning that Sulla was master of Rome and the party of Marius and Carbo ruined, and expecting the arrival of a general with an army to fight him, Sertorius sent Livius Salinator with six thousand infantry to hold the line of the Pyrenees. Not long after this Gaius Annius arrived, sent by Sulla. Seeing that Livius' position was unassailable, he settled down on the lower slopes not knowing what to do. But a certain Calpurnius Lanarius murdered Livius, and his army abandoned the heights. Annius advanced, brushing aside resistance with his powerful force. Sertorius could not match his strength in battle and so retreated to Cartagena with 3,000 men, where he took ship and sailed across the sea to Africa, landing in the Maurusian region.

OROSIUS 5.23

Sertorius was a bold and cunning man, who had been on the Marian side.

* The date may be either 81 or 80 BC. Pompey was born in 106 BC.

Escaping from Sulla, he slipped into Spain from Africa and stirred the most warlike peoples to arms.

FLORUS 2.10 *(3.22)*

He tried his luck first in Africa, then in the Balearic Islands. His plans stretched even to the Atlantic and the Azores. In the end he called Spain to arms.

(i) Egypt

APPIAN, *Civil Wars* 1.102

Sulla gave the throne of Egypt to Alexander, son of Alexander, the former king. He had been brought up in Cos, and surrendered by the people there to Mithridates. He escaped from Mithridates, fled to Sulla, and got on well with him.

80 BC   Consuls: L. Cornelius Sulla Felix II; Q. Caecilius Metellus Pius

(a) Sulla dictator and consul

APPIAN, *Civil Wars* 1.103

Next year Sulla, though dictator, deigned to become consul along with Metellus Pius to provide a specious façade of constitutional government.

(b) Metellus Pius sent to Spain

APPIAN, *Civil Wars* 1.97

Sulla sent Metellus to Spain to fight Sertorius.

(c) Cicero defends Roscius of Ameria

AULUS GELLIUS, *Attic Nights* 15.28.5

Nor is there any doubt that in the year following his defence of Quinctius (*dated to 81 BC by Gellius* A.N, *15.28.3 and Eusebius* Chron.) Cicero spoke in defence of Sextus Roscius at his trial for parricide. He was then 27, and L. Sulla Felix and Q. Metellus Pius were consuls, the former for the second time.

PLUTARCH, *Cicero* 3

Cicero undertook the defence and won an amazing success.

(d) Nola falls

EPITOME OF LIVY, Bk. 89

Sulla captured Nola.

LICINIANUS p.32F

The year before (*here* = *80 BC*) the Samnites at Nola followed suit and capitulated.

(e) Surrender of Volaterrae

EPITOME OF LIVY, Bk. 89

Sulla received the surrender of the besieged town of Volaterrae, which was still in arms.

CICERO, *de domo* **79** (57 BC)

Even though they had gone on fighting, the victorious Sulla could not rob the people of Volaterrae of their citizenship through the centuriate assembly. Today the Volaterrans are Roman citizens and share our state with us.

(f) The East and the Aegean

APPIAN, *Mithridatica* **67**

With no other distractions, Mithridates reduced the Crimean Bosporus, and made his son Machares king there.

EPITOME OF LIVY, Bk. 89

In Asia, Mitylene, the only city still fighting after Mithridates' defeat, was stormed and plundered.

SUETONIUS, *Julius Caesar* **2**

Caesar saw his first military service in Asia....At the storming of Mitylene he was awarded the civic crown by Thermus.

(g) Spain

PLUTARCH, *Sertorius* **11**

Sertorius sailed from Africa to Spain, at the request of the Lusitanians. He became their supreme commander, and set about subduing the neighbouring parts of Spain.

EPITOME OF LIVY, Bk. 90

The proscribed Q. Sertorius set a huge war ablaze in Further Spain.

PLUTARCH, *Sertorius* **12**

Sertorius won a naval battle against Cotta in the Mellerian Strait, and by the River Baetis (*Guadalquivir*) put Fufidius the governor of Baetica to flight with the loss of two thousand Roman troops.

In 79 BC Sulla divested himself of his dictatorship and retired into private life. A year later he was dead.

INDEX OF PASSAGES QUOTED

(ANONYMUS)
De Viris Illustribus (66) 111, 114, 117–118; (68) 153; (69) 147; (70) 144–145, 147; (72) 65; (73) 84, 87, 92, 95, 97–98; (75) 108, 159; (76) 147; (77) 162, 172; (80) 116

APPIAN
Celtica (13) 67–68
Civil Wars (1.7–1.8) 14–15; (1.9) 16, 17; (1.10) 18; (1.11) 17; (1.12) 19; (1.13) 20, 21; (1.14–1.16) 22–23; (1.18–1.20) 30–31; (1.21) 35, 36; (1.21–1.23) 38–39; (1.23–1.24) 51; (1.24–1.26) 54–55; (1.27) 60–61; (1.28) 87; (1.29–1.31) 93; (1.32) 97; (1.33) 100, 102; (1.34) 35; (1.35–1.36) 114–115; (1.37) 119; (1.38–1.39) 121–122; (1.40) 126; (1.48) 129; (1.49) 123; (1.50) 129; (1.50–1.52) 131; (1.52) 130; (1.54) 127; (1.55) 134; (1.55–1.56) 134–135; (1.59) 136; (1.60–1.61) 136; (1.63) 137; (1.64–1.66) 138–139; (1.67) 141; (1.68) 141; (1.71–1.75) 142; (1.75) 143; (1.76–1.78) 148; (1.79) 150; (1.80) 151; (1.86) 150, 152; (1.87) 159; (1.87–1.88) 153; (1.89) 154, 160; (1.91) 160; (1.92) 160; (1.94) 161; (1.95) 154, 161; (1.96) 156, 157; (1.97) 159, 173; (1.99) 157–158; (1.100) 159, 164, 165, 166; (1.101) 159; (1.102) 167–168, 173; (1.103) 173; (1.104) 166; (1.108) 162
Iberica (99) 104
Mithridatica (10) 122; (11) 132; (22) 138; (29) 138; (30) 142; (54) 146; (55) 146, 147; (60) 147; (61) 149; (62) 167; (63) 150; (64–65) 152; (65) 162; (66) 171; (67) 174

ASCONIUS
(Clark) (3) 124; (14) 130; (17) 35–36; (21) 81, 82–83, 90, 111; (22) 119–120; (25) 133; (45) 66–67; (57) 107; (67) 105, 106; (68–69) 71–72; (78) 80; (79) 127; (80) 81; (84) 156

ATHENAEUS
(6.104, p. 272 e) 83.

(AUCTOR)
Ad Herennium (1.21) 84; (1.24) 85; (1.25) 76; (2.17) 99; (2.21) 99; (2.45) 135

AULUS GELLIUS
Attic Nights (1.6) 28; (1.7.6) 45; (2.24.11) 170; (2.24.12) 65; (2.27.2) 104; (4.4.3) 123; (11.10) 37–38; (15.12) 37; (15.28.3,5) 173; (16.10.10) 75

CAESAR
African War (56) 86
Civil War (1.7) 164
Gallic War (1.7) 76

CASSIODORUS
Chronicle 76, 148, 151

CASSIUS HEMINA
(fr. 17p) 15

CATO THE ELDER
For The Rhodians 15

CASSIUS DIO
(fr. 83) 25; (fr. 83.2) 32; (fr. 87.5) 66; (fr. 94) 88; (fr. 95.3) 102; (fr. 97) 110; (fr. 100) 128; (fr. 102.2) 137; (fr. 102.7) 141; (fr. 102.8) 141; (fr. 104.1) 145; (fr.109.4) 161; (37.37) 165

CICERO (*see also* Asconius)
Brutus (95) 22; (99 100) 53; (103) 16; (106) 49; (109) 33; (115) 110; (125–6) 43; (128) 49, 60, 71; (159) 61, 67; (160) 62; (162) 105; (164) 77, 110; (168) 136; (203) 133; (205) 120; (222) 84, 112; (224) 82, 90, 97; (226) 133; (304) 120, 122; (305) 128; (308) 144; (311) 154
De Amicitia (1–2) 134; (37) 26; (95) 28
De Divinatione (1.56) 34; (1.72) 131

De Domo (24) 47; (41) 118; (43) 155; (50) 118; (53) 102; (79) 167, 174; (82) 45, 94; (84) 143; (91) 25

De Finibus (4.66) 54

De Haruspicum Responsis (41) 133; (43) 16, 82, 133; (54) 158

De Inventione (1.43) 67; (1.92) 76

De Lege Agraria (2.35) 171; (2.78) 167; (2.80) 122; (2.81) 18, 47, 156; (2.89) 150; (3.5) 158

De Legibus (1.42) 158; (2.12–14) 98; (2.14) 118; (2.31) 118; (3.22) 163; (3.24) 22; (3.26) 45; (3.27) 166; (3.35) 27–28; (3.36) 76; (3.38) 62

De Natura Deorum (3.74) 170; (3.81) 128

De Officiis (1.108) 112; (2.49) 85; (2.72) 46, 84; (2.73) 81; (2.75) 120; (3.47) 33, 105; (3.80) 143–144

De Oratore (1.24) 112; (1.25) 130; (1.255) 77; (2.48) 102; (2.106) 28, 60; (2.107) 85; (2.124) 85; (2.132) 60; (2.165) 60; (2.170) 27, 60; (2.195) 101; (2.196) 103; (2.197) 85; (2.198–201) 105; (2.199) 77; (2.227) 110; (2.257) 106; (2.274) 104; (2.285) 25; (3.2–6) 116–117; (3.8) 142; (3.24) 109; (3.93) 109

De Provinciis Consularibus (17) 47; (19) 80

De Re Publica (1.6) 26; (1.31) 32; (3.41) 32; (4.2) 33

Divinatio in Caecilium (67) 81

Epistulae ad Atticum (1.17.9) 50; (1.19.4) 166; (5.17.5) 108; (6.1.15) 108; (8.11.2) 158; (9.15.2) 158; (12.36.1) 170–171

Epistulae ad M. Brutum (1.5.3) 101

Epistulae ad Familiares (1.7.10) 47; (1.9.16) 101; (1.9.25) 164; (1.9.26) 108; (3.6.3.) 164; (3.6.6) 165; (3.10.6) 165; (3.11.2) 170; (8.4.1) 165; (9.21.3) 32, 61

Epistulae ad Quintum Fratrem (1.1.33) 148; (2.3.3) 32

In Catilinam (1.4) 59; (1.8) 167; (2.20) 166; (3.9) 151; (3.14) 166; (4.10) 44

In Pisonem (50) 169

Lucullus (13) 16

Paradoxa Stoicorum (6.2.46) 157

Philippics (5.8) 102; (8.7) 139; (8.14) 59; (11.18) 29; (12.27) 129–130, 152; (13.2) 152

Post Reditum ad Quirites (11) 100

Post Reditum in Senatu (25) 100

Pro Archia (7) 124; (11) 124

Pro Balbo (11) 77; (21) 123; (46) 89; (48) 95, 106; (54) 91, 106

Pro Caecina (97) 167

Pro Cluentio (97) 169–170; (104) 45, 169; (110) 164; (140) 62, 76; (144) 45; (147) 170; (148) 45, 169; (151) 46; (153) 115; (154) 46; (157) 46

Pro Flacco (32) 149; (98) 103

Pro Fonteio (13) 62; (24) 85; (38) 110; (43) 126

Pro Lege Manilia (8) 171; (14) 50; (19) 50

Pro Milone (8) 28; (16) 112

Pro Murena (49) 166

Pro Plancio (Scholiast p 157 St) 50; (12) 78; (33) 118; (51) 63; (69) 101

Pro Publio Sulla (72) 155

Pro. C. Rabirio Perduellionis Reo (12) 44; (20) 91; (20–21) 96–97; (24) 102; (28) 98

Pro Rabirio Postumo (8) 82, 90–91, 169; (16) 115

Pro Roscio Amerino (33) 143; (125) 163; (128) 163; (130) 155; (136) 163; (149) 163

Pro Sestio (30) 106; (37) 94; (61) 44–45; (101) 87; (103) 18, 46; (140) 60

Tusculan Disputations (3.48) 46

Verrines (1.26) 90; (1.30) 168; (1.37) 168; (1.38) 49; (2.1.26) 82; (2.1.77) 168; (2.1.79) 168; (2.1.108) 169; (2.1.155) 163–164; (2.2.3) 61; (2.2.12) 50; (2.2.184) 67; (2.5.3) 103

CICERO Quintus,
De Petitione Consulatus (9) 155–156

DESSAU *ILS* (23) 27; (49) 111–112; (59) 82, 98; (8770) 132; (8888) 125, 130

DIODORUS SICULUS (24.2.23)
27; (34.2.26) 29; (34/35.25–27) 42;
(34/35.28a) 58–59; (36.2) 83; (36.3–8)
87; (36.9) 88; (36.10) 92, 101; (36.15)
91; (36.16) 100; (37.2) 120, 126, 128,
131–132; (37.3) 138; (37.5) 107;
(37.9) 42; (37.10) 112, 118–119;
(37.11) 116; (37.12) 133; (37.13) 116,
122

DIONYSIUS OF
HALICARNASSUS
(4.62) 151; (5.77) 165

EUSEBIUS
Chronicle (p 233) 143

EUTROPIUS
(4.12) 48; (4.20) 30; (5.8–9) 161–162;
(6.14) 150

FESTUS
(p 267L) 83; (p 345L) 83; (p 388L)
33; (p 464L) 136; (p 728L) 47

FLORUS
(1.35) 33; (1.38) 73; (1.40) 132, 138,
146; (2.1) 50; (2.4) 92, 97; (2.5) 113,
117; (2.6) 121, 128, 129; (2.7) 88;
(2.9) 157; (2.10) 173

FRONTINUS
Stratagems (1.11.11) 159; (4.2.2.) 78

JULIUS VICTOR
(6.4) 53–54

JUSTIN
(32.3.10) 77; (34.4.8) 30; (36.4.6) 29;
(37.4.3) 83; (38.1.2) 92; (38.2.3) 107;
(38.3.1) 107; (38.3.3) 109; (38.3.4)
122; (38.3.6) 86; (38.4.13) 121; (40
prologue) 150; (40.1.3) 150

JUSTINIAN
Institutes (4.4.8) 170; (4.18.7) 169

LICINIANUS
(p11F) 79; (p13F) 85; (p14F) 80;
(p16F) 140; (p20F) 141; (p21F) 141;
(p26F) 146; (p27F) 147; (p28F) 149;
(p31F) 172; (p32F) 173; (p34F) 166;
(p35F) 125

LIVY
(6.35.5) 15; (10.13.14) 15; (35.10.11–
12) 15; *Epitome* (58) 18, 22; (59) 28,
29, 31–32; (60) 34, 35, 38, 41–42, 125;
(61) 57, 59, 60; (62) 63, 65; (63) 65,
67; (64) 69, 70; (65) 73, 75; (67) 78,
80, 86; (68) 88, 89; (69) 90, 91, 93, 96,
101; (70) 104, 110, 111, 114; (71) 114;
(72) 121; (74) 127, 128, 132; (75) 128,
129, 131; (76) 130, 131, 138; (77) 135,
136, 137; (78) 138; (79–80) 139–140;
(80) 141, 142, 143; (82) 142; (83) 144,
145; (84) 125, 147, 148; (85) 152; (86)
153, 160; (88) 156, 160, 161; (89) 158,
161, 164, 165, 171, 172, 173, 174; (90)
174.

MACROBIUS
Satires (1.12.34) 99; (3.17.11) 170

MEMNON
(22 Jac) 138; (25 Jac) 146, 147

OBSEQUENS
(37) 67; (41) 76; (44) 88; (45) 101; (46)
100; (114–15) 122

OROSIUS
(5.9.7) 27; (5.12) 48, 53; (5.15)66, 77;
(5.17) 87, 96, 97, 98 99; (5.18.24)
129; (5.18.30) 132; (5.21) 154; (5.23)
172–173; (6.18.22) 130–131

PAUSANIAS (1.20.5) 138

PLINY THE ELDER
Natural History (3.5.52) 166; (3.6.80)
99; (3.17.123) 99; (3.70) 130; (7.135)
130; (8.16.53) 108; (8.223) 65; (10.16)
83; (14.6.62) 167; (17.1) 110; (25.52)
113; (30.3.12) 103; (33.3.46) 120;
(33.20) 113; (33.34) 49; (33.132) 144;
(36.116) 157; (37.1.9) 79

PLUTARCH
Cato Minor (2) 115–116
Cicero (3) 173
*Comparison of Agis and Cleomenes
and the two Gracchi* (2.1) 50
Comparison of Lysander and Sulla (3)
171
Crassus (6) 148
Gaius Gracchus (1–2) 34; (2) 35; (2.3–

3.2) 36; (3.2–8.2) 39–41; (8.2–12.3) 51–53; (9.2) 47; (10) 32, 47–48; (13.1–17.5) 55–57

Lucullus (2) 142; (3) 145–146; (4) 149

Marius (4) 61–62; (5) 63; (6) 65, 66; (8) 72; (8–9) 73; (10) 79; (14) 83, 86; (15) 88; (25) 83, 89; (28) 90; (29) 93–94; (30) 104; (31) 100, 101; (33) 128; (35) 134, 135; (41) 140–141

Pompey (5) 147–148; (8) 151; (11) 162; (12) 171; (13) 171; (14) 172

Roman Questions (50) 71; (83) 66

Sertorius (5) 140; (7) 172; (11) 174; (12) 174

Sulla (3) 75, 135; (4) 83, 89; (5) 108, 111; (6) 128; (10) 136, 137; (11) 138; (22) 146; (24) 146; (25) 149; (27) 151, 152; (28) 160; (29) 160; (31) 155, 156; (33) 158; (34) 159, 163; (35) 170

Tiberius Gracchus (8.1–3) 13–14; (8.3–9.1) 15; (9.2) 18; (9.4) 17; (10–12) 19–20; (13.1) 20; (14–15) 21; (16–19) 23–24; (20.2–3) 26–27; (21.1–3) 25

POLYBIUS (6.16.5) 19

POMPONIUS

Digest (1.2.2.32) 164, 168; (48.1.1) 168, 169

QUINTILIAN

Institutio Oratoria (6.3.75) 133; (11.1.12) 110

SALLUST

Ad Caesarem Senem (2.8) 53

Bellum Jugurthinum (11–12) 63; (13–16) 64–65; (20) 66; (21–27) 68; (25.4) 65; (27.3–4) 47; (28–35) 69; (31.7) 26; (36) 70; (37) 70; (40) 70–71; (41.2–42.1) 13; (43–69) 72; (64–73) 73–74; (85) 74–75; (86) 75; (92–100) 78; (104) 79–80; (114) 78

Catilina (33) 143; (37) 166

Histories (1.20M) 106; (1.55.6M) 156; (1.55.11M) 166; (1.55.12M) 167; (1.55.17M) 156–157; (1.55.18M) 179; (2.21M) 137; (4.69.10M) 132

SENECA THE YOUNGER

Ad Helviam (7.9) 99

Ad Marciam (16.4) 114

De Beneficiis (6.34.2) 112

De Brevitate Vitae (6.1–2) 112; (13.6) 108; (13.8) 163

SISENNA

(fr.17P) 123

STRABO

(4.6.7) 99; (4.8) 83; (5.1.11) 65; (5.4.2) 125; (5.4.11) 162; (12.2.11) 107; (13) 145; (14.1.38) 29, 33

SUETONIUS

De Grammaticis (25) 109

Julius Caesar (2) 174; (88) 99

Nero Caesar (2) 59, 81

Tiberius Caesar (3) 54

TACITUS

Annals (11.22) 164, 168; (12.60) 49, 76

Dialogus De Oratoribus (35) 109

VALERIUS MAXIMUS

(2.3.2) 78; (2.9.5) 104; (2.10.5) 110–111; (3.2.18) 96; (3.7.8) 111; (4.1.12) 32; (4.7.1) 26; (4.7.3) 84; (5.2.7) 101; (5.2.8) 89; (5.3.2e) 26; (6.9.6) 75; (6.9.9) 130; (6.9.14) 64; (7.6.4) 153; (8.1.11) 82; (8.5.2) 85; (8.6.4) 120; (8.13.4) 143; (9.5.1) 34–35; (9.5.2) 118; (9.7.1) 92; (9.7.2) 87, 137; (9.7.3) 92; (9.7.4) 127; (9.13.2) 161 (8 Damnati 2) 102; (8 Damnati 3) 100

VELLEIUS PATERCULUS

(1.15) 36, 48, 99; (2.2–3) 24–25; (2.4) 28; (2.6) 43, 57–58; (2.7) 62; (2.8) 67; (2.11) 73; (2.12) 81, 90; (2.13) 49, 110, 113; (2.14) 112; (2.15) 120; (2.16) 123, 125–126, 131; (2.18) 135; (2.20) 124, 139; (2.21) 129, 141; (2.23) 143; (2.24) 147; (2.26) 153; (2.27) 159, 160, 161, 163; (2.28) 154, 156, 158; (2.30) 163; (2.32) 49, 168

INDEX OF NAMES AND PLACES

Abella 167
Abellinum 48
Achaea 95
Acilius Glabrio (lex Acilia) 50
M'. Acilius Balbus (*cos*. 114) 66
Adherbal 63–65, 66, 68
Aebutius 140
Aeculanum 131
Aedui 59
Aegritomari 81
L. Aelius 120
Q. Aelius (*cos* 167) 33
Aemilia (Vestal) 66
M. Aemilius Lepidus (*cos*. 187) 15
M. Aemilius Lepidus (*cos*. 126) 33
L. Aemilius Paullus (*cos*. 182) 15
M. Aemilius Scaurus (*cos*. 115) 65, 69, 71, 79–81, 83, 85, 90, 96, 111, 119, 159
Aesernia 131, 162
Aesis (River) 159
Africa 34, 38, 48, 51, 52, 64, 66, 69–70, 75, 77, 84, 87, 136, 139–40, 161, 171–173, 174
Albinovanus 136
Aleria 99
Alexander I of Egypt 173
Alexandria 95
Allobroges 59
Alps 35, 43, 67
Amastris 132
Ambrones 88
Q. Ancharius 142
Ancona 147
C. Annius 172
L. Annius (*tr*. 110) 70
T. Annius Luscus (*cos*. 153) 21–22
T. Annius Rufus (*cos*. 128) 27
Antioch 150
P. Antistius 133, 144, 153, 154
Antium 140
M. Antonius (*cos*. 99) 85, 88, 95, 97, 100, 102–105, 110, 122, 139, 140
Q. Antullius 54, 56

Apollonia 29
C. Aponius Motylus 126
C. Appuleius Decianus 102
L. Appuleius Saturninus (*tr*. 103, 100) 82, 84–87, 91–94, 96–98, 100, 102, 106, 134
Aquae Sextiae 88
Aquileia 123
M'. Aquillius (*cos*. 129) 29, 30, 33, 38
M'. Aquillius (*cos*. 101) 89, 92, 101, 103, 138, 146
Arausio 78–80, 105
Archelaus 138, 142, 144, 146
Ariarathes 30, 122
Aricia 140
Ariminum 159, 161
Ariobarzanes 107, 109, 111, 122, 132, 146–147, 171
Armenia 107, 111, 150
Arretium 166–167
Arsaces 111
Arverni 59
Asculum 113, 121–122, 129–131, 152
Asia 25–27, 29–30, 33, 38, 44, 50–51, 83, 86–87, 95, 101, 107–108, 110–111, 134–135, 142, 143, 144–146, 148–150, 167, 172, 174
Asinius Herius 125–6
Athenion 88, 92
Athens 138, 142, 144
Attalus Philometer 21, 22, 29
Attica 83, 142
Atticus (*see* Pomponius)
C. Attilius Serranus (*cos*. 106) 76, 78, 142
Aufeius 37
Augustus Caesar 28
Aulis 146
C. Aurelius Cotta (*cos*. 75) 110, 119–120, 122, 133, 142, 154, 167, 174
L. Aurelius Cotta (*cos*. 119) 38, 61, 85
L. Aurelius Orestes (*cos*. 126) 33–36
L. Aurelius Orestes (*cos*. 103) 84

C. Aurelius Scaurus 78
M. Aurelius Scaurus (*cos. suf.* 108) 73, 78

C. Baebius 69, 84
M. Baebius 142
Bagoas 122
Balearic Islands 173
Baetica 174
Baetis 174
Beneventum 162
Bithynia 29–30, 83, 92, 122, 132, 138, 145–147, 149
Bituitus 59
C. Blossius 16, 26
Bocchus 74, 78–79, 108
Boiorix 78, 89
Brundisium 150
Bruttius Sura 138
Byzantium 145

Cadatia 48
Q. Caecilius 155
M. Caecilius Metellus (*cos.* 115) 65
Q. Caecilius Metellus Balearicus (*cos.* 123) 38, 48, 60
C. Caecilius Metellus Caprarius (*cos.* 113) 66, 87, 100
L. Caecilius Metellus Delmaticus (*cos.* 119) 61, 66
L. Caecilius Metellus Diadematus (*cos.* 117) 63, 65, 100
Q, Caecilius Metellus Macedonicus (*cos.* 143) 21, 27, 28–29, 32
Q. Caecilius Metellus Nepos (*cos.* 98) 100, 101
Q. Caecilius Metellus Numidicus (*cos.* 109) 61–62, 71–75, 77, 80, 87, 93–94, 98–102
Q. Caecilius Metellus Pius (*cos.* 80) 100, 101–102, 130, 140–141, 150–151, 155, 159–160, 173
Caepio (*see* Servilius)
Caesar (*see* Julius)
Cales 44, 152
Q. Calidius 101–102, 162
L. Calpurnius Bestia (*cos.* 111) 47, 49, 60, 68–69, 71, 119
P. Calpurnius Lanarius 172

L. Calpurnius Piso (*pr.* 74) 123, 144
L. Calpurnius Piso Caesoninus (*cos,* 112) 68
L. Calpurnius Piso Frugi (*cos.* 133) 13, 46, 49, 60, 120
Camertini 89
Campania 18, 21, 47–48, 122, 156
Cannae 131
C. Canuleius (*tr.* 98) 102
Cappadocia 29–30, 92, 101, 107, 111, 122, 132, 145, 147, 152, 165
Capua 21, 27, 41, 134, 139, 150, 152, 167
Carbo (*see* Papirius)
Carinas 159
Cartagena 172
Carthage/Junonia 13, 31, 48, 52, 54–55, 60, 63
Cassius (*legate* 89) 132
L. Cassius (*cos.* 107) 69, 74, 75
L. Cassius (*tr.* 104) 80
L. Cassius (*tr.* 89) 127
C. Cassius Longinus (*cos.* 124) 36, 48
C. Cassius Longinus (*cos.* 96) 104
L. Cassius Longinus Ravilla (*cos.* 127) 28, 34, 66–67
Cato (*see* Porcius)
Caunos 149
Celtiberi 86, 104, 109, 162, 172
Censorinus (*see* Marcius)
Cercina 86–87
Chaeroneia 138, 144
Charisius 48
Chios 149
Cicero (*see* Tullius)
Cilicia 88, 95, 108, 164–5
Cimbri 67–68, 73, 75, 78–81, 83, 84, 86, 88–89, 93, 156
Cirta 68
Claudia 16
Claudius (Emperor) 49, 76
App. Claudius Pulcher (*cos.* 143) 16, 20–21, 22, 25, 30, 32
App. Claudius Pulcher (*cos.* 130) 30
App. Claudius Pulcher (*cos.* 79) 139
App. Claudius Pulcher (*cos.* 54) 164–165
C. Claudius Pulcher (*cos.* 92) 109

P. Clodius Pulcher (*tr.* 58) 25, 47
Clusium 154, 160, 166
C. Coelius Caldus (*cos.* 94) 76, 107
Cnidos 95
Colchis 152
Comana 152
Compsa 131
Conusium 131
Corfinium 123, 125–126
Cornelia 16, 31, 40, 42
C. Cornelius (*tr.* 67) 107
P. Cornelius Cethegus 136, 151
L. Cornelius Cinna (*cos.* 87, 86, 84) 124, 125, 126, 130, 137–148
Cn. Cornelius Dolabella 97
Cn. Cornelius Dolabella (*cos.* 81) 159, 163
L. Cornelius Dolabella 103
P. Cornelius Dolabella (*cos. suf.* 44) 165
Cn. Cornelius Lentulus (*cos.* 130) 30
Cn. Cornelius Lentulus (*cos.* 97) 103
Cn. Cornelius Lentulus Clodianus (*cos.* 72) 144
P. Cornelius Lentulus Sura (*cos.* 71) 144
L. Cornelius Merula (*cos. suf.* 87) 138–139, 142
P. Cornelius Scipio Africanus (*cos.* 205, 194) 26, 40, 43
P. Cornelius Scipio Africanus Aemilianus (*cos* 147, 134) 14, 16, 21, 26, 27, 28, 31–32, 35, 51, 63, 64
L. Cornelius Scipio Asiaticus (*cos.* 83) 150, 152, 154
P. Cornelius Scipio Nasica (*cos.* 138) 23–26
P. Cornelius Scipio Nasica (*cos.* 111) 47, 68, 69
L. Cornelius Sulla Felix (*cos.* 88, 80) 18, 46, 47, 49, 75, 78–79, 82, 86, 89, 99, 108, 125, 126, 128, 130–131, 133–139, 142, 144–174
P. Cornelius Sulla 110, 155
M. (Caecilius) Cornutus 126
Corsica 99
Cos 173
C. Cosconius 131

Cossura 161
Crassus (*see* Licinius)
Cremona 123
Crete 107
Critolaus 37
Cyclades 138
Cyprus 95
Cyrene 95, 104
L. (Junius Brutus) Damasippus (*pr.* 82) 136, 140, 153
Dardanelles 144
Dardanus 146
P. Decius (*tr.* 120) 60, 65
Delos 119, 146
Delphi 94–95
Demades 37
Demosthenes 37
Dertona 65
T. Didius (*cos.* 98) 85, 101–102, 104, 109, 126, 131
Diophanes 15, 26
C. Domitius 116
Cn. Domitius 162, 171
Cn. Domitius Ahenobarbus (*cos.* 122) 51, 59, 65
Cn. Domitius Ahenobarbus (*tr.* 104, *cos.* 96) 81, 101, 104, 109
L. Domitius Ahenobarbus (*cos.* 94) 107, 153
Dorylaus 144
M. Duronius 104
Egypt 95, 142, 173
Ephesus 29, 149, 167
Eporedia 99
L. Equitius 87, 92, 96
Eretria 138
Erythrac 151
Etruria 16, 115, 123, 128, 140–141
Euboea 138
Eudemus 21
Eumenes 29
Euphrates (River) 111
Euporus 58
Q. Fabius Maximus (*cos.* 116) 63
Q. Fabius Maximus Allobrogicus (*cos.* 121) 54, 59
Fabrateria 36, 48

Faesulae 166
C. Fannius (*cos.* 122) 41, 51, 52–53
Faventia 160
Ferentinum 44, 48, 122
Fidiculanius 45
C. Flavius Fimbria (*cos.* 104) 78, 80, 85–86, 97
C. Flavius Fimbria (son of above) 141, 143–147
Florentia 157
Fonteius 113, 121
Forum Popillii 27
Fregellae 35–36
Fucine Lake 129
Fufidius 155
Ser. Fulvius 67
M. Fulvius Flaccus (*cos.* 125) 24, 25–26, 31, 34–35, 38, 51–52, 54–58
P. Furius (*tr.* 99) 97, 99, 102
L. Fursidius 154

A. Gabinius (*tr.* 139) 27
A. Gabinius 131, 171
Gaetuli 74, 86
Galatia 84, 101, 162
Gallograeci 86, 146
Gantisci 65
Gaul 62, 68, 77–80, 83, 86
L. Giganius 97
Gordius 111, 162
Gracchus (*see* Sempronius)
Granius 118
Cn. Granius
Q. Granius
Greece, Greeks 132, 138

Hadria 167
Hadrian (Emperor) 121
Hannibal 158
Helvetii 75
Henna 27
Heraclia 123
Herculaneum 131

Iapyges 122
Ilium 132, 145, 149
Illyricum 31, 67
Insteius Cato 126
Interamna 157

Interamnia (Praetuttian) 167
Italica 123–125
Italy, Italians *passim*

Jugurtha 63–79
C. Julius Caesar (*cos.* 59, *dictator*) 44, 47, 76, 82, 90–91, 99, 165, 174
L. Julius Caesar (*cos.* 90) 113, 122–126
S. Julius Caesar (*cos.* 91) 111, 118, 121, 126
C. Julius Caesar Strabo 87, 133–134, 141–142
L. Junius Brutus Damasippus (*pr.* 82) 136, 140, 153
D. Junius Brutus (*cos.* 138) 58
M. Junius Brutus (tyrannicide) 33
M. Junius Brutus (*tr.* 83) 150, 161
M. Junius Pennus (*tr.* 126) 33, 105
M. Junius Silanus (*cos.* 109) 71, 73, 81
Junonia (*see* Carthage)

T. Labienus (*tr.* 63) 165
Q. Labienus 96–97
C. Laelius Sapiens (*cos.* 140) 14, 26, 28, 32
P. Laetorius 58
M. Laetorius 136
T. Lafrenius 126
M. Lamponius 126
Lanuvium 140
Larinum 131
Latini 32, 41, 51–54, 118, 167
Lavinium 81
Lepidus (*see* Aemilius)
Leucae 29
Liburnia 148
Licinia 25, 57
Licinia (Vestal) 66, 67
C. Licinius (*tr.* 367) 15, 43
L. Licinius 157
L. Licinius Crassus (*cos.* 95) 27, 33, 61, 67, 76–77, 80, 105–106, 109–110, 116–117, 132, 142
M. Licinius Crassus (*cos.* 70, 55) 144, 148, 154
P. Licinius Crassus (*cos.* 97) 103, 124, 127, 139, 140, 142

P. Licinius Crassus Mucianus (*cos.* 131) 16, 25, 27, 29–30, 32
L. Licinius Lucullus (*cos.* 74) 142, 145–146, 149
L. Licinius Lucullus 88
P. Licinius Lucullus (*tr.* 110) 70
Liguria 35, 65, 88, 99
Lilybaeum 161
Liris (River) 122
M. Livius Drusus (*tr.* 122, *cos.* 112, *cens.* 109) 51–54, 68, 71
M. Livius Drusus (*tr.* 91) 49, 98, 111–121, 128, 133
Livius Salinator 172
Lucania 27, 122, 128, 138
Lucceius 131
Q. Lucretius Ofella 159, 161
Lucullus (*see* Licinius)
Luna 65
Lusitania 103, 109
Q. Lutatius Catulus (*cos.* 102) 78, 87–89, 97, 126, 139, 142
Q. Lutatius Catulus (*cos.* 78) 154
Lycia 149

Macedonia 47, 67, 95, 132, 146, 150
Machares 174
Magnesia 149
Malaga 148
Cn. Mallius Maximus (*cos.* 105) 78–79, 85
C. Mamilius Limetanus (*tr.* 110) 49, 70–71, 74
M'. Manilius (*cos.* 149) 49
P. Manilius (*cos.* 120) 60
Manius 66
T. Manlius Mancinus (*tr.* 108) 74
Marcia 66, 67
L. Marcius Censorinus (*cos.* 149) 49
C. Marcius Censorinus 154
L. Marcius Philippus (*cos.* 91) 81, 111, 116–118, 121, 143, 144
Q. Marcius Rex (*cos.* 118) 62
C. Marius (*cos.* 107 etc.) 49, 61–66, 72–75, 78–101, 103–104, 106, 123, 126, 128, 134–136, 138–143, 147, 151

C. Marius (*cos.* 82) 129, 135–136, 139, 153–154, 156, 159–161, 172
M. Marius (of Teanum) 43–44
M. Marius Egnatius 126, 131
M. Marius Gratidianus 144, 156
Marrucini 122, 130
Marsi 113, 116, 122, 125–126, 128–130, 133
Masinissa 69
Massilia 35, 77, 83
Massiva 69
T. Matrinius 106
Mauretania 65
Mellerian Strait 174
Memmius 162
C. Memmius (*tr.* 112) 68–69, 86, 96–97
Metella 159, 170
Metellus (*see* Caecilius)
P. Mettius 96
Micipsa 34, 63–64
C. Milonius 140
Minatius Magius 131
Minucius 23
M. Minucius Rufus (*cos.* 110) 58, 70
Misenum 58
Mithraas 122
Mithridates 30, 37, 83–84, 86, 91, 92, 107, 109, 111, 122, 132, 134–135, 138, 142, 145–147, 149, 152–153, 162, 171, 174
Mucius 23
P. Mucius Scaevola (*cos.* 133) 13, 16, 24, 25, 26, 32
Q. Mucius Scaevola (*cos.* 117) 63, 96
Q. Mucius Scaevola (*cos.* 95) 33, 105–106, 107–108, 110, 143, 153
Q. Mummius (*tr.* 133) 19, 22, 23
(Licinius) Murena 150, 152–153, 154, 162, 172
Mutilus (*see* Papius)
Mytilene 16, 174

Nannius 155
Naples 123
Narbo Martius 62–63
C. Nemetorius 142

Nicomedes 29, 37, 83–84, 92, 107, 122
Nicomedes (son of above) 122, 132, 146–147, 149
Nitiobriges 75
Nola 131, 135, 138–139, 167, 173
C. Norbanus (*cos.* 83) 85, 105, 150, 152, 154, 156, 160
Noricum 67, 88
Numantia 16, 21, 64
Numidia 47, 63–72
A. Nunnius 92

Cn. Octavius (*cos.* 87) 137–142
M. Octavius 84
M. Octavius (*tr.* 133) 19–23, 39–40
L. Opimius (*cos.* 121) 27, 35–36, 49, 52–60, 64–65, 71
Q. Opimius (*tr.* 75) 163–164
Q. Oppius 146
Orchomenus 144, 146
Orobazus 111
Ostia 139–140

Padus (Po) 65, 123–124
Paeligni 121, 125, 130
Panna 162
Paphlagonia 30, 83, 107, 146, 149
C. Papirius Carbo (*cos.* 120) 27–32, 49, 60–61
C. Papirius Carbo (*tr.* 89) 124
Cn. Papirius Carbo (*cos* 113) 66–67
Cn. Papirius Carbo (*cos.* 85) 144, 147, 150, 153–154, 156, 159, 161–162, 172
C. Papirius Carbo Arvina (*tr.* 90) 128, 139–140, 142, 153
C. Papius (*tr.* 65) 105
C. Papius Mutilus 126, 131
Parma 65
Parthia 107, 111, 130
Patrae 150
S. Peducaeus (*tr.* 113) 66
Pergamum 21–22, 25, 30, 145–147
C. Perperna 126
M. Perperna (*cos.* 130) 29–30
M. Perperna (*cos.* 92) 109, 143
C. Persius 53
Philocrates 57

Phrygia 162
Picenum 122, 130, 151
Piraeus 138, 142, 150
Pisa 65
Piso (*see* Calpurnius)
Pitana 145
Cn. Plancius 50
M. Plautius Hypsaeus (*cos.* 125) 34
M. Plautius Silvanus (*tr.* 89) 124, 127
Poediculi 131
Polybius 19
Q. Pompaedius Silo 116, 121, 125–126, 131, 138
Pompeii 122, 131, 167
A. Pompeius 157
Q. Pompeius 135
Q. Pompeius (*cos.* 141) 21, 27
Cn. Pompeius Magnus (*cos.* 70, 55, 52) 124, 126, 129, 137, 147–149, 150–152, 154, 159–162, 171–172
Q. Pompeius Rufus (*cos.* 88) 128, 133–135, 136–138
Cn. Pompeius Strabo (*cos.* 89) 124–130, 137–141, 151
Pomponius 58
Cn. Pomponius (*tr.* 90?) 127, 133–134, 154
T. Pomponius Atticus 53
C. Pontidius (?Pontilius) 126
Pontius Telesinus 126, 160–161, 163
Pontus 30, 135, 146, 152
C. Popillius Laenas 76
P. Popillius Laenas (*cos.* 132) 26–27, 39–40, 42, 45, 60
C. Porcius Cato (*cos.* 114) 49, 66, 67
L. Porcius Cato (*cos.* 89) 123, 127–130
M. Porcius Cato (*cos.* 118) 62
M. Porcius Cato (Minor) 44–45, 116
Posidonius 83
C. Postumius 131
A. Postumius Albinus (*cos.* 99) 70, 100, 131
Sp. Postumius Albinus (*cos.* 110) 16, 49, 69–71
Praeneste 157, 159, 161, 167
Ptolemy Apion 104
Pylaemenes 84

Pyrenees 172

Quinctius 173
T. Quinctius Flamininus (*cos.* 123) 38, 44

C. Rabirius 96–98
Ravenna 160
L. (Antistius) Reginus (*tr.* 103) 84
Regium 27
Rhodes 93, 138, 149
Rome, Romans *passim*
S. Roscius 163, 173
Rubrius (*tr.* 133) 22–23
Rubrius (*tr.* 123) 47–48, 52
Q. Rubrius Varro 136
L. Rufus 24
P. Rupilius (*cos.* 132) 26–27
P. Rutilius Lupus (*cos.* 90) 113, 122, 123, 126
P. Rutilius Rufus (*cos.* 105) 75, 78, 80, 82, 90, 94, 97, 107, 110–111

Sabata (Lake) 65
Salapia 131
Salassi 99
Salluvii 35, 59
Samnium, Samnites 122, 128, 131, 138, 139, 141, 159–163
Sardinia 35–37
Sarmatians 86
P. Satureius 24
Saturninus (*see* Appuleius)
C. Saufeius 96–97
Scaevola (*see* Mucius)
Scipio (*see* Cornelius)
Scolacium 48
Seleucia 150
Sempronia 31, 87
A. Sempronius Asellio 127
C. Sempronius Gracchus (*tr.* 123–2) 13, 16, 18, 20, 22, 25, 28, 30–61, 65, 69–71, 76, 84, 112, 113, 168
Ti. Sempronius Gracchus (*cos.* 177, 163) 21, 43
Ti. Sempronius Gracchus (*tr.* 133) 13, 15–32, 36, 39–41, 43, 47, 49, 56, 57, 60, 69, 87, 92, 113
C. Sempronius Tuditanus (*cos.* 129) 30–31

C. Sentius 132
L. Sergius Catilina 130, 155–156
Q. Sertorius 104, 139–140, 154, 162, 172–174
Cn. Servilius Caepio (*cos.* 141) 34
Q. Servilius Caepio (*cos.* 106) 76–80, 84–85, 95, 105
Q. Servilius Caepio (*pr.* 91) 82–84, 90, 99, 105, 111, 113, 117–119, 121–122, 126
C. Servilius Glaucia (*pr.* 100) 82–83, 87, 90–91, 93, 96–98, 106, 111
L. Sextius (*tr.* 367) 15
C. Sextius Calvinus (*cos.* 124) 36, 48
Sicily 17, 27, 50, 83, 88, 92, 95, 101, 103, 114, 159, 161–162
Smyrna 85
Sothimus 132
Spain 40, 66, 83, 86, 104, 109, 125, 140, 148, 162, 172–174
Sparta 138
Spoletium 106, 157, 167
Stabiae 130
Stratoniccia 30
Suessa Aurunca 48, 162
Suessula 167
Sulla (*see* Cornelius)
C. Sulpicius Galba 60, 71
Ser. Sulpicius Galba (*cos.* 108) 73, 97
P. Sulpicius Rufus (*tr.* 88) 85, 122, 124, 125, 133–137, 139
Sunium 83
Synnada 149
Syria 47, 95, 108, 150

Tanusius 155
Tarentum/Neptunia 41, 48, 152
Tarquinii 48
Tarquinius Superbus 80
Tauromenium 27
Teanum Sidicinum 43, 152
Telamon 140
Telesia 162
M. Terentius Varro 151
Teutones 67–68, 73, 84, 86, 88–89
Thermus (M. Minucius) 174
Sp. Thorius (*tr. pl.* ?119, 118) 61
Thrace 132, 145, 147

Thyateira 29, 149
Tigranes 107, 109, 150
Tigurini 68, 73, 75
Titinius 155
C. Titius 128
S. Titius (*tr.* 99) 98, 100, 102
Tolosa 77, 80, 95
Toutomotulus 59
Troas 146
Tryphon 88
M. Tullius Cicero (*cos.* 63) 44, 49, 98
Q. Tullius Cicero (*pr.* 62) 98
M. Tullius Decula (*cos.* 81) 159, 163
Tunisia 161
T. Turpilius Silanus 72–73

Umbria 115
Urbana 167
Utica 74, 75, 171

Vaga 72
Valerius Corvinus 90

C. Valerius Flaccus (*cos.* 93) 108
L. Valerius Flaccus (*cos.* 131) 27, 29
L. Valerius Flaccus (*cos.* 100) 90, 93, 96, 99, 103–104
L. Valerius Flaccus (*cos. suf.* 86) 143–145, 158, 172
M. Valerius Messala 126
Q. Varius Hybrida (*tr.* 90) 119–120, 121, 122, 128, 135
Veliocassi 86
Vellitrae 48
Venafrum 162
P. Ventidius (*cos. suf.* 43) 130
Venusia 44, 122, 131, 162
Vercellae 89
Vestini 121, 130
P. Vettius Scato 126, 129
L. Veturius 66
C. Vidacilius 126, 129
Vindalium 59
Volaterrae 166–167, 174

Printed in the United States
by Baker & Taylor Publisher Services